Thought as Experience in Bataille, Cioran, and Rosset

Thought as Experience in Bataille, Cioran, and Rosset

Joseph Acquisto

BLOOMSBURY ACADEMIC
NEW YORK • LONDON • OXFORD • NEW DELHI • SYDNEY

BLOOMSBURY ACADEMIC

Bloomsbury Publishing Inc, 1359 Broadway, New York, NY 10018, USA
Bloomsbury Publishing Plc, 50 Bedford Square, London, WC1B 3DP, UK
Bloomsbury Publishing Ireland, 29 Earlsfort Terrace, Dublin 2, D02 AY28, Ireland

BLOOMSBURY, BLOOMSBURY ACADEMIC and the Diana logo are trademarks of
Bloomsbury Publishing Plc

First published in the United States of America 2024
Paperback edition published 2026

Copyright © Joseph Acquisto, 2024

Cover design: Eleanor Rose
Cover image: Caesura © Megan Holmberg

All rights reserved. No part of this publication may be: i) reproduced or transmitted in any form, electronic or mechanical, including photocopying, recording or by means of any information storage or retrieval system without prior permission in writing from the publishers; or ii) used or reproduced in any way for the training, development or operation of artificial intelligence (AI) technologies, including generative AI technologies. The rights holders expressly reserve this publication from the text and data mining exception as per Article 4(3) of the Digital Single Market Directive (EU) 2019/790.

Bloomsbury Publishing Inc does not have any control over, or responsibility for, any third-party websites referred to or in this book. All internet addresses given in this book were correct at the time of going to press. The author and publisher regret any inconvenience caused if addresses have changed or sites have ceased to exist, but can accept no responsibility for any such changes.

Library of Congress Cataloging-in-Publication Data
Names: Acquisto, Joseph, 1975- author.
Title: Thought as experience in Bataille, Cioran, and Rosset / Joseph Acquisto.
Description: New York : Bloomsbury Academic, 2024. | Includes bibliographical references and index.
Identifiers: LCCN 2023050007 (print) | LCCN 2023050008 (ebook) | ISBN 9798765111239 (hardback) | ISBN 9798765111475 (paperback) | ISBN 9798765111482 (ebook) | ISBN 9798765111499 (pdf)
Subjects: LCSH: French literature–20th century History and criticism. | Thought and thinking in literature. | Self in literature. | Bataille, Georges, 1897–1962–Criticism and interpretation. | Cioran, E. M. (Emile M.), 1911–1995–Criticism and interpretation. | Rosset, Clément–Criticism and interpretation. | LCGFT: Literary criticism.
Classification: LCC PQ307.T46 A37 2024 (print) | LCC PQ307.T46 (ebook) | DDC 840.9/00912–dc23/eng/20240202
LC record available at https://lccn.loc.gov/2023050007
LC ebook record available at https://lccn.loc.gov/2023050008

ISBN:		
	HB:	979-8-7651-1123-9
	PB:	979-8-7651-1147-5
	ePDF:	979-8-7651-1149-9
	eBook:	979-8-7651-1148-2

Typeset by Integra Software Services Pvt. Ltd.

For product safety related questions contact productsafety@bloomsbury.com.

To find out more about our authors and books visit www.bloomsbury.com and sign up for our newsletters.

Contents

Introduction 1

1 Georges Bataille: Thinking as Anguished Adventure 45
2 Emil Cioran: Thinking against Oneself 97
3 Clément Rosset: Thinking the Real 149

Conclusion 187

Notes 192
Bibliography 204
Index 209

Introduction

In *Précis de décomposition*, his first book published in French (1949), Emil Cioran writes:

> Tout problème, si on en touche le fond, mène à la banqueroute [...] : plus de questions et plus de réponses dans un espace sans horizon. Les interrogations se tournent contre l'esprit qui les a conçues : il devient leur victime. Tout lui est hostile : sa propre solitude, sa propre audace, l'absolu opaque, les dieux invérifiables, et le néant manifeste.
>
> (*Œuvres* 652–3)

> [Every problem, if we go down to the depths of it, leads to bankruptcy [...]: no more questions and no more answers in a space without horizon. Questionings turn against the mind which conceived them: it becomes their victim. Everything is hostile to it: its own solitude, its own audacity, the opaque absolute, unverifiable deities, and the manifest nothingness.]

He stages thinking as a kind of drama, with both thought and the thinker as recognizable characters with intentional states, engaged in a hostile interaction. Any sense of calm philosophical contemplation vanishes in something like a scene of horror and division between thinker and what we usually think of as the thinker's own thought as a part of his consciousness. Neither completely unified nor totally divided, thinker and thought reconfigure subject-object relations that had formed a basic dichotomy at least since Descartes.

This study examines three writers in the years during and shortly after the Second World War who address the question of what it means to think, what it means to constitute oneself as a thinking subject, at a time that seems to come "after everything," with the ruins of attacked cities seeming to echo, as a culmination, the dismal remains of a philosophical tradition confident in its establishment of human beings as rational, of reason leading inevitably to progress, and of the self and the world as knowable. The war figures not at all explicitly in any of the writings I will examine here—indeed, Georges Bataille was criticized for writing a book such as *L'Expérience intérieure* in wartime, given the perceived distance of its concerns from the immediate political reality—and yet these writings seem preoccupied with finding a way to pick up and carry on, to take what is salvageable from a tradition of thought and reshape it into a not-yet-determined way of reconfiguring the relation of self to world, if it still even made sense to speak of the self as if it were coherent.

There is a fundamental uncertainty and consequent anguish to the process of writing about thought, precisely because so many past assumptions could no longer be taken for granted, but nor could they simply be jettisoned wholesale. A remarkable feature of the writings I will examine is the way they call into question the classic distinction between the *vita activa* and the *vita contemplativa*. While experience is a notoriously fraught term to define, let me offer a basic working definition for our purposes.[1] By "experience" I mean, at one level, acting in the world or having sensations or perceptions, a pre-reflective moment devoid of inherent meaning but calling out to a human subject for reflection and, perhaps, the assigning of meaning to the perception or action. It is not itself a given, but is characterized after the fact by its sense of immediacy, a perception of being unmediated. At first glance, then, experience is distinguished from thought by coming before it and sparking reflection on it in a later moment that is distinct from the initial experience. But a major premise of my argument is that such a tidy distinction between experience and thought is necessary but insufficient for these writers as they navigate the relationship of thought to experience. While they hold out a place for the sensory or perceptual aspect of experience, their reflection on that experience is not simply removed from it or posterior to it. What I hope to demonstrate is that, for these writers, thinking is *itself* an experience, a fact that requires them to remap understandings of the relationship of thought to experience and to the notion of immediacy or mediation, and of thinking subjects to themselves and to their writing. Thinking about experience, which becomes thinking *as* experience, thus also implies a renegotiation, but can never accomplish a cancelation, of the subject-object relation inherent in thinking about the relation of self and world. There is, as we have already seen, a certain hostility, exasperation, or melancholy built into this reconfiguration, an enactment of the sense that the thinker is never at home in the world, and if that world is the thinker's own mind, then thought turns thinkers away from themselves, but in a way that never gets them past a notion of self as subject. And so several kinds of questions are already beginning to come into focus: how to persist in writing and thinking when one has the sense of having arrived at its end? What would thinking look like under such circumstances? What is the relation of the thinker to the thought? How to cope with the persistence of the subject even in moments when one actively desires its annihilation? What can be taken from the ruins of thought? And what is the role of writing in mediating or even creating the experience of thought and the thinker?

Those questions suggest an intimate relationship between thinking and a strong personal investment in thought by the thinker, with an important affective dimension. And it is my contention that the thinkers I examine highlight the extent to which what might seem like abstract conceptual problems are infused with an important personal immediacy, something that Robyn Marasco has called "the play of passions that accompany the restlessness of the negative" (84). These philosophical concerns relate to questions such as the distance from the thing-in-itself which has animated philosophy since Kant and the question of the possibility of representing the world as it "really is" in an externally verifiable sense. Such considerations give rise not only to questions about how to live, as ethics had always conceived that question, but also of how to think, how thinking might still be possible, and how to conceive of thought *as* a way of living, not as a second-order reflection on life. The realization of our distance from things in themselves and from meaningful objective descriptions of reality could be said to give birth both to a crisis for thought and to new possibilities stemming from the anguish of a reimagined role for thought in relation to experience and a new relationship to, and role for, language.

I use "thought" rather than "philosophy" to characterize the activity of these writers to mark the anti-systematic nature of their enterprise, their status as writers rather than philosophers in most senses of the term, and the shifting, ephemeral, and dialectical nature of their thought, as well as the intimate relation between thinker and thought along with the emphasis on the lived, engaged, experiential nature of that thought. Part of what animates their writing is the impossibility of tracking thought as experience precisely because to do so would be to conceptualize it in the immediacy of the moment and to assume a relationship of identity between the experience and the conceptual representation of it. Thought is always non-identical to itself, precisely because even in the moment of thought as experience, thought is mediated by its representation, even of itself, as we can see in Hegel's *Phenomenology of Spirit*:

> Experience is the name we give to just this movement, in which the immediate, the unexperienced, i.e. the abstract, whether it be of sensuous being, or only thought of as simple, becomes alienated from itself and then returns to itself from this alienation, and is only then revealed for the first time in its actuality and truth, just as it then has become a property of consciousness also. (21)

This relationship to thought as experience plays out in these writers as something akin to a drama animated by the realization that we can never get beyond the concept, whether our attempts be through action, laughter, eroticism, intoxication, or willful ignorance. Insofar as thought is known to be impossible when it attempts pure immediacy or the perception of a unified self, it could be said to be the object of a kind of fiction, operating in the realm of the "as if" in the writings of thinkers who are aware of that fictional status but who are sometimes unable fully to embrace the fictive nature of the unified subject in a clearly defined relation to the external world. It is perhaps in part because of this that many of the writings I examine here have an undeniably literary character, which is another reason I use "thought" rather than "philosophy" to characterize them. Since we can speak of the thinking subject as a "character" and of its relations to its own thought as operating as a kind of drama, there is an inherently narrative quality to these writings, where the subjects and their thoughts are created through its language and not merely reflected by it.

There are political stakes in conceiving thought as experience, and here too, these authors challenge an overly simplistic approach that would associate isolated contemplation with a refusal to engage politically. The very removal from daily activity and from contact with others which is required for thought has the potential to negate the status quo of an affirmative, nonreflective engagement with the busy-ness of the world. As I will show by appeal to Hannah Arendt and Theodor Adorno, thought is essential in order to avoid the calamity provoked by a culture of non-thought, of a non-critical acceptance of the world as it is that gives rise all too easily to an enthusiasm for, or at least a passive acceptance of, authoritarianism. The withdrawal of thought, in its non-participation in non-reflective daily life, allows for the cultivation of a subject at odds with the world as it is, and in the very non-belonging that the non-participation engenders can be found an essential kind of belonging through the insight gained in thought.

The solitary thinker has a crucial role to play not despite, but because of, his removal from the social world insofar as the removal allows for the darkness of the moment to be perceived as an object of critical reflection and a non-participation in collective evil.

The writers I examine thus engage by non-engagement, if by engagement we mean only direct nonreflective political action. As their very approach to reflective thought reveals, however, redefining concepts such as "action" and "engagement" in a way that forces a critical reevaluation of commonplaces is central to their thinking and writing, and the revisiting of commonplaces in light of a more accurate perception of the world is a political action at its very heart, insofar as it resists the ideology of passively repeated conceptions of the social world. What seems like an apolitical removal from the world becomes inherently political as soon as we consider the importance of thinking for resisting evil and refusing to succumb to ideology. The reconfiguration of the subject-object relation, which moves in the direction of mutually constituting subjects and objects rather than a simple subject-object divide, is of course fully political given the relation of dominance that is presupposed by a model whereby a subject stands removed from, and in a stance of knowledge and power over, an object.

Already several themes are emerging that will be prominent throughout this study: the importance of non-identity, in terms of the relation of both the writing subject to the world and the writing subjects to themselves, whose working through forms a major component of these writings, the fragmentariness and nonsystematic nature of the writings that both mirror and create that sense of the non-identical self, the importance of contradiction to the movement of thought, and anguish as a necessary component of working through the consequences of contradiction in the experience of thought.[2] The movement of thinking, as it intertwines with the written expression that produces it, reflects the new self-consciousness of thinking on the part of the living, experiencing subject who cannot be abstracted from the thought process itself. This implication of the thinking and writing subject constituted by that act of thinking and writing marks a further distinction between thought and systematic philosophy insofar as it questions the separation of the subject from the world "out there" to be perceived in order to posit a dialectical, mutually constituting relation between the two.

Inherent in dialectical thought since Hegel is the kind of plot structure that I have already referred to as a drama, one which, contrary to some understandings of Hegel, does not and cannot aim at synthesis.[3] As Todd McGowan has argued:

> Rather than synthesizing, the logic of the movement in Hegel's works is one of dramatizing opposition in order to make its contradiction apparent. In the drama that his philosophy unleashes, every position reveals its own undoing, exhibiting that rather than being self-identical it is at odds with itself. Dramatization exposes each position to its own crisis. When the contradiction becomes evident, Hegel moves on to a subsequent position that avoids this specific contradiction. The new position is not a synthesis but another perspective from which the earlier contradiction ceases to be contradictory. This gives rise to a more recalcitrant contradiction, not the elimination of contradiction. Through the development of Hegel's system, contradiction does not become increasingly easy to resolve but increasingly more difficult, until the final recognition that thought itself—and ultimately being—is contradictory. (14)

We can see the writings I will consider here as a working out and working through of this drama of contradiction and the consequences for both thought and the thinker in terms of the way we talk about and construct subjectivity. As I am about to suggest in more detail, the thought of Theodor Adorno can help us grasp what is at stake in thinking via contradiction as opposed to attempting to move toward resolution. In his lectures on Kant, Adorno indicates that "the depth of a philosophy does not lie in the extent to which this philosophy can reconcile contradictions, but rather in the extent to which it is able to make contradictions manifest which are inherent in the matter [*Sache*] itself" (*Kant's Critique* 128). He writes in "Why Still Philosophy?" that contemporary thought renounces traditional metaphysical claims to totality known through a philosophical system, but this renunciation puts thought into "conflict with its entire tradition" (*Critical* 7). Thus contradiction becomes central to the role of thinking:

> After everything, the only responsible philosophy is one that no longer imagines it had the Absolute at its command; indeed philosophy must forbid the thought of it in order not to betray that thought, and at the same time it must not bargain away anything of the emphatic concept of truth. This contradiction is philosophy's element. It defines philosophy as negative. (7)[4]

This nonsystematic attempt to think via contradiction is what I am calling thought in what follows; I reserve the term "philosophy" for approaches that proceed systematically and/or with an attempt to account for totality by aiming to resolve contradiction, even while I recognize that such neat distinctions between philosophy and dialectical thought do not apply unilaterally. Thought as I understand it establishes itself via the negation of systematic approaches, as Adorno suggests here, and is often characterized in my study as dialectical, another term which I will now attempt to characterize.

Michael Rosen, in his study of Hegel, highlights the impossibility of assigning a clear and decisive definition to dialectics and, importantly for our purposes, links it to experience:

> [I]t is a specific feature of the dialectical movement that we cannot answer such questions as "what does the dialectical movement consist in?" by giving an argumentative equivalent in ordinary discourse; the *experience* of Thought is an ineliminable feature of the dialectical progress, and, moreover, cannot be given an equivalent in the ordinary propositional form. It is only open to the critic and commentator to *characterize* the experience, not to give an equivalent which might substitute for or translate it. (92)

Rosen goes on to elucidate the problem this raises:

> [W]hen we characterize an experience we try to answer the question "what is it like?" But this experience of Thought is an experience which is *sui generis*; the point is that it is not *like* finite experience at all, and it was the extension of such finite ways of thinking to the transcendental realm that led to the self-contradictions of traditional metaphysical philosophy. (92)

So what would it mean to think via contradiction rather than attempting to move toward resolution? It is worth tarrying a bit with Adorno to get a better sense of how we might characterize dialectical thinking in its relation to the thinker, to the object of its thought, and to experience. Adorno offers no precise or concise definition of dialectical thought, and with good reason. To define it precisely and systematically would be to betray the nature of dialectical thought itself, as Adorno indicates in a 1957 lecture: "it would be a denial of all my philosophical views if I sought to advance a definition of what dialectics or a dialectical approach actually means" (*New* 147). Nevertheless, he provides a characterization of dialectics as:

> the method of investigating its own truth and falsehood within the matter itself, without referencing anything foreign to it, anything predetermined, without positing something abstractly external. In this sense, dialectics [...] is not an approach [...] that brings along some ready-made concepts and undertakes some more or less rabulistic manipulations of the matter via the medium of abstraction; on the contrary dialectics is, as Hegel formulated it, 'simply watching'—that is, leaving the matter to itself and trusting that it has its standards, its criteria within itself. (147)

The following year in another set of lectures, Adorno underscores the importance of reciprocal relation for dialectics; his particular example is that of the whole and the part, which do not stand opposed so much as they are mutually constitutive: "it is a dynamic relation, one where both moments reciprocally produce one another" (*Introduction* 88). In a similar vein, Susan Buck-Morss indicates that "the meat-and-potatoes principle of dialectical logic was, of course, that what appeared to be one thing was essentially its opposite" (100).

In short, most characterizations of dialectical thinking end up being restrictively specific, such as the definition by mutually constitutive categories that we have just considered, or frustratingly vague. My own characterization, which draws significantly on Adorno's, will be no exception, and I go about it tentatively, but I will add, by way of a working characterization, and in the spirit of an *essai*, that in addition to its being a method whereby terms depend on each other in a mutually constitutive relation, dialectical thought is in perpetual motion by virtue of its resistance to definitive conclusion. Building on that characterization by negation, I would add that dialectical thinking is nonlinear, nonsystematic, and nonteleological, and is accompanied by a self-conscious awareness of its own processes and their potential limitations. Some more specific engagement with Adorno's method will, I hope, elucidate some important characteristics of what I will mean when I call the thinking of the writers I consider in this study dialectical. To be sure, the thinkers I address in this introduction and throughout this study differ on important particulars, and I am not suggesting otherwise. Still, I claim that writers as varied as Adorno, Arendt, Valéry, Fondane, Bataille, and Cioran could be said to share in the broad outlines of the characterization I have just proposed and that this characterization of dialectical thinking is a helpful way to understand their respective intellectual projects in their variety.

It is to the credit of the essay form, according to Adorno, that it "rebels against the doctrine, deeply rooted since Plato, that what is transient and ephemeral is unworthy of philosophy" (*Notes* 10). It is in that very transitoriness that the essay and similarly constructed forms reveal and participate in the historically situated notion of truth, which is another way in which I would contend that the authors here can never be exploring "merely" their own individual inner experience:

> The relationship to experience—and the essay invests experience with as much substance as traditional theory does mere categories—is the relationship to all of history. Merely individual experience, which consciousness takes as

its point of departure, since it is what is closest to it, is itself mediated by the overarching experience of historical humankind. The notion that the latter is mediated and one's own experience unmediated is mere self-deception on the part of an individualistic society and ideology. (*Notes* 10)

Dialectical thought is thus situated, tentative, and in a reciprocally mediated relationship to the thinker and to its historical moment, a supremely self-conscious mode of thought, since it is "thought's attempt to recognize its limitations by recourse to the matter at issue itself" (Adorno *Introduction* 3). Commenting on this characterization, Richard Leppert identifies an implicit distinction in Adorno between the limits of thought and the limitations of thought:

> The limits of thought are those places in life where we stop making sense to ourselves. Logic, for example, forms the limits of thought in that whatever violates the rules of logic […] has not so much violated a norm (or committed a foul in the language game) as it has stopped playing the game altogether. […] Limitations, on the other hand, express contingent barriers to thought. One may be limited in one's thoughts simply because one lacks the imagination to think otherwise, or has not had the right education, but not because what one is trying to think simply cannot be thought. Limitations can be overcome. Limits cannot. (Leppert 459)

The potential of dialectical thought, then, is to attempt to think past the limitations, to open up new possibilities for thinking otherwise and thinking oneself otherwise, at the risk of the anguish of that newly multiplied set of possibilities created or revealed when one sees beyond a limitation. Part of thinking beyond limitation is to think by and through contradiction rather than seeking to eliminate or resolve it, a situation that derives in part from the subject that takes itself for its own object by representing itself to itself conceptually. As McGowan puts it, "contradiction is the name for the necessary impurity of every identity—its inability to just be itself" (8); Adorno's term for this is non-identity. To see objects, including the concept, as mobile is to set dialectical thinking in motion and to establish a fundamental opposition between it and a Cartesian approach to subject-object relations that had been dominant before Hegel. In his *Introduction to Dialectics*, Adorno develops a critique of Descartes on the grounds of the impossibility of a static object of knowledge:

> We can only arrive at [Descartes'] *clara et distincta perceptio* in the first place if the objects of knowledge are indeed static, distinct and clearly delimited in

themselves, if they are so isolated from all others that they can be separated from the whole and can be treated as individual objects without violating their intrinsic truth. (Adorno *Introduction* 102)

The relation of thinking to knowledge becomes even more complex when knowledge itself becomes an object. Adorno outlines how any attempt to know *something* automatically implicates knowledge itself as an object of knowledge:

> If we want to know something, then [...] we want to know *something*, and not just stay with the act of knowing. In other words, we want to advance beyond the domain of our thought, Yet, on the other hand, precisely in wanting to know this something, the latter itself also becomes a moment of our thinking, becomes itself knowledge, and also becomes itself mind or sprit. (*Introduction* 83)

This process by which knowledge becomes an object creates a situation of non-identity in the moment when the non-identical object of knowledge is then taken up by the consciousness of the knower as simultaneously part and not part of that consciousness, in a process which Adorno describes as "translating something into identity" while also maintaining its status as non-identical so that we can continue to talk about an object of knowledge:

> To know or to cognize something always resembles a process where something other or non-identical which confronts us is taken up into our own consciousness, is appropriated in a certain sense or made into something of our own. And this paradox—that knowing means translating something into identity, while yet relating to something which is non-identical, since otherwise there would be no process of knowing at all—this otherwise irresolvable paradox is precisely what calls for the labor of the concept for that process of both self-unfolding truth and self-unfolding thought which we understand by the name of "dialectic." (*Introduction* 83)

The complex relation between the thinker and the thought, as the writers I examine here conceive it, is beginning to come into focus. Dialectical thought calls into question the dichotomy between subject and object not by abolishing the notion of the subject but by identifying and drawing the consequences of a mutually constitutive relationship between thinker and thought.[5] In that relationship, each forms the other in a process that can have no definitive end nor any clearly defined self-identical relationship outside the process of constant mutual determination.

Such an approach to thought, while seemingly abstract and somewhat detached from lived experience at first glance, is in fact totally bound up with it.

Adorno goes on to specify how happiness and suffering are intricately bound to thought itself, and are not just a post facto reaction to it:

> For the essential task here, as I see it, is not to logicize language, as the positivists want to do, but rather to bring logic to speak—and this precisely captures Hegel's intention, namely that happiness and suffering may be revealed as an immanent condition, as an immanent content of thought itself, that thought and life alike maybe redefined and reinterpreted, that this task be undertaken with all possible rigor and seriousness. And it is of course precisely this aspect which is completely misunderstood as mere intellectualism in the standard hostility to dialectical thought. [...] But the essence of dialectic lies precisely in this: that it tries by means of thought itself to undo that separation of spheres which is pre-eminently reflected in the common or garden cliché of the three faculties of thinking, feeling, and willing. (*Introduction* 44)[6]

By reshaping the object of thought, we are reshaping thought itself in a process which automatically involves a reshaping of the thinking subjectivity at the same time. Insofar as writing is a record of thought at the same time that it is the working out of thought itself, we can understand writing as involved in a similarly dynamic relationship to thought. The dialectical approach forces us to see writing as constituting thought as an object in the very act of attempting to capture it in fixed form. The inscription of a first-person subject in most of the writings I examine is thus an integral part of the writing and the thought, as is the affective dimension of the anguish of attempting to articulate a dynamic process in something more akin to a stable form.

What may look like a constantly shifting set of undeveloped thoughts thus become the process of dialectical thought itself, which cannot be expressed in fixed or simple form without becoming frozen into the appearance of an identity which in fact hides the fundamental non-identity of the word or concept to the thing it seeks to represent. The urge for some kind of coincidence between the knowing subject and the object is thwarted by the dynamic character of both the subject and the object of knowledge:

> I would say that the epistemological-dialectical place of what I have called the mobility of thought, i contrast to all merely indicative or merely deductive intellectual procedures, is precisely the attempt of thought—now abiding with itself, now moving beyond itself—ultimately to bring the knowing subject that approaches from without together with the movement of the matter itself. This is something which is necessarily involved in the dialectical method. (Adorno *Introduction* 155)

This non-coincidence produces a different kind of subject and object of knowledge which take their reshaping by the process into account. The paradox is that a particular moment of thinking or writing needs to freeze the dialectical moment temporarily, so that a moment may then present itself as an object for the further work of dialectical thought as it continues to unfold. As Adorno indicates in "The Essay as Form," in a remark that can be generalized to the kind of writing I consider here, "discontinuity is essential to the essay; its subject matter is always a conflict brought to a standstill" (*Notes* 16). Dialectical thinking and writing is thus a negative practice in that it operates against itself in order to unleash the dynamic potential in the subject and object.

What Adorno claims about the essay is true of dialectical thinking and writing more broadly: "The essay, however, is concerned with what is blind in its objects. It wants to use concepts to pry open the aspect of its objects that cannot be accommodated by concepts, the aspect that reveals, through the contradictions in which concepts become entangled, that the net of their objectivity is a merely subjective arrangement" (*Notes* 23). The essay shares this negative conception with thought itself as Adorno characterizes it in *Negative Dialectics*: "Thought as such, before all particular contents, is an act of negation, of resistance to that which is forced upon it [...]. The effort implied in the concept of thought itself, as the counterpart of passive contemplation, is negative already—a revolt against being importuned to bow to every immediate thing" (*Negative* 19). Out of negation, and following on the act of its "doing violence to the object of [thinking's] syntheses," Adorno claims that thinking "heeds a potential that waits in the object" (19). His description of the operation of dialectical thought takes on the character of drama that we have already evoked, whereby thought itself could be said to take on some sort of intentional state and agency.

> [Thinking] unconsciously obeys the idea of making amends to the pieces for what it has done. In philosophy, this unconscious tendency becomes conscious. Accompanying irreconcilable thoughts is the hope for reconcilement, because the resistance of thought to mere things in being, the commanding freedom of the subject, intends in the object even that of which the object was deprived by objectification. (19)

While the hope for reconciliation is an essential part of the drama, we know that such reconciliation is ultimately impossible and would need to be undone by a further act of negation in order to prevent dialectics from coming to a standstill that would mean an end to thought. What is most necessary in order to keep thought alive is also a chief source of the anguish it produces, since the unconfigured subject can take no comfort in a possibility of reconciliation.

And yet, in the process of its own disintegration, the subject comes upon what Adorno would describe as a truer subjectivity by negation, a subjectivity all the more human for seeming inhuman by the common-sense view of what humanity is:

> Thinking men [sic] and artists have not infrequently described a sense of being not quite there, of not playing along, a feeling as if they were not themselves at all, but a kind of spectator. Others often find this repulsive; it was the basis of Kierkegaard's polemic against what he called the esthetic sphere. A critique of philosophical personalism indicates, however, that this attitude toward immediacy, this disavowal of every existential posture, has a moment of objective truth that goes beyond the appearance of the self-preserving motive. [...] The inhuman part of it, the ability to keep one's distance as a spectator and to rise above things, is in the final analysis the human part, the very part resisted by its ideologists. (*Negative* 363)

What had seemed to be a flaw or an error turns out to be an important move toward truth. The importance of language to the process shines forth yet again as Adorno affirms that "dialectics appropriates for the power of thought what historically seemed to be a flaw in thinking: its link with language, which nothing can wholly break" (*Negative* 56). Language, in its own non-identity with the thing it names, reveals a similar fissure between concepts and their objects which is realized in a moment of non-coincidence between the thinker and the thought and between thinkers and their own subjectivity. Writing thus comes to assume a central role in fashioning thought rather than merely recording it, even as writing brings out the non-identity between word and concept just as thought brings out the non-identity between concept and thing.[7] What emerges is something else, thought as a mediated object between the subject and the world which participates in their mutual constitution.

That mutual constitution is thought as experience, and accounting for that mutual constitution means we cannot see experience as primary. Rather, experience becomes possible only as mediated by thought when it is brought into the realm of the thinkable: "Intellectual experience can be expressed only by being reflected in its mediation—that is, actively thought. There is no way to make the intellectual experience expressed and the medium of thought irrelevant to one another" (*Hegel* 138). Adorno puts us on guard against pre-determining experience with clichéd or common-sense categories of thought by which experience would come to us in a pre-digested form. Rather, theory exists as a sort of potential through which we are able to have a mediated and mediating experience:

> [I]f someone wants to gain knowledge of something rather than cover it up within categories, he will have to surrender to it without reservation, without the cover of preconceptions, but he will not succeed unless the potential of the knowledge that is actualized only through immersion in the object is already waiting in him as theory. (*Hegel* 81)

And to understand experience and thought this way is to preserve the notion of the subject, as Adorno never ceases to insist. What Hegel establishes, according to Adorno, is not "an irrational unity of subject and object"; rather, Hegel "preserves the distinct moments of the subjective and the objective while grasping them as mediated by one another" (Adorno *Hegel* 7). By that process, dialectical thought yields the beginning of philosophical knowledge "only where it opens things up that traditional thought has considered opaque, impenetrable, and the mere products of individuation" (*Hegel* 81). To do this is to create a language that would differ from traditional philosophical language, which would use words against themselves, so to speak, in order to attempt to create the concept in a new way and in a new relationship to the subject. Writing thus plays a central role in the experience of thought as it gives voice to the experience of a subject navigating a terrain of common words with which there may be a new set of uncommon possibilities, in ways that cannot be clearly articulated through the language passed down to us and which can emerge only through an emptying and reimagining of the possibilities of those words and concepts:

> Philosophy is faced with a paradox: to say clearly something that is unclear, that has no firm outline, that does not accommodate itself to reification [...] This demand is paradoxical because language and the process of reification are interlocked. The very form of the copula, the "is," pursues the aim of pinpointing its object, an aim to which philosophy ought to provide a corrective; in this sense all philosophical language is a language in opposition to language, marked with the stigma of its own impossibility. (*Hegel* 100)

Rather than philosophy providing a clear correlative to other kinds of more creative language use by laying out logical arguments, philosophy here would take its cue from esthetically inflected writing, with its subject as a character and the drama of thought as thoroughly emplotted. The esthetic becomes a kind of safeguard against philosophy's tendency toward a false sense of totality based on identity thinking rather than being nourished by the richness of non-identity that sits more comfortably in the esthetic realm. For Adorno, the esthetic and the philosophical are not rigidly separated; rather, the esthetic can serve as a model of sorts for dialectical thinking:

> But if art is not an idea separate from philosophy and guiding it as a prototype, if philosophy as such wants to accomplish what is not accomplished in art, as illusion, then the philosophical totality thereby becomes esthetic, an arena for the semblance of absolute identity. This semblance is less harmful in art insofar as art posits itself as semblance and not as actualized reason. (*Hegel* 137)

By paying serious attention to writing which does not explicitly provide straightforward arguments, we can begin to do the work on language that the dialectical approach requires. The writers I examine respond to this newfound need to say something that cannot be clearly said because it requires a sometimes unspoken work on both the subject and the language the subjects have at their disposal. In the meanderings and contradictions of their writing, these writers activate the dialectical subject as it acts on, and is acted upon by, the calling into question of the common vocabulary of the concept and by emphasizing the non-identity of the concept to itself as an object of knowledge.

The difficulty of reshaping the subject-object relation is often what gives rise to the anguish often portrayed in the texts I consider in this study, which hesitate between the tone of a voice "from nowhere," so to speak, and the highly particularized tone of autobiographical or journal writing. These are authors who have read widely and digested much in the Western intellectual tradition but who leave relatively few traces of that reading in terms of explicit mentions of, or engagement with, other writers, with the effect that what sometimes seems to be a voice rising up ex nihilo from the page actually contains a heavy past of other writers and thinkers with and against whom these writing subjects are operating. Their thinking is thus dialogic not only with themselves as a split subject of intellectual experience but also with many silent partners whose ghostly presence makes itself felt in the texts. That hidden reading life comes to take its more or less silent place in the fragmentary drama of thought that is played out in these texts which both reject and depend on much of what has come before. The mix of implicit rejection and engagement is part of the way thought is constructed as experience in the texts, as these sources of implicit dialogue are not the object of some sort of academic study but come to bear on the thought experiments that these texts sometimes seem to record and at other times seem to create in and through the writing itself.

If the engagement with dialectical contradiction could be said to be a modern approach to thinking since Hegel, the sense in which this kind of thought is a work on the self, to the point of the potential undoing of the self, is much older. Anguish as these thinkers enter it is not an unbridled passionate state but rather the result of a something that takes at least some inspiration from older spiritual traditions. As Evelyne Grossman indicates, "To think oneself into anguish requires a patient asceticism, an experience that Bataille readily compares to the *Spiritual Exercises* of Ignatius of Loyola" (3). It is not that anguish is associated with death or nothingness but rather its opposite, an excess of possibilities for thought which overwhelm the thinker: "The void reveals itself [...] for what it is: not an absence of life but an astounding swarming of energies, an infinite vibrational movement" (19). Once again, this drama is inherent in the act of thinking itself, and not because thinking rejects the world outside thought but precisely because it claims status as a source of experience just like the external world, which puts the dialectical energy of thought in motion and contributes to that "swarming of energies," putting the thinker in the position of incorporating or somehow managing the excess. This happens in a way that does not maintain the full agency of the thinker, however. As I have suggested, part of rethinking the subject-object relation of thinker and thought is to accord some kind of agency to thought itself, without simply emptying out the subject entirely as some kind of mere vessel of thought. This is a position that Adorno characterizes in "The Essay as Form":

> The thinker does not actually think but rather makes himself into an arena for intellectual experience, without unraveling it. While even traditional thought is fed by impulses from such experience, it eliminates the memory of the process by virtue of its form. The essay, however, takes this experience as its model without, as reflected for, simply imitating it. The experience is mediated through the essay's own conceptual organization; the essay proceeds, so to speak, methodically unmethodically. (*Notes* 13)[8]

The work of thinking remains visible in the writing rather than being erased from it once the process has been completed, suggesting that the processual element is central to the enterprise of dialectical thinking in ways that de-emphasize the notion of an end-goal for that precisely because such a goal, synthesis, or resolution would betray the process itself. The thought is made through the writing and not merely recorded there, leaving the thinker with a sense of unpredictability in terms of the direction of the thought which contributes to the sense of overwhelming possibility contained even in a thought that seeks to meditate on nothingness.

Another mid-century thinker who informs my work in this study is Hannah Arendt, whose reflections on thinking form an intriguing play of same and difference with Adorno's. In what follows I outline key aspects of those reflections that will complement Adorno's dialectical thinking via non-identity and expand the role of thinkers in relation to the world of which they are a part. Arendt and Adorno's shared historical moment, the catastrophe of the mid-twentieth century, dictates their need to revisit but also reevaluate past traditions of thought in the West, articulating what might remain from those traditions in the ruins of catastrophe and seeing how those traditions unfold historically in such a way that only much later can we come to see the power of non-identity potentially inherent even in approaches that predate dialectical thinking in historical terms.[9]

Arendt looks back to Enlightenment figures such as Kant and ancient philosophers including Aristotle, Plato, and Socrates in her account of thinking and willing, *The Life of the Mind*. She establishes thinking as a removal from the busy-ness of acting in the world which, like Adorno's conception of thought, removes the thinker from the realm of "common sense" so that received opinions no longer hold up to scrutiny, no longer account meaningfully for the world. To withdraw from the busy-ness of goal-oriented nonreflective work in society is also to withdraw from the potentially false world of appearances that manifest themselves in the rationally irrational pursuit of, for instance, profit and power. For Arendt, there remains something crucial from Plato's division of the world into the realm of appearances and reality, but in a significantly altered sense; attempting to discern what separates appearance from reality is a crucial task of thinking, and thus withdrawal is a key condition of possibility for it. Arendt states this forcefully: "For thinking, [...] withdrawal from the world of appearances is the only essential precondition" (78). To remove oneself from the world is thus also to see the world differently, to yield perspective unavailable to those caught up in the unreason of daily activities, and thus to become a stranger to that world, both literally and figuratively. This capacity to think is not reserved for "professional thinkers" but is available to anyone who undertakes what Arendt calls the "two in one" of internal dialogue, modeled on Socrates.[10] These will live, at least for the time in which they are thinking, "the life of a stranger," a term Arendt borrows from Aristotle (Arendt 53). The thinker thus becomes alienated from the rest of the world by virtue of the way a period of thought catalyzes a change in understanding of what had been previously taken for granted, including, as I have already indicated, what it means to be a subject and how we might evaluate our claims to knowledge of the world. The temporary removal from the world of the given, of the society in which one lives, of the common sense that guides it, transforms thinkers in ways that mean that they can no longer return to that world in the same way as before, since thinking acts on judgment and impedes the smooth functioning of an unreflective social or political life. This is what makes thinking inherently political, even though, or precisely because, it involves removal from the world of the status quo.[11]

Like Adorno's, Arendt's model of thought is both creative and destructive. The destruction is primary; she compares knowing to an act of construction and thought to an act of destruction. But she reserves a creative power for thinking as well, which means that, as for Adorno, there is an affinity between thinking and esthetics. By turning answers into questions, thinking destabilizes knowledge and gives questioning primacy over any answers one may find, given that these answers are necessarily provisional and subject to change over time. To be aware of the need for new questions is a major task for thinking; this need removes thinking from the instrumental realm of the search for answers to a set of predetermined questions. To lose such awareness is to lose a sense of the vitality of thinking and art-making alike for Arendt:

> Behind all the cognitive questions for which men [sic] find answers, there lurk the unanswerable ones that seem entirely idle and have always been denounced as such. It is more than likely that men, if they were ever to lose the appetite for meaning we call thinking and cease to ask unanswerable questions, would lose not only the ability to produce those thought-things that we call works of art but also the capacity to ask all the answerable questions upon which every civilization is founded. (62)

To attempt to give voice to as-yet unarticulated questions requires a work on language that has something to do with the creativity of the esthetic, a creativity that is still mindful of thought's destructive role. To be able to say what is not yet sayable requires us to reach beyond the words and concepts available to us, and by doing so we recognize, in ways Adorno articulated, the necessary and productive failure of our words to match up to our concepts, which leads us on to identifying the fissure between the identity of concepts to the world and the fissure and division at the heart of subjectivity itself.

Put another way, thinking yields the negative presence of what Arendt does not hesitate to call the void. She arrives at the void by means of an initial move whereby she, again following Aristotle, identifies the "condition of homelessness as being natural to the thinking activity" (199). Unsettled and restless, the thinker cannot be grounded, literally or figuratively. The thinker's limitlessness in terms of imagining time and space brings the thinker to a kind of plenitude that Arendt labels a "nowhere," a negation of time and space that recreates time and space as a mediated product of, and condition of, thought:

> [I]t may well be that we were posing a wrong, inappropriate question when we asked for the location of the thinking ego. Looked at from the perspective of the everyday world of appearances, the everywhere of the thinking ego—summoning into its presence whatever it pleases from any distance in time or space, which thought traverses with a velocity greater than light's—is a *nowhere*. (200)

To articulate a "nowhere" in which the thinker is situated calls to mind for Arendt "the twofold nowhere from which we suddenly appear at birth and into which almost as suddenly we disappear in death," but she stresses that the nowhere of thinking "is by no means identical" with the nowhere of before birth and after death. The void that is thinking's nowhere "can be a limiting boundary concept; though not inconceivable, it is unthinkable" (200). This experience of the limit, along with a continued questioning of how we might be sure of our assertion of limits, is essential to the act of thinking; this limit, by being absolute negativity, paradoxically furthers thought in that a subjectivity forced to confront this limit cannot help but attempt to make meaning from it, in conditions that produce the anguish I have already evoked in terms of thought conceived as an experience.

While not synonymous with death, as Arendt indicates, this approach to thinking as being nowhere inevitably invites comparison to a kind of death:

> "Take on the color of the dead"—so indeed the philosopher's absent-mindedness and the style of life of the *professional* who devotes his entire life to thinking, thus monopolizing and raising to an absolute what is but one of the many human faculties, must appear to the common sense of common men, since we normally move in a world where the most radical experience of disappearing is death and withdrawal from appearance is dying. The very fact that there have always—at least since Parmenides—been men who chose this way of life deliberately without being candidates for suicide shows that this sense of an affinity with death does not come from the thinking activity and the experiences of the thinking ego itself. It is, rather, the philosopher's own common sense—his

being "a man like you and me"—that makes him aware of being "out of order" while engaged in thinking. (80)

To think likely means to discover the kind of "wrong life" that, as Adorno famously put it, cannot be "lived rightly" (*Minima* 43); being "out of order" in a world which reveals itself, by thinking, to be out of order is to define oneself negatively to that world, to commit to another kind of possibility while at the same time refusing to give positive content to that vision of how things could be otherwise, since to do so would be to fill up the void that thinking leaves open. If the texts I examine in this study do not always seem at first glance to "make sense," it is because they engage the kind of thinking activity that is to some extent aware of itself as going beyond conventional approaches to meaning-making.

The very lack of meaning-making that emerges from seeming to use the same words as those who make recourse to common sense points up the divide between the thinker and a potential audience, in a negative work on language: "since thinking itself is helpless against the arguments of common-sense reasoning and the insistence on the 'meaninglessness' of its quest for meaning, the philosopher is prone to answer in common-sense terms, which he simply turns upside down for the purpose" (Arendt 80). What emerges, once again, in this new emphasis on the rift between thought and the commonplace is the emphasis on thought as experience as opposed to a focus on the objects of thought.

> The whole history of philosophy, which tells us so much about the objects of thought and so little about the process of thinking and the experiences of the thinking ego, is shot through with an *intramural warfare* between man's common sense, this sixth sense that fits our five senses into a common world, and man's faculty of thought and need of reason, which determine him to remove himself for considerable periods from it. (81)

The removal from the common, again in a spatial and conceptual sense, makes of thought itself an object of thought in that move toward the non-identity of both subject and object; from this non-identity emerges the reorientation of subjectivity and objectivity that makes thought possible and prevents its ever coming to definitive resolution.

Such a process can only draw the thinker further and further from the world since the world would presumably line up less and less with the way thought mediates its experiences of the world, to the point where what had been taken for truth risks being revealed as utterly false, within a conceptual scheme whereby no positive truth content could be definitively articulated. This is an important aspect of thought's destructive nature as Arendt conceives it:

> And not only is the quest for meaning absent from and good for nothing in the ordinary course of human affairs, while at the same time its results remain uncertain and unverifiable; thinking is also somehow self-destructive [...] The business of thinking is like Penelope's web; it undoes every morning what it has finished the night before. (88)

Thinking thus constructs its own world, which is not to say that it is unrelated to the external world. Rather, it is to say that it creates the mediation by which, within the context of thinking, we might know a world which is, at the same time, constructed by that mediation. What seems like immediate or intuitive knowledge of an external reality can only be, on this view, a non-realization of the creative-destructive work of thinking.

Thinking cannot be frozen partly because to solidify the thought is to end the thought, to make it into an object, which would then need to be subsumed into the subject in a mutually constitutive relationship in order to remain in existence, at which point thought has begun its work of mediation once again. To describe thinking this way is also to create it through language, as Arendt underscores:

> [F]or thinking itself—whose language is entirely metaphorical and whose conceptual framework depends entirely on the gift of the metaphor, which bridges the gulf between the visible and the invisible, the world of appearances and the thinking ego—there exists no metaphor that could plausibly illuminate this special activity of the mind, in which something invisible within us deals with the invisibles of the world. (123)

And so we are back to language, with metaphors serving as a direct reminder that even supposedly non-metaphorical language is mediated insofar as words mediate, and to that extent determine, their concepts in dialectical relationship with the thinkers themselves. Thought is left to identify its own meaning or lack thereof, but the interpretation by thought of itself will not leave the original thought unaltered. It will always be out of step with its own meaning; it will never coincide completely with it: "Thinking is out of order because the quest for meaning produces no end result that will survive the activity, that will make sense after the activity has come to its end" (123).[12] This sense of being out of order has personal resonance in terms of what we have been calling the non-identity of the subject to itself as both revealed and advanced through writing and thinking. It has temporal resonance in terms of the way we think about linearity and permanence, and for Arendt it has political resonance as well.

Reflection on the limits of thought, conceived together with the limits of thought, yields as imaginative space that allows thinkers to transcend their own particular lifetime, their own limited temporality: "whenever I transcend the limits of my own life span and begin to reflect on this past, judging it, and this future, forming projects of the will, thinking ceases to be a politically marginal activity. And such reflections will inevitably arise in political emergencies" (192). Arendt's remark illustrates the inherently political stakes in thought, an activity carried out in solitude and withdrawal. Thinking on this model necessarily reveals itself to be intimately connected with political relations on account of the insight that temporary removal from the status quo reveals. By liberating the faculty of judgment, thinking allows for a refusal of the status quo that has potential to be critical by negation. To think is to be committed politically, but otherwise than engaging in direct action. While this stance is not without paradox and remains open to potential criticism, it is important to highlight that a withdrawal from the world in order to engage in thought as I have been characterizing it here is far from a reactionary activity or one that would seek to ignore the political world in which one is situated. To be a thinker is to be situated *otherwise* in terms of politics, to open up the kind of creative destruction that political change ultimately demands.[13] And it is to do so in the act of writing, whose work of creative destruction may surpass or contradict the personal political views of the author.

Just as personally conservative authors such as Honoré de Balzac and Charles Baudelaire's literary works are now often read, via the way mimesis and irony function in them, in ways that question or contest the views of their biographical authors, the thinking enacted by the writerly personae in the text I examine has contestatory potential by virtue of a refusal of active engagement as antithetical to thinking. What Kevin Attell says about Herman Meville's Bartleby, as he has been deployed by thinkers such as Gilles Deleuze, Giorgio Agamben, and Slavoj Zizek, aptly characterizes thought's implicitly contestatory power: "the 'violence' of Bartleby's comedy is the linguistic—*literal*—violence that this formula ['I would prefer not to'] wreaks on all hegemonic and majoritarian linguistic and political formations" (Attell 196). Thus Bartleby's is "not a passivity and acceptance of the hegemony of the ruling order, but rather a passive aggressiveness whose radicalness renders it more threatening to that order than any direct resistance" (Attell 222). This action of non-action is, in all its paradox, what operates in the way thought manifests itself in the work of the three authors I consider. That work creates the space for the refusal of fascism and totalitarianism by withdrawal from a world whose smooth functioning risks leading to unthinking commitment to reactionary causes.

In the chapters of this book, I look at the historical moment of the years in and soon after the Second World War, in order to shed light on an approach to thinking and writing in this period that tends to be marginalized in terms of the *grandes lignes* of intellectual and literary history of this period, which tends to underscore the hugely influential contributions of Jean-Paul Sartre and Albert Camus. I would not claim that Bataille, Cioran, and Rosset represent a countertradition to the existentialists, although Sartre famously attacks Bataille in a scathing review of *L'Expérience intérieure*, which I address in Chapter 1. Rather, the thinkers I engage emerge in parallel, though hardly ever in dialogue, with the existentialists, and they also share an attention to, and show some degree of influence from, predecessors such as Soren Kierkegaard and Friedrich Nietzsche.[14] Uninterested in developing a systematic philosophy, their writing sits uneasily in any well-established set of literary or philosophical genres. My contention is that interpreting these writers in light of the characterization of thinking elaborated in this same period by Adorno and Arendt will allow us a foothold in these writings, to better understand their contradictory and paradoxical nature as well as the way they negotiate between literature and philosophy by situating themselves outside both in the usual sense.

My readings are literary in that they attempt to do justice to the ways these authors give voice to thought in shifting contexts and sometimes contradictory formulations that emphasize the imperative to interpret, to focus on language as it constructs a complex speaking subject who is constructed through its language. To attempt to articulate arguments emerging from the texts is to miss their literary character and thereby obscure the way that productive contradiction emerges from the very style that these authors deploy. The working out of inherent contradictions thus forms a sort of plot structure that is a crucial aspect of these texts and that invites the reader into the drama of the text, accompanying the writing subject, probing, interpreting, and resisting conclusive or totalizing meanings. Such a literary or quasi-narrative approach may be fruitful even in more systematic philosophical texts; it is absolutely crucial when mining the potential of the works I consider here. My readings are also "inter-historical" in that, while they attempt to do justice to the specificity of the historical moment that gave rise to the texts, my claim is that the import of the dialectical thinking modeled in these texts suggests a continuity with our own time that does not transcend its historical moment so much as it suggests some important sources of continuity that would see our own moment as still struggling to assign a role to thought as experience and as a way of intervening dialectically in the world.

These texts can serve as illustrations of the working out of dialectical thought, especially as it pertains to knowledge and subjectivity in light of a reimagined subject-object relationship that transforms both self-knowledge and knowledge of the subject's relationship to the world. This work is often carried out as a kind of creative destruction of commonplaces and past intellectual history, as I have indicated is necessarily the case for dialectical thought. In the rest of this introduction I would like to explore two immediate precursors in France to the approach to thought that we have been exploring, Paul Valéry and Benjamin Fondane, who illustrate, each in his own way, the emergence of a new orientation that is similar in some respects to dialectical thinking and that emphasizes thinking as kind of experience.[15] In his *Cahiers*, Valéry explores, in aphorism-like sections, ideas on a wide variety of topics in the day-to-day journaling that makes up the text. Valéry could sometimes be justifiably identified as an apostle of clarity. An often-repeated theme in the *Cahiers* is the view, analogous to the stance of analytical philosophy, that what seem to be conceptual problems are simply the result of a sloppy vocabulary and that by seeking a quasi-mathematical clarity in the expression of concepts, what seem to be a set of paradoxes and contradictions simply melt away in the act of clarification: "Toute la philosophie est née d'illusions sur le savoir qui sont illusions sur le langage" ["All philosophy is born of illusions about knowledge which are illusions about language"] (Valéry *Cahiers* 1: 413). Many other moments in the *Cahiers*, however, give the lie to this denigration of contradiction by indicating a thinking subjectivity that is mobile rather than grounded. In that sense, the writing subject in the *Cahiers* has its predecessor in Michel de Montaigne and conforms to the portrait of thought, and the play of thought and its expression, outlined in Adorno's "The Essay as Form."[16] These moments in Valéry foreshadow the complexity of dialectical subject-object relationships that play out in thinkers writing shortly after Valéry, and a brief consideration of some of these moments in the *Cahiers* will serve to illustrate a number of features of dialectical thought in terms of the methods it adopts (explicitly or implicitly) and the kind of tentative and sometimes paradoxical conclusions to which it gives rise.

Valéry highlights the tension between thought and work insofar as the latter denotes a polished, finished, unalterable final product: "En ce qui concerne la « pensée », les œuvres sont des falsifications, puisqu'elles éliminent le provisoire et le non-réiterable, l'instantané, et le mélange pur et impur, désordre et ordre" ["As for 'thought,' works are falsifications, because they eliminate the provisional and the non-reiterable, the instantaneous, and mix of pure and impure, disorder and order"] (1: 12). An important implication here is that the provisional is not antithetical to the truth but rather a key part of it; what emerges is a new set of criteria for thought that seeks to include and account for the momentary and to embrace it as part of a dialectical process rather than seeing the moment instrumentally as a step toward an ultimate goal of decisive truth. Likewise, Valéry's idea of the thinking subject involves a similar recognition of an illusion of unity whose illusory character is only visible at certain privileged moments: "L'homme sort de lui-même le temps de s'apercevoir comme bizarrerie, manies, personnage à habitudes et caractère de comédie, puis il rentre dans la croyance de son unicité et dans l'illusion de sa généralité" ["Man leaves himself for just enough time to notice himself as oddity, manias, a character with comedic habits and character, then he goes back within the belief in his unity and the illusion of his generality"] (2: 1376). This model for thought and for the thinker is also shown to have esthetic implications in that Valéry challenges a traditional goal of a work as stable and definitive; instead, he leaves room not just for a work that can accommodate the mix of order and disorder but whose very form itself may carry implications for the thought, now seen not as the "content" of which the form is merely the container, but rather as a dialectical interplay. Valéry's comments on subjectivity also prefigure the split and the complexity of the subject-object relation that I will explore in what follows:

> Il y a un imbécile en moi et il faut que je profite de ses fautes. Dehors il faut que je les masque, les excuse.[17] Mais dedans je ne les nie pas, j'essaye de les utiliser. C'est une éternelle bataille contre les lacunes, les oublis, les dispersions, les coups de vent. Mais qui est moi, s'ils ne sont pas moi ? (1: 49)
>
> [There is an imbecile in me and I must take advantage of his faults. Outside I need to mask them, to excuse them. But inside I do not deny them; I try to use them. It is an eternal battle against lacunae, forgettings, dispersions, gusts of wind. But who is I, if they are not I?][18]

Subjectivity is figured here as an inner struggle against oneself, with the self-constituted not as fighting against its lacunae but rather constituted both by those lacunae and by the aspect of the subject that resists them. The point is not to synthesize those two aspects of the subject into some higher unified subject but rather to attempt to think the subject as constituted by the contradiction itself and to de-emphasize the unified subject in favor of privileging the lapses as constitutive of the subject rather than an aberrance, as Valéry implies by identifying himself with those lapses.

In addition to being constituted to an important extent by its lapses, Valéry describes the subject as unstable on account of its constant change, a changing for which any description of the self would have to account:

> Mon premier point est toujours la *self-variance*. Tout ce qui semble stable dans la conscience ou capable de retours aussi fréquents et aussi aisés que l'on voudra, est pourtant soumis à une instabilité essentielle. L'esprit est ce qui change et qui ne réside que dans le changement.
>
> Mais ce changement se fait par plusieurs modes mêlés. Et aux dépens de ce changement d'ensemble se font des changements partiels réglés. (1: 960)
>
> [My first point is always self-variance. Everything that seems stable in consciousness or capable of such frequent and easy returns as one wants, is nonetheless subjected to an essential instability. The mind is what changes and what resides only in change.
>
> But this change is made by several mixed modes. And partial, regulated changes are made at the expense of this total change.]

The fragmentary form of the *Cahiers* does not allow for the full elaboration of the consequences of the view of subjectivity that is suggested here, but that too is part of the point: the disappearance of this very thought itself, the lapses that cannot simply be filled in by editing out the lapse or by attempting to smooth it over, constructs by its form the challenge that the thought poses to the writer and reader: any attempt to work out the consequences of this view of subjectivity will give rise to further contradiction and perhaps to a notion of self as constituted by that contradiction. Subjectivity thus plays a game of hiding and revealing itself here, containing the seed of a complex model of subjectivity but suggesting in the very brevity of the passage here that to work out that account systematically would do violence to the kind of subjectivity that it posits.

A third characteristic of dialectical subjecthood present in Valéry's notebooks is the extension of the notion of foreignness to self to include foreignness to the world more broadly:

> Il y a en moi un étranger à toutes choses humaines, toujours prêt à ne rien comprendre à ce qu'il vit, et à tout regarder comme particularité, curiosité, formation locale et arbitraire ; et qu'il s'agisse de ma nation, de ma langue, de

ma vie, de ma pensée, de mon physique, de mon histoire, il n'est rien que je ne trouve, cent fois par jour, accidentel, fragmentaire, extrait d'une infinité de possibles—comme un échantillon— (1: 187)

[There is in me a stranger to all human things, always ready to understand nothing of what he lives, to regard everything as a particularity, a curiosity, a local and arbitrary formation; and whether it's my nation, my language, my life, my thought, my physique, my history, there is nothing that I do not find, a hundred times a day, accidental, fragmentary, extracted from an infinity of possible things—like a sample—]

Here again, what might otherwise be considered a weakness, the inability to see things as other than the particular, is a strength from the perspective of an approach that privileges the historically situated and dynamic nature of the external world and the way in which its status as object of knowledge is mediated by the subject, in this case the subject self-identified as foreign to the world. The idea is not that the subject is radically cut off, in the isolation of thought, from everyone and everything around him; rather, the separation that he posits is in fact a relation based on a contingency and variability that a more common-sense variety of unity with others may smooth over. By identifying himself as separate from everything human, he is in fact asserting a more thoroughly radical kind of humanity, one that is "out of order" in Arendt's sense, available only through this kind of removal that imbricates him all the more in a humanity understood differently from what we often might mean by the label "human."

Valéry also develops an approach to truth that situates it as something to be made and unmade, in a kind of program he establishes for himself in this passage structured by imperatives:

Ne cherche pas la « vérité »—Mais cherche à développer ces forces qui font et défont les vérités.

Cherche à penser à plus de choses simultanées—à penser plus longtemps, plus rigoureusement à la même—à te surprendre en flagrant délit [...]. Propose-toi des coordinations. Essaie tes idées en tant que fonctions et moyens.

(1: 328–9)

[Do not look for "truth"—but seek to develop those forces that make and unmake truths.

Seek to think of more simultaneous things—to think longer, more rigorously of the same thing—to catch yourself red-handed [...]. Propose coordinations to yourself. Try out your ideas as functions and means.]

Valéry calls for a layered approach to thought that superimposes thoughts on one another in simultaneity, disrupting a linear model of thought, and distances himself from any notion of conclusion except in a provisional sense. This exhortation also preserves the thinking subject as divided against itself, taking itself for both subject and object, self and other in a relation of surprise to itself, all of which figures thought as an openness and a welcome strangeness.

In another exuberantly lyric passage, Valéry evokes the thinker as entirely separable from the object of thought, so that the thinker becomes pure object to himself in a vibrant process where he seems to observe his own self-absorption in thought. Valéry employs a kinetic comparison to a dancer in this description which emphasizes something akin to the freedom a thinker might enjoy if detached from an instrumentalized use of reason bound to definitive conclusions:

> *Penseur* ! Ce nom ridicule—Pourtant il est possible de trouver un homme, ni philosophe, ni poète, non définissable par l'objet de sa pensée, ni par la recherche d'un résultat extérieur, livre, doctrine, science, *vérité* ... mais qui soit *penseur* comme on est *danseur*, et usant de son esprit comme celui-ci de ses muscles et nerfs ; qui, percevant ses images et ses attentes, ses langages et ses possibles, ses écoutes, ses indépendances, ses vagues, ses nettetés—distingue, prévoie, précise ou laisse, se lâche ou refuse—circonscrive, dessine, se possède, se perde ... artiste non tant de la connaissance que de soi—qu'il préfère à toute connaissance ; *elle*, n'étant jamais que l'acte particulier que *lui* peut, en somme, rendre toujours plus fin, plus *vrai*, plus élégant, plus étonnant, plus universel ou plus singulier—etc. (1: 334)

> [*Thinker!* That ridiculous name—And yet it is possible to find a man, neither philosopher, nor poet, definable neither by the object of his thought, nor by the search for an exterior result, book, doctrine, science, *truth* ... but who would be a *thinker* as one is a *dancer*, and using one's mind as a dancer would use his muscles and nerves; who, perceiving his images and his expectations, his languages and his possibilities, his listenings, his independences, his vaguenesses, his clarities—distinguishes, foresees, specifies or leaves, lets go of himself or refuses—circumscribes, draws, possesses himself, loses himself ... artist not so much of knowledge as of himself—which he prefers to all knowledge, the latter never being anything but the particular act that he can, all told, render always finer, *truer*, more elegant, more surprising, more universal or more particular—etc.]

There is, then, a veritable art of thinking for Valéry, which I would claim is linked to the way in which the writers we consider pay attention to form, and sometimes adopt unusual forms, in order to do the work on language that would be involved in wresting it free from the commonplace in a way that makes room for dialectical thought. Such a clearing out or destruction makes space for both the thinker and the thought to operate in a space in which they can be mutually constitutive. Valéry explicitly evokes the relation of philosophy to destruction:

> Le commencement d'une « philosophie » est toujours et nécessairement la destruction de quelque chose—qui est ou bien ce que pensait celui qui constitue sa « philosophie » avant qu'il s'y soit mis ; ou bien ce qui était pensé par d'autres.
> Il n'y a pas de vraie philosophie sans cette réaction et destruction initiale, à laquelle quelques-uns s'arrêtent.
> —J'observe, à côté de ceci—que toute Science se détache progressivement—en tant que vocabulaire, du langage commun et en tant que manière de penser ou d'agir, de la manière commune ; et d'abord, en instituant entre le *penser* et l'*agir*, une relation toute particulière (1: 721)
>
> [The beginning of a "philosophy" is always and necessarily the destruction of something—which is either what the one who is constituting his "philosophy" thought before he started, or what was thought by others.
> There is no true philosophy without that reaction and initial destruction, at which point some stop.
> —I observe, alongside this—that all Science progressively detaches itself—in terms of vocabulary, from common language and, as a manner of speaking or acting, from the common manner, and first, by instituting between *thinking* and *acting* a very particular relation.]

It is not that the object of thought vanishes and that the thinker escapes to some putatively "pure" space of thought, but that the object is freed to constitute the thinking subject by means of the very distinction that is initially seen as separating them. Such a move calls for removal, not from the world generally, but from the realm of common language and the frozen concepts that thinking seeks to reanimate by rethinking the subject-object relationships inherent in the act of knowing.

Valéry calls for a new approach to philosophy on the grounds of the inadequacy of what has hitherto passed for observation. Prefiguring Bataille's notion of *expérience intérieure*, Valéry writes: "Je dis que la philosophie est forcément fondée sur l'observation et l'expérience intérieure—et je dis que cette observation a été généralement insuffisante ; et que les moyens de fixer ces observations ont été géneralement grossiers" ["I say that philosophy is necessarily founded on observation and inner experience—and I say that this observation has generally been insufficient; and that the means of establishing these observations have been generally crude"] (1: 482). Here too, Valéry could be read as setting out a program for a new approach to thought that writers like Bataille will take up, in ways theorized more extensively and explicitly by thinkers such as Adorno. He challenges us to attempt to articulate what it would mean for observation (including the kind of self-observation involved in inner experience) to be adequate to the task. To begin to explore this kind of thought involves reorienting not only the answers we give to our questions about thought and its relation to the subject and the world but also the nature of the questions themselves. The work of creative destruction of thought eventually yields that ground zero from which one must begin to articulate the questions differently, or revaluate what questions could or should be asked at all: "La plus grande ignorance est de ne savoir quelles questions ne se doivent poser. C'est confondre les faux avec les vrais problémes" ["The biggest ignorance is not to know which questions should not be asked. It means confounding true and false problems"] (505). The one example he adds of a poorly articulated question is about self-identity: "Que suis-je ? Tu crois que c'est un problème ? Ce n'est qu'un non-sens" ["What am I? You think that that's a problem? It is only meaningless nonsense"] (1: 505). This affirmation invites questions of its own: is it nonsensical to ask the question of self-identity because such a thing cannot be named or articulated, or because that kind of identity does not exist at all, even beyond questions of its naming or articulation, or because the articulation of identity is so complex as to make asking the question useless insofar as the question seems to propose a straightforward or unified answer?

Poet and critic Benjamin Fondane, writing in the 1930s and 1940s before perishing at the Birkenau concentration camp, works from a rather different set of assumptions about the life of the mind, influenced by his mentor Léon Chestov, which emphasizes irrationalism and appeals to an existential line of thought that includes thinkers such as Pascal, Kierkegaard, and Nietzsche.[19] I will suggest, through a consideration of some of Fondane's essays, that we can see him ultimately as calling for a new kind of reason, a new approach to the relation between thinking and experience, rather than advocating the abolition of reason altogether. His critiques of reason, as it was defended by a certain reading of Hegel in his time, outline the problem of linking reason to instrumentality and a notion of linear progress. In the logic of the either-or that is present in his writings, we can see the problem to which dialectical thought as I have been describing it emerges as at least a potential and partial response. His emphasis on what he labels the real and his fundamentally tragic orientation to characterizing human experience prefigure the ideas of Clément Rosset. It is possible, and here Fondane's own preferred thinkers could be said to be historical models of this, to infuse thinking itself with the vitality of lived experience and, in so doing, address the critique of reason as cold, calculated, abstract, and removed from key aspects of human affectivity.

In "La conscience malheureuse," an essay originally published in *Cahiers du sud* in 1935 and later included in Fondane's *Le Lundi existential et le dimanche de l'histoire*, Fondane establishes a tension between the real and hope, with the former exerting resistance to a human tendency to preserve the latter through conceptual or imaginative strategies of various kinds:

> Entre le réel—qui est nécessité—et l'espoir—qui est liberté—il noue une action réciproque et quotidienne d'autant plus significative qu'elle s'avère efficace à la longue et que l'espoir, sous le nom d'idée, d'absurdité ou d'utopie, témoigne d'une mystérieuse capacité à dominer le réel, à le domestiquer et à lui imprimer des modifications certaines et salutaires.
>
> Cependant, l'espoir journalier de millions d'êtres humains, le rayonnement qui en émane et le rendement qu'on en obtient, ne sauraient guère suffire. Quelle que soit la puissance motrice de notre espoir, le réel ne cède pas, il résiste, il multiplie autour de nous ses pièges, ses pressions. (*Lundi* 93)

> [Between the real—which is necessity—and hope—which is freedom—there is a reciprocal and everyday action which is all the more meaningful given that it seems effective in the long run and that hope, under the name of an idea, or an absurdity, or a utopia, testifies to a mysterious capacity to dominate the real, to domesticate it and imprint salutary and certain modifications on it.
>
> However, the daily hope of millions of human beings, the shine emanating from it and the yield we get would hardly suffice. Whatever the motor of our hope, the real does not yield; it resists, it multiplies its traps and pressure around us.]

This tension leads Fondane to a series of reflections about unity and division, as he claims that philosophy and religion offer competing understandings of the real even as both claim that the real is unified:

> Au déchirement de la pensée humaine en croyance philosophique et en croyance religieuse, correspondrait-il, quelque part, une déchirure objective du Réel lui-même ? Il est étrange de voir, pour une fois, pensée philosophique et pensée religieuse complètement d'accord ; toutes deux se refusent à une conclusion semblable ; toutes deux pensent que le réel est un—le leur bien entendu. (*Lundi* 96)

[Would an objective splitting of the Real itself correspond, somewhere, to the splitting of human thought in philosophical and religious belief? It is strange to see, for once, philosophical and religious thought in complete agreement; both refuse such a conclusion; both think that the real is one— their own, of course.]

Without claiming that one or the other version of the real is the true one, we are left with a split in the real whereby those who affirm its unity in fact contribute to its division, and this participation in enforcing the division is what temporarily united the two poles of religion and philosophy which are otherwise construed in opposition to each other. Fondane questions such a neat division between philosophical and religious thought and goes on to suggest that such a split, which seems to be between camps of people, is in fact indicative of an inner division of the human subject itself:

> Croire que pensée religieuse et pensée philosophique sont profondément et nettement séparées, c'est simplifier bien des choses. En fait, la déchirure n'est pas seulement de l'homme à l'homme, mais dans l'homme même. En chaque homme il y a un philosophe et un croyant. Il y a un croyant dans un philosophe et un philosophe dans le croyant. (*Lundi* 96)

> [To believe that religious thought and philosophical thought are profoundly and clearly separated is to simplify many things. In fact, the split is not only from man to man but within man himself. In each man there is a philosopher and a believer. There is a believer in the philosopher and a philosopher in the believer.]

Through this indication of tension and the construction of one kind of thought as construed by, and therefore dependent on, its opposite, Fondane suggests the foundation of dialectical thought without actually making the move to affirm it as a way to account for and engage with the kind of complexity he is identifying when it comes to the relationship of thought to the real.

Fondane likewise hints at what I have been identifying as a conception of thought as experience when he suggests that in the face of the real's force that imposes suffering and meaninglessness, the basic human tendency is to resist rather than accepting it with resignation:

> Si la déchéance et la misère de l'homme ont été voulues, qu'à ce destin il se résigne donc une fois pour toutes ! Néanmoins, l'homme ne peut pas se résigner. Il sent qu'à ne pas se résigner, il joue sa chance. Peut-être l'aime-t-on violent, téméraire, capricieux, obstiné, despotique ? Que doit-il, en ce cas, détruire, tuer, assassiner, forcer ? Serait-ce le tour de l'homme théorique, du décadent,

de l'*homo philosophicus*? Doit-il hâter l'événement, ou doit-il attendre que ce mystère s'accomplisse sans lui ? Mais est-il chose qui puisse s'accomplir au monde sans qu'il y ait, même infinitésimale, une collaboration effective de l'homme ? (*Lundi* 98)

[If the decline and misery of man were intentional, he should resign himself to that destiny once and for all! Nevertheless, man cannot resign himself. He senses that by not resigning, he plays his luck. Maybe we like it to be violent, reckless, capricious, obstinate, despotic? In that case, what should he destroy, kill, assassinate, force? Would it be the turn of the theoretical man, the decadent, *homo philosophicus*? Should he hasten the event, or should he wait for this mystery to happen without him? But is there something he could accomplish in the world without there being even just an infinitesimal collaboration of man?]

Fondane's critique of what he labels philosophy's approach to understanding the world is that it supposes a view of reason that establishes a supposedly fixed, immobile universe that is false because it denies the indeterminacy and changing nature of the world in favor of a simplified and unified portrayal:

Ce monde assis par le philosophe sur une Raison, un Esprit, un Logos immuable, déraille toutes les nuits sur un principe d'indétermination, sur un tremblement de terre, conçu et posé là par le poète. Sans doute, tout comme le philosophe, le poète cherche-t-il, ce qui est le plus important ; mais si, pour le philosophe, noblement, n'est importante que la conservation de la matière, le cosmos de l'atome, les structures idéales, le poète, lui, honteusement, parle de souffrance, d'ennui, de mystère. La folie, méprisée par le philosophe et l'immortalité de l'âme qu'il foule à ses pieds, sont rattrapées avec avidité par le poète. (*Lundi* 99)

[This world planted by the philosopher on Reason, or a Spirit, or an immutable Logos, goes astray each night on a principle of indetermination or an earthquake conceived and put there by the poet. Without a doubt, just like the philosopher, the poet seeks what is most important. But if, for the philosopher, nobly, the only important thing is the conservation of matter, the cosmos of the atom, ideal structures, the poet speaks, shamefully, of suffering, ennui, mystery. Insanity, despised by the philosopher, and the immortality of the soul which he casts at his feet, are avidly retried by the poet.]

One could suggest, however, that Fondane is trapped in the very kind of logic that he criticizes here. By maintaining a rather rigid view of what a "philosophical" view of the world entails, he seems committed to an unhelpful opposition between a unified world obeying identifiable laws of logic and the irrational world of imaginative extreme mental states such as insanity. Articulating other ways of conceiving the world in its relationship to thought can get us out of both such an opposition and a bland and unhelpful approach that would call for some sort of synthesis or middle state that encourages a moderate approach that avoids the pitfalls of either extreme. A dialectical approach would not settle into such an unhelpful compromise but would keep the productive tension between the views alive in ways that illuminate the way in which they are mutually constitutive and in which they both represent a mediated view of the reality they claim to represent.

Intriguingly, what Fondane calls "poetic" experience comes close to such a move, based on a creative act of the imagination. It is the poet who embodies humanity's revolt against the given by refusing the resignation that Fondane associates with the philosophers broadly speaking:

> Que ferait le poète de la réalité telle quelle ? Il n'y a pour lui réel, que du possible ; possible que de l'espoir ; espoir, que dans la tension la plus haute, la passion, le déchirement ; il boude la résignation ; c'est là qu'il joint et parfois sans s'en douter, les frontières de la vie, les prémices du transcendant. [...] La présence du monde ne le touche qu'en tant qu'absence—une absence dont il a faim et soif. (*Lundi* 100)

> [What would the poet do with reality as it is? The only real for him is the possible, the only possible is hope; the only hope is in the highest tension, passion, tearing apart; he scorns resignation; that is where he links, and sometimes without realizing it, the borders of life, the premises of the transcendent. [...] The presence of the world only touches him as absence—an absence for which he hungers and thirsts.]

By appealing to a sense of the poetic as associated with lived reality and imagination, Fondane poses a challenge to thought that does not seek to reject it but to reconfigure the relation between thought and experience. Fondane's model of a tragic hero, as well as of an existential thinker, is the biblical figure of Job:

> les œuvres les plus hautes de la pensée existentielle ont-elles toujours non seulement revêtu, mais signifié, une grande activité lyrique : poésie, le Livre de Job ; [...] poésie, la pensée, toute passion ne peut, en dernier ressort, prendre d'autre figure que lyrique. C'est ainsi qu'à défaut d'exemples plus hauts et qui nous sont interdits, la poésie par sa démarche, sa tension, sa technique et jusque par cet inachèvement en système, en vase clos, qui est son lot sur la terre, si elle ne se confond avec l'existant, du moins l'épouse-t-elle et exprime son déchirement, sa liberté. (100-1)

[The highest works of existential thought always have not only adopted, but also signified, a great lyric activity: the Book of Job is poetry; [...] thought is poetry; every passion can, in the end, take no kind of form other than lyric. Thus it is that, lacking higher examples which are forbidden us, poetry by its processes, its tension, its technique and even by its inability to be finished off in a system, in a closed container, which is its lot on earth, if it does not mix with the existent, at least it espouses it and expresses its tearing apart, its freedom.][20]

The description of what "poetry," figuratively speaking, brings to thought resembles in some important ways what we have been identifying as dialectical thought, most notably its inability to be codified into a system and the unresolved tension which remains its motor, along with the sense that thought in this sense mirrors the tension inscribed into a lived experience conscious of the presence of suffering in an indifferent world along with a faculty of imagination that encourages us to conceive how things might be otherwise. And yet poetry cannot simply be assimilated to philosophy or to thought more broadly: "Cependant, la poésie ne dispose que d'affirmations passionnées, de rapprochements ineffables ; elle vit, mais ne décrit pas ; vit et ne conclut guère" ["However, poetry only has at its disposal passionate affirmations, ineffable relations; it lives but does not describe; it lives and hardly concludes"] (101). This affirmation suggests another productive, unresolvable tension, that between art and philosophy, which stand in a mutually constitutive relationship whereby philosophy is completed by art but in a way that cannot reduce what art has to say to the clear language of philosophy. To attempt to articulate the ways the "poetic" as Fondane figures it here can inform the experience of thought is to realize the inadequacy of any straightforward articulation of that relation between thought and experience. At that point, the attempt to account for the poetic alters thought and draws the thinker into an experience that is not simply a reaction to, or mirror of, other kinds of lived experience but rather becomes part of the experience itself. The challenge becomes one of letting ourselves be perpetually disturbed by this "poetic" element of thought rather than reverting to the perhaps more comforting, straightforward, but ultimately false world of systematic philosophy: "À l'issue d'une lecture, la plus fiévreuse, le lecteur un instant séduit par le réel vivant, retombe entre les mailles de la logique quotidienne; il a été ému par le poème, mais convient-il de confondre l'émotion avec la créance ?" ["After emerging from reading, the most feverish kind, the reader, seduced for an instant by the living real, falls back into the net of everyday logic; he had been moved by the poem, but is it appropriate to conflate emotion with credibility?"] (101).

Fondane does distinguish between the poet and the existential thinker; while existential thought emerges from poetic experience and is, like poetic experience, "une pensée de passion, de dilatation" ["a thought of passion and expansion"] (102), the poet "affirme, sans donner un but à sa passion" ["affirms, without giving an objective to his passion"], whereas an existential thinker, and here Fondane mentions Job and Kierkegaard, situates thought "au centre d'un conflit, du conflit qui oppose la raison à l'existence et l'immanence à la transcendance" ["at the center of a conflict, of the conflict that opposes reason to existence and immanence to transcendence"] (102). While he emphasizes unresolvable conflict, he does not situate existential thought within historical development, claiming rather that existential thought is "aussi vieille que le monde" ["as old as the world"] (102). Even so, Fondane's call for revolt rather than passive acceptance of the unresolvable conflict, a revolt he associates with a philosophy of tragedy and sees as an "exhortation à la liberté" ["exhortation to freedom"], is perhaps not incompatible with a view of thought that sees it as anchored in history, as positing an eternal aspect that is in tension with a historical approach in a way that calls that eternal aspect itself into dialectical tension.

Fondane rejects that sort of historical view partly on account of his rejection of Marxism and Hegelianism, but this strong anti-Hegelian stance is based on an understanding of Hegel that emphasizes the resolution of the dialectic, which Fondane rightly sees as opposing the perpetual tension that he outlines in his existential philosophy. Given what he claims is the permanent nature of the metaphysical tensions of human existence, he is committed to a critique of Marx on the grounds that even if Marx's historical materialist dialectic were to be resolved historically, the improved material conditions of humanity would not impact the metaphysical tensions. According to Fondane, writing in the preface to the collection of his essays, *La conscience malheureuse* (1936), "Nous sommes à la fois, en tant que citoyens du malheur social, des êtres politiques, et en tant que citoyens du malheur humain, des êtres métaphysiques" ["We are at the same time, as citizens of social unhappiness, political beings, and as citizens of human unhappiness, metaphysical beings"] (*Conscience* 20). Fondane claims that Marx dismisses the absurd as mere abstraction and thus offers an incomplete account of human existence:

> Nous nous froissons à notre tour de ce que la dialectique définisse l'homme, « dans sa réalité », comme « l'ensemble des rapports sociaux » (Marx) et sacrifie à la légère les « abstractions » qui ne sont que les états vécus de la conscience,

bien qu'il lui faille reconnaître d'autre part « que la production en général est une abstraction » aussi. (*Conscience* 24)

[We take umbrage in turn that the dialectic defines man, "in his reality," as "the totality of social relations" (Marx) and sacrifices lightly the "abstractions" that are only the lived states of consciousness, even though he must recognize on the other hand "that production in general is an abstraction" too.]

Alleviation of material need would, according to Fondane, reinforce a society's awareness of, and suffering from, the metaphysics of absurdity and the drama of revolt against it, which we can perhaps ignore but never overcome:

> Il est même vraisemblable qu'une société absolument débarrassée de tout souci matériel—si jamais cela arrive—soit autrement plus propre que la nôtre à se livrer totalement et sans arrière-pensée à l'angoisse métaphysique. [...] Tant que la réalité sera telle qu'elle est, de manière ou d'autre—par le poème, par le cri, par la foi ou par le suicide—l'homme témoignera de son irrésignation, dût cette irrésignation être—ou paraître—absurdité et folie. Il n'est pas dit, en effet, que la folie ne doive jamais finir par avoir raison de la raison. (*Conscience* 25)
>
> [It is even implausible that a society absolutely free of all material concern—if that were ever to happen—would be otherwise in better stead than ours to give itself over totally and without a second thought to metaphysical anguish. [...] As long as reality is what it is, one way or another—by the poem, by a shout, by faith or by suicide—man will affirm his refusal to resign himself, even if this non-resignation be—or seem—to be absurdity or insanity. It is not said, in fact, that insanity must not end up by besting reason.]

Fondane's critique of Marx is thus closely aligned with his critique of philosophy in that both, according to Fondane, seek, by systematic means, to overcome contradiction by way of a universalizing, unifying logic that achieves its result at the cost of minimizing or forgetting key aspects of the tragedy of finitude and the drama of revolt:

> Quoi de plus *naturel* que de vouloir bâtir un édifice de certitude qui soit hors d'atteinte ? [...] Il y avait là une grande clarté, si grande, que l'idée nous est venue sur le tard que, derrière cette clarté, se dissimulait une peur atroce—la peur que ces évidences ne fussent ni vraies, ni premières, ni absolues—la peur que la philosophie ne fût autre chose qu'un acte manqué, une névrose obsessionnelle, un secret honteux qu'à tout prix il fallait taire—sous peine de sombrer, de toucher du pied l'angoisse, l'absurdité et la folie. Sans doute, avant d'élever son édifice, un Husserl *a vu* cela ; c'est parce qu'il *a vu* cela qu'il a tenté, avec une

audace et une puissance incroyables, le plus désespéré des systèmes rationalistes; c'est parce qu'il a abordé de face la peur et le danger que le danger et la peur l'ont marqué si profondément—si indélébilement—lorsqu'il nous semble que, chez lui, la Raison elle-même est devenue folle. (26)

[What is more *natural* than to want to build an edifice of certainty that would be invincible? [...] There was such great clarity there that the idea came late to us that, behind that clarity was hiding an atrocious fear—fear that these clarities were neither true, nor primary, nor absolute—fear that philosophy was nothing other than a missed action, an obsessional neurosis, a shameful secret that one would have to keep quiet about at all costs—to avoid falling under, to touch on anguish, absurdity, and insanity. Without a doubt, before constructing his edifice, a Husserl *saw* that; it is because he *saw* that that he attempted, with an incredible audacity and power, the most desperate of rationalist systems; it is because he directly confronted fear and danger that danger and fear marked him so profoundly—so indelibly—when it seems to us that, in his case, Reason itself became insane.]

If Fondane had had recourse to a model of negative dialectics, it would appear, based on what he writes in this preface, that he would have found more common ground between political struggle and what he calls "la vie intérieure." He rightly criticizes those who resist metaphysical concerns on the grounds that there are pressing world-historical acts to be performed in the service of revolution. Such a position denies the negative dialectical force that would oppose itself to any definitive end, which for a thinker like Adorno can only end in the stasis of a totalitarian situation. What I have been trying to suggest is that the anguish and restlessness of thought understood in this light are also subject to mediation by the thinker's historical situation and thus can become an act of resistance by opposing simplistic notions of definitive political solutions. To oppose thinking on the grounds that it opposes itself to political action is to misunderstand thinking as a private and superfluous concern that implicitly reinforces the political status quo, and to understand politics as a simple definitive cancelation of past injustice in a quasi-utopian social transformation:

> Trop de gens, à l'heure actuelle, proclament à tue-tête que soulever la moindre poussière métaphysique équivaut au vouloir sournois de défendre l'ordre des valeurs compromises et rendent solidaire le cri angoissé et profond de l'être du maintien d'un état de choses aussi délabré qu'inique, dont il est le premier à souffrir.

Combien que soit juste l'insurrection collective dressée contre la réalité économique, éthique et politique, pourquoi faut-il absolument qu'on veuille nous la faire payer par l'abandon forcé des sollicitations de notre vie intérieure et par le refoulement aussi angoissant qu'inutile d'une réalité qui ne se donne et n'est présente qu'au plus intime et au plus secret de l'individu. [...] A la catégorie éthique collective que l'on appelle : « injustice », répond, sur un autre registre humain, la catégorie métaphysique, aussi peu claire que la première, et qu'on appellee : « le malheur ». (20–21)

[Too many people, at the present time, proclaim loudly that kicking up the least metaphysical dust is equivalent to the unseemly desire to defend the order of compromised values and render the anguished and profound cry of being in solidarity with the maintenance of an order of things that is as dilapidated as it is iniquitous, of which it is the first to suffer.

As justified as collective insurrection against economic, ethical, and political reality may be, why must we absolutely want to pay the cost by the forced abandonment of the solicitations of our interior life and by the repression, as anguishing as it is useless, of a reality that only gives itself and makes itself present to the most intimate and secret aspects of the individual. [...] To the collective ethical category that we call: "injustice", responds, on another human level, the metaphysical category, just as unclear clear as the first, which we call: "unhappiness".]

Fondane underscores the synergy between what he calls metaphysical and dialectical concerns, or what I am labeling thought and politics. He indicates, in a way that echoes Adorno and Arendt's conception of thinking as never fixed and eternally subject to revision in light of the way it is mediated by other kinds of historical experience, that both thinking and politics enact a refusal of letting what currently is stand in for what must always necessarily be. In other words, he accuses what he calls dialectics of being undialectical in Adorno's sense: "Refuser à *ce qui est* le droit d'être éternellement « ce qui est », refuser à « ce qui est » le prédicat de la vérité, telle est en somme, du moins telle devrait être, la double démarche dialectique et métaphysique" ["To refuse to *what is* the right to be eternally 'what is,' to refuse to 'what is' the predicate of truth, that is, or at least that is what should be, the double process of dialectics and metaphysics"] (23). True thinking and true politics thus reveal the lie of what we might assume to be eternal or fixed, whether that be metaphysical truth or historical reality. The point seems to be, according to Fondane, to disrupt both the affirmation of and the desire for such impermanence:

> L'homme ne pourra pas se dérober au besoin de remette éternellement en question la signification de son existence, pour la simple raison qu'il ne peut s'imposer à son existence et que c'est l'existence qui s'impose à lui ; il ne peut renoncer à vouloir posséder la vérité, pour la simple raison que c'est la vérité qui ne renonce pas à lui. (24)
>
> [Man cannot shirk the need to question eternally the meaning of his existence, for the simple reason that he cannot impose himself on his existence and that existence imposes itself on him; he cannot renounce wanting to possess truth, for the simple reason that truth does not renounce him.]

To affirm a thinking of this sort is not to turn one's back on politics but to see both as united by a common desire to reject the temptation of easy answers or definitive solutions, a path which ends in dogmatism for the one and totalitarianism or fascism for the other. The anguish of thought as Fondane conceives it can thus be made to render a possible world thinkable politically in ways that emphasize the continuity of thought and politics rather than enforcing an artificial separation between them. Rather than separating the thinker from the world, thought serves to bring him all the more deeply into it but the instability and uncertainty that it catalyzes:

> Merveilleuse et atroce nuit ! Nuit étouffante où tout s'effondre, ou la pensée ne trouve rien à quoi s'accrocher, sinon à elle-même ; « pensée accrochant de la pensée et tirant » (Rimbaud, Lettre du voyant). Cette pensée angoissée n'est pas encore *libre*, mais la liberté est parmi ses *possibles*. […] Ce n'est plus une pensée *autonome* mais une pensée solidaire de l'existence, qui « participe » à l'existence. (29)
>
> [Marvelous and atrocious night! Stifling night where everything melts, where thought finds nothing to grasp onto besides itself; "thought holding onto itself and pulling" (Rimbaud, Lettre du voyant). That anguished thought is not yet *free*, but freedom is among its *possibilities*. […] It is no longer an *autonomous* thought in solidarity with existence, which "participates" in existence.]

The thinkers with whom I engage in this study reshape what it might mean to participate in existence via thought, and to live in the contradictions of its unending process of reimagining what it means to live the drama of the reconfigured subject-object relations that emerge from that process.

Chapter 1 explores the complex phenomenon of what Georges Bataille calls "inner experience" as he characterizes it in the book of that name, which proceeds via a fragmented and dialogical form and establishes a paradoxical, and at times contradictory, evocation of the writing of inner experience as both a record of experience and as the experience itself. By conceiving the kind of writing that Bataille undertakes in the book as akin to fiction, we can see the esthetic as a mediating factor between concepts and experience and the site of a transformed experience by and through concepts. What is at stake is not getting beyond conceptual notions such as "knowledge" or "self" but rather changing them via a process that alters them as it attempts to capture or reflect on them, an experience which brings an affective dimension of anguish to the dialectical thought process. In Bataille, thought reveals the falsity of a reasoned totality and of a unified subject. Like the category of thought itself, the notion of subject and object is not canceled in inner experience but understood differently, as the subject of dialectical thought becomes both subject and object of the experience. While Bataille occasionally suggests the desirability of the obliteration of the subject or the attainment of the void, to accomplish this would be to assign to thought a goal or endpoint, which would cancel inner experience altogether. The persistence of the reimagined dialectical subject thus becomes a key feature of the drama of inner experience as it plays itself out in Bataille's work.

Chapter 2 traces the nature and role of thought in the early work in French of Emil Cioran, beginning with the paradox that the failure of his oft-repeated desire for quietism and resignation brings him repeatedly back to the anguish and unease of thought in a way that leads his written reflections to become a thinking about the stakes of the refusal of thought. Cioran's notion of "thinking against oneself" captures a division both within thought itself and within the thinking subject; it serves to highlight that to achieve passivity or quietude by canceling thought would necessarily cancel the thinking subject at the same time, which means that passivity depends on its own cancelation in order to continue playing its role as an aspirational ideal in Cioran's writing. If it were not to cancel its own possibility of realization, it would become a goal for thought, which would install a teleological orientation to thought that Cioran opposes. The tension between skepticism and dogmatic conviction is what can prevent historical violence and catastrophe by never allowing the subject either to abandon the project of thought and pass into action on account of the dead end of skepticism or to advance strong political convictions untempered by the reflection that reveals the divided subject to itself. A similar dynamic is at play in the form of Cioran's writings themselves, where the sometimes strong assertions of a point of view are tempered by other moments that call for skepticism in the face of strongly held convictions. The impossibility of an Archimedean point by which one might evaluate truth claims about experience turns Cioran's thought away from an orientation to the goal of truth, which liberates thought from its object so that it becomes its own object in relation to the thinker. The final part of the chapter examines how thought and the form of Cioran's writing undo claims he sometimes makes about the eternal sameness of experience. Cioran's frequent evocation of insomnia illustrates the non-identity of the supposedly same with itself: the purportedly undifferentiated night reveals itself to the insomniac as the truth of the day, thus setting into motion the dialectical process of thought that breaks down the day-night opposition in order to reveal both the potential nothingness of the activity of waking life and the content-rich dynamism of a night that was supposedly the space of non-differentiated void. The non-undifferentiated night thus becomes the stage on which the drama of thought plays itself out in Cioran and allows readers to articulate, by reading not within but across his aphorisms, the dynamics of a thought that claims to be committed to what turns out to be an impossible quietude.

Chapter 3 engages the work of philosopher Clément Rosset on tragedy and the real, beginning with his claim that the real, which is ultimately unknowable, becomes a source of suffering. Rosset takes his distance from both optimism and pessimism by claiming that they, like Christianity, are united in their unwarranted assumptions about the nature of reality. His emphasis on dissonance stands in contradiction with an urge to reconcile the rift between thought and experience by positing what he calls joy or grace, but his refusal to engage that contradiction by means of thought leads to a potential meaninglessness in those affective relations which he posits. To call reality unknowable and therefore to claim that attempts to interpret or assign meaning to it are futile is to incite a dialectical relation between meaning and meaninglessness to which Rosset responds by shutting it down rather than engaging it. His unconditional affirmation of the real calls out for thought to engage with the contradictions such a position entails, but Rosset has recourse instead to the notion of tautology whereby all we can posit is that the real is equal to itself. To argue, as Rosset does, that the real is unrepresentable is to theorize the real and make interpretive claims about it, just as to claim that tragedy is meaninglessness is to make a claim about meaning. Rosset ultimately reinforces a totalizing conceptual vision to which dialectical engagement with these contradictions gives the lie, and he is forced to posit a rift between thinking and experience rather than the dialectically constituted establishment of thought as a kind of experience.

His attempt to account for dissonance in a gesture toward reconciliation with the tragic by an experience of secularized grace reveals the redemptive logic to which he is ultimately led. I argue that the persistence of dissonance in that redemptive framework necessitates a more dialectical approach than Rosset is willing to grant to the mutually constituting categories of dissonance and consonance, of the real and its interpretation, and of thought and experience.

1

Georges Bataille: Thinking as Anguished Adventure

Is it possible to conceive of thought as a kind of fiction, as the account of an attempt to push thought to the very limits of the mind? We could call Georges Bataille's writing of what he calls "inner experience" the attempt to grab hold of our inability to grab hold of thought, to freeze its movement in order to represent it in a way that does not alter the thought in the very act of attempting to represent it. In this chapter, I explore the ways in which Bataille's attempts to work through, name, or seize inner experience end up showing that to seize it would be unfaithful to it, because it would cancel the goal-less feature that is constitutive of inner experience to begin with. By not capturing or representing inner experience, the process by which he sets out to do so reveals instead something else about the nature of the dialectical subject and about how writing about inner experience becomes itself the experience of thought. To learn how we might read *L'Expérience intérieure* involves the same sort of working-through that the first-person subject of the book undertakes; it requires the reader to consider familiar categories such as thinking or the subject-object relation in new and unexpected ways as readers enter the experience described by the writing subject but go beyond it at the same time. To do so is to risk our own undoing as readers, and this becomes an important aspect of attempting to read *L'Expérience intérieure* in the sense of both understanding the text and reflecting on the mediated and mediating nature of the thought into which that interpretive act takes us.

L'Expérience intérieure is a largely unclassifiable book. It consists of five parts, the first four of which are composed largely of paragraph-length short sections, sometimes alternating with passages in italics that provide later commentary by the author on the passages in Roman font; the last section is a short series of free verse poems. The first section is an "Ebauche d'introduction à l'expérience intérieure" ["Draft of an Introduction to Inner Experience"] while the middle three sections are structured around "Le Supplice" ["Torture"], the title of the second section, with the third part entitled "Antécédents du supplice" and the fourth "Post-scriptum au supplice" ["Post-Scriptum to the Torture"]. It is perhaps easier to say what this book is not than to say what it is: despite what first impressions of the book's title may suggest, it is not a series of calm reflections on contemplation, or a record of the wanderings of a frivolous mind in solitude closing itself off to the world. Exactly what it is, however, is harder to say. *L'Expérience intérieure* poses itself above all as a text that challenges readers to figure out how to read it, and to recognize that that effort is itself folded into the notion of inner experience, such that reading becomes not an act of discovery of the author's experience but itself an experience for both author and reader.[1] In fact, one could argue that if readers claim to have figured out how to read the book, they have understood nothing of it; the failure to make definitive claims about how to read it is, like the author's failure to establish a definitive characterization of inner experience itself, part of the experience.[2]

By affirming that claiming to understand inner experience is to have understood nothing about it, we are already in the realm of paradox that guides most of Bataille's writing about it. While it is impossible to communicate inner experience, it has no existence except in the words Bataille uses to characterize it and, in that sense, it exists as a purely verbal phenomenon, an experience of language in both the subjective and objective senses of the genitive "of." Giving verbal form to the experience is itself the experience in an important sense, as is the process of reading that text, and yet the text does not entirely lose its status as, at the same time, some kind of record of some other experience that the text is seeking to describe or report. If inner experience precedes or surpasses language while, at the same time, it can only be constituted as language in a process which itself becomes experience, then inner experience becomes inaccessible because the words the author uses to evoke it would kill precisely the experience the words aim to represent. I would claim that the text could helpfully be understood as a fiction, a verbal rendering that constructs an experience from the basic paradox that inner experience can only be brought to consciousness through reading and writing in the construction of the text that Bataille writes, on which he himself comments as a reader in the passages in italics, and with which his other readers enter in their own variant of the kind of experience he constructs in the text and to which that text invites anyone who tries to make sense of it.

To see the text as a kind of fiction is also to establish its relationship to philosophy. While Bataille is staunchly anti-systematic in his approach (precisely because thought cannot be adequately accounted for in a philosophical system), the implied relation between words and experience, whether that be a role of mediating or constituting the experience, and the role of rational thought and concepts in understanding or impeding our understanding of experience, initiates a dialogue with philosophical reflection on those questions and implies a set of philosophical assumptions undergirding the writing and setting the course for the interpretive moves that readers will make. As Kane Faucher indicates:

> Bataille defines his inner experience as a "project," and as such, he commits himself to a view that concepts do not condition experience. [...] Explanations are post facto denominations on real experience, and as such are only symptoms of experience. It is the error of rational thought to believe that words adequately explain experience or objects, especially since words rely on concepts, and concepts can be too baggy or loose to account for the minute variations, nuances and differences manifest in experience and objects. (168)

Likewise, Leslie Hill argues about Bataille, Pierre Klossowski, and Maurice Blanchot that if they:

> may be found at times to substitute literary fiction for philosophical discourse, it is not in order to abandon philosophy. Nor is it to abandon philosophy to itself. On the contrary, it is to pursue a philosophical project, albeit one that is incompatible with his philosophy's own image of itself as an authoritative telling of universal truths; and by pursuing the question of literature—the question asked by literature—to the limit, it is to begin to question philosophy from a place that is at one and the same time within its boundaries yet beyond them. (Hill 20-1)

I will argue that considering *L'Expérience intérieure* as a kind of fiction allows us to position the esthetic as a middle ground between concepts and experience. The "error of rational thought" by which words are taken adequately to represent concepts means that there is a kind of remainder in effect, a surplus of meaning even within the context of the inadequacy of the words vis-à-vis concepts, and the esthetic, in its attention to the way form mediates and helps constitute meaning, allows us to address that gap or remainder that is in play when we examine a book like *L'Expérience intérieure* from a perspective that would only seek to account for its conceptual content.

This attention to the esthetic carves out a place of central importance for words and meaning in the elaboration of inner experience and makes it impossible for explanations to remain mere "symptoms of experience." By according words a key role in the constitution of experience itself, we get past the impasse of the inaccessibility of a purportedly nonverbal experience of which a written record can be at best an imperfect copy or representation. The unconventional form of Bataille's book gestures toward the essay and the personal journal, but in its ultimate refusal to map completely onto any established genre, Bataille performs a kind of solution to the problem of words and experience by opening inner experience to the realm of the esthetic and allowing us to see his words *as* experience without, for all that, sacrificing the complexity of the question of words' relationship to experience.

If words not only represent but also create the real, in a way that calls out for interpretation in ways akin to the processes at play in a work of fiction where words go beyond a merely communicative function, then seeing words as part of experience, and reading *L'Expérience intérieure* accordingly, helps address the aspect of Bataille's project that Faucher has identified: "Discursive Reason […] is not the entirety of the real, and it is precisely Bataille's project to demonstrate Reason's limit, to expose exactly where Reason expires and ecstasy of life in stochastic rapture begins" (169). Rather than limiting the potential of a book like *L'Expérience intérieure*, this identification of the limit of discursive reason and of the ineffability of something like rapture opens new possibilities for seeing Bataille's project itself, and the text which forms a crucial part of that project, as a kind of experience. There is an important kinship here between Bataille's intellectual and affective exploration of the limit and Adorno's conception of it within the context of his characterization of dialectical thought:

> The limit must be at once posited and transcended. And in this moment—that the limit is acknowledged in all seriousness as unavoidably posited but as one that must nonetheless be transcended—you have the simple form of logical contradiction which this thinking encounters once it no longer moves naively within the realm of either formal-logical or merely empirical knowledge, but actually becomes a philosophy of reflection—in other words, once it moves to a realm where the empirical moment and the formal moment can be recognized as mediated with one another. (Adorno *Introduction* 67)

As I have suggested in the introduction, Bataille's writing on inner experience can be characterized as dialectical if we retain emphasis on the negative capacity of dialectics, its focus on contradiction and movement rather than resolution. According to Asgar Sorensen, "Bataille's dialectics can be said to be the result of a determinate negation of Hegel" (598). He argues that "for Bataille, it is

[...] possible to criticize Hegel and Kojève very strongly and still (or perhaps precisely therefore) consider his own thinking dialectical in the same sense as those criticized, i.e. those negated" (600).[3] This results in a Bataillean dialectics which is "neither the ancient conception nor the Hegelian conception" and which offers "a comprehension of the material *flux* of life as a historical process, i.e. grasping it with concepts that do not degrade it to, at best, a deficient mode of being" (604).

Bataille's text could be seen above all as the drama of playing out the positing and transcendence of the limit through the dialectical movement of thought. Given that the form, genre, and structure are crucial to the effect this text has upon its readers, its thematic concerns, which include mysticism, absolute knowledge, laughter, and eroticism in their relation to inner experience, may be the least interesting aspect of the book. If we are to see the first-person voice in the book as a kind of character, an important part of the "plot" of the book is the continual constitution, destruction, and reconstitution of the self through thought, writing, and reading. While Bataille often engages in what Jean-Luc Nancy has called a "writing *against* meaning" (336), this is not to say that meaning is unavailable or that the text absolutely resists it. In fact, Bataille's affirmation of paradox and contradiction implies that we need to preserve the possibility of a meaning that would somehow account for the text's own resistance to it. Succumbing to the temptation to eliminate meaning as a category is too simplistic an approach and is unfaithful to the complex contradictions which Bataille's texts elicit. Nancy affirms that, in the case of Bataille, reading "must remain weighty, hampered, and, without ceasing to decode, must stay just this side of decoding" (336). Puzzling out what such a thing could mean, or what kinds of reading practices it could engender, is the main task of the reader of *L'Expérience intérieure*.

Like inner experience itself, which can never be grasped and completely defined, the self constituted in and through inner experience is the negation of a definitive and bounded self. As Julia Kristeva indicates in her essay on experience in Bataille:

> Loin de se fixer dans le savoir, le « moi » dans l'expérience intérieure démontre que ce que Hegel visait par le « savoir absolu » [...] est un savoir impossible. Pourquoi ? Parce que demandant une traversée du « voir », il ne peut sa-voir aucun objet fixe, mais n'aperçoit à la place de l'objet qu'une « catastrophe », une contradiction, une lutte non localisable et non identifiable. (290)[4]

[Far from fixing itself in knowledge, the "self" in inner experience demonstrates that what Hegel aimed at with his "absolute knowledge" [...] is an impossible knowledge. Why? Because by asking for a penetration of "seeing," he cannot know any fixed object, but notices only, in place of the object, a "catastrophe," a contradiction, an unlocalizable and unidentifiable fight.]

This is not to say that the self and inner experience should simply be dismissed as non-knowable. As Allan Stoekl indicates, in Bataille "knowing implies a dialectical advance: not-knowing can be overturned and lost in knowing, but this will be a (necessarily dialectical) knowing that is conscious of the phenomenon of not-knowing, that recognizes it, that studies its effects in the world (and which, consequently, betrays it)" (290). It is not a case of getting "beyond" knowledge or the concept but rather of redefining what we consider knowledge to be along the lines of a more dynamic model.[5] The reading and writing of *L'Expérience intérieure* thus set in motion a "plot" whereby such categories are emptied and redefined in an always unstable way by a dynamic reading or writing subject who becomes the stage whereby the anguish of the perpetual unseizable nature of experience is played out. As I will show in greater detail, there is thus a kind of dramatic structure to the "plot" that plays out in *L'Expérience intérieure* that allows us to see it as a drama of thought, a sort of narrative journey on which we accompany the speaking subject and which we also undertake ourselves through the act of making meaning from the parts of the text in relation to what we attempt to construct as its whole, all in the context of the eternally shifting terrain of defining the terms of the drama and the way they construct and are constructed by the subject who is the main character.[6]

L'Expérience intérieure is, as I have suggested, an unusual book, heterogeneous and multilayered. As Bataille's most recent translator puts it: "The book that emerges [from the process of writing], if it is a book, contains prose and poetry, argument and autobiography, analysis and exegesis, as well as the jargons of distinct discourses: religion, philosophy, and poetics most prominently" (Kendall xiv). The book's publication history reflects this heterogeneity as well. The first edition appeared in February 1943 and included some sections that had appeared prior. The second edition, which also included *Méthode de Méditation* and a post-script, was published in 1954, now within the context of a larger multivolume project that Bataille planned to entitle *La Somme athéologique*, a term he first used in a letter to Raymond Queneau in March 1950.[7] The version that appears in Bataille's *Œuvres complètes* is accompanied by more than a hundred pages of Bataille's notes about the project and a variety of plans about what texts it would include. *L'Expérience intérieure* is thus a finished and unfinished work, in dialogue both in the main text and in the notes with its author's rereading of and commentary on the text. The book is structured, as I have indicated, around the section called "Le Supplice"; for Stuart Kendall, Bataille enacts torture upon the text itself and "tears it apart":

> He interrupts his arguments with autobiographical reminiscences and flights of poetic language. He abandons his outlines, leaves things unfinished. He makes a mockery of rhetorical modes of persuasion: combines forms and registers, interjects quotations to the point of self-effacement, shifts between temporal moments—past and present—and personal and impersonal modes of discourse. (Kendall xiv)[8]

In a similar vein, Denis Hollier claims that "*L'Expérience intérieure* is no more than a string of prefaces indicating something foreign to the book, that perhaps plays within the book, but only as something making fun of it" (45). Text and commentary, reading and writing, seriousness and playfulness are inseparable in the experience of reading and writing *L'Expérience intérieure*, the instability of its form mirroring the instability of the kind of thought it enacts and, more in fact than mirroring, underscoring the impossibility of separating the thought from the form in which it takes shape.

This impossible separation further calls into question the distinction between words and concepts and indicating the ever-shifting nature of both so that any laying out of concepts in words can only be temporary. The words provide a snapshot of a concept at a given moment in time that can be looked on and analyzed at a different moment, in an act of interpretation that changes the character of the original concept itself such that meaning always occurs in an unseizable and dynamic present. An act of reading that looks back at a past text transforms it by intervening in its purported stability on the page. Bataille inscribes the difficulty of reading and writing the text into the text itself: "Je traine en moi comme un fardeau le souci d'écrire ce livre. [...] Je compose avec [l'idée] à tel pont qu'on m'enlèverait un membre plus facilement" ["I carry within me like a burden the concern for writing this book. [...] I create with [the idea] to such a degree that one could remove one of my limbs more easily" (65, translation modified)] (5: 75).[9] If he characterizes writing the text as painfully difficult, he claims near the outset that reading his own text is akin to revisiting a moment of intoxication from a later standpoint of sobriety: "Mais qu'en est-il de nous quand, désintoxiqués, nous apprenons ce que nous sommes ? perdus entre des bavards, dans une nuit où nous ne pouvons que haïr l'apparence de lumière qui vient des bavardages. La souffrance s'avouant du désintoxiqué est l'objet de ce livre" (5: 10) ["But what happens to us when, disintoxicated, we learn what we are? Lost among babblers, in a night wherein we can only hate the appearance of light that comes from babbling. The self-acknowledged suffering of the disintoxicated is the object of this book" (4)]. Observing a state of intoxication after the fact changes the initial experience, however; it is not a mere report on a prior state but an intervention in it that transforms the static past event into a dynamic one or rekindles the dynamism that had been present in the original experience, but now transformed in light of the reading and interpreting that is no less of an experience itself: "Si je disais décidément : « j'ai vu Dieu », ce que je vois changerait" (5: 16) ["If I said decisively: 'I have seen God,' that which I have seen would change"]. Bataille thus underscores from the outset the experiential nature of looking back or reporting on experience, an act he sees as a reply: "L'expression de l'expérience intérieure doit de quelque façon répondre à son mouvement, ne peut être une sèche traduction verbale, exécutable en ordre" (5: 18) ["The expression of inner experience must in some way respond to its movement, cannot be a dry verbal translation, executed on command" (13)].

Bataille's preliminary remarks implicate the reader in what is to follow; they establish both a kinship and distance between writer and reader: "L'esprit se meut dans un monde étrange où l'angoisse et l'extase se composent. Une telle expérience n'est pas ineffable, mais je la communique à qui l'ignore : sa tradition [...] exige d'autrui angoisse et désir préalables" ["The mind moves in a strange world where anguish and ecstasy take shape" (4)] and there is "rien d'apaisant" ["nothing calming"] in the experience (5: 10); indeed he characterizes the book as "le récit d'un désespoir" (5: 11) ["the narrative of a despair" (4)]. On the last page of this "Foreword," Bataille establishes the world as given to humans "ainsi qu'une énigme à résoudre" (5: 11) ["as if it were an enigma to resolve" (4)] but traces the process by which he realizes that the enigma is unresolvable, which itself comes as a kind of revelation from the experience of thought. This, however, is not his ending point but rather the start, the sign under which we enter the book that follows, one that commits us to the impossibility of resolution and the perpetual instability of thought without at the same time giving ourselves over to the irrational, which remains incomplete without the reflection on potentially irrational experience. Such reflection transforms the event, brings it within at least the possibility of partial communication, and encourages us to draw conclusions from the necessary failure of mapping either concepts or nonrational experience onto words. I am not simply trying to "tame" Bataille or discredit his emphasis on the intensity of violence or sacrifice by claiming that such phenomena always exist in and as writing by a subject in his works. Irrationality, which potentially leads to sterile, stable-seeming but dead and inaccessible past experience, is ultimately just one element in Bataille's thought that can never conclude, that draws on nonrational experience but surpasses it by engaging it as a term in the process of thinking. This kind of dynamic thought leads Bataille to "une énigme nouvelle, et celle-là, je le sus aussitôt, insoluble" (5: 11) ["a new enigma, and I quickly knew that one was unsolvable" (5)]. The preface ends with Bataille's indication that, in the face of the discovery of the impossible solution of the enigma, he abandoned the text he had planned, which had been intended to present that solution, and wrote "Le Supplice" ["Torture"] instead. Thus, the non-solution of the enigma leads not to an abandonment of thought generally but to its transformation into something more faithful to non-resolution of thought.[10] While such an irresolvable enigma is "amère" ["bitter"] and inspires feelings of impotence, the experience of thought drives him on not despite but because of the fact that the thought can bring no definitive resolution unless it were to be unfaithful to the experience that it provokes. It is no wonder, then, that all of the writing that follows will have an unfinished quality, will feature a mind turning back on itself in order to bring past thought into the present by its very transformation or negation.

In the first large section of the work, "Ebauche d'une introduction à l'expérience intérieure" ["Draft of an Introduction to Inner Experience"], Bataille turns his attention to questions of definition of inner experience, whose very characterization seems to be an unsolvable enigma both in this first attempt at definition and in other contrasting descriptions that he offers throughout the book:

> J'entends par *expérience intérieure* ce que d'habitude on nomme *expérience mystique* : les états d'extase, de ravissement, au moins d'émotion méditée. Mais je songe moins à l'expérience *confessionnelle* [...] qu'à une expérience nue, libre d'attaches, même d'origine, à quelque confession que ce soit. C'est pourquoi je n'aime pas le mot *mystique*.
>
> Je n'aime pas non plus les définitions étroites. (5: 15)
>
> [By *inner experience*, I understand what one usually calls *mystical experience*, states of ecstasy, of ravishment, at least of meditated emotion. But I am thinking

less of *confessional* experience [...] than of a bare experience, free of ties, even of an origin, to any confession whatsoever. This is why I don't like the word *mystical*.

Nor do I like narrow definitions. (9)]

The introduction of the mystical blurs the definition more than it clarifies it, since Bataille proposes it as a synonym of inner experience before immediately identifying ways in which it is distinct from it, inviting misunderstanding from the outset. This definition communicates above all the slipperiness of the attempt to define the notion of inner experience and seems to set up a distinction between the kind of immediacy that ecstasy implies and intellectual experience.[11] As I have suggested, reflection on experience becomes itself a kind of experience, which calls into question any distinction one might have wanted to draw between inner experience and thought based on this definition.

A note that did not make it into the final text of the book expands and qualifies the initial definition. After a variant on the definition above, Bataille adds:

> Je ne proposerai pas de définition plus serrée. En dernier lieu je montrerai l'expérience intérieure liée à la nécessité, pour l'esprit, de tout mettre en question—sans trêve ni repos concevables. [...] Rien de plus loin des possibilités qui m'appartiennent—ou des intentions de ce livre—qu'un mysticisme quelconque [...]. (5: 427)

> [I will not propose a tighter definition. At the end I will show that inner experience is linked to the mind's need to put everything in question—ceaselessly and without a break. [...] Nothing farther from the possibilities available to me—or from the intentions of this book—than some mysticism [...].][12]

By aligning inner experience with the need to put all into question, Bataille places it solidly within the domain of thinking that seemed excluded from experiences such as mysticism and ecstasy. What he suggests here is not a move away from thinking but rather an understanding of it as distinct from the philosophical operation of the systematic development of concepts. Thinking here is of the kind that turns answers into questions but does not renounce the life of the mind in favor of some more immediate experience incompatible with or irreducible to words.[13] So, taken together, the note and the published text establish that inner experience is a mysticism and also very far from any sort of mysticism. The act of puzzling out how these contradictions can coexist, and what that might imply about the relationship between words, their common definitions, and the possibility of radically questioning what we could mean by those words becomes, in all its anguishing complexity, precisely the kind of experience Bataille describes by claiming inner experience as the act of putting all in question.

In fact, inner experience of this thought-filled type becomes opposed to mysticism entirely according to this same note, precisely on the grounds of the mystic's relation to pre-established knowledge and familiar conclusions:

> Un « mystique » voit ce qu'il veut [...]. Et de même il découvre—ce qu'il savait. Sans doute il est des volontés, des croyances inégalement favorables, mais en tel [*homme ?*] l'expérience n'introduit rien qui n'ait d'abord été dans l'entendement—*sinon la contestation de l'entendement comme origine des croyances.* (5: 428)

> [A "mystic" sees what he wants [...]. And similarly he discovers—what he knew. No doubt there are wills and beliefs unequally favorable, but in such [*a man?*] experience introduces not that was not first in the understanding—*except for the realization that the understanding is the origin of beliefs.*]

On this view, writing becomes more akin to inner experience than mysticism because it is in and through writing that conclusions are questioned and paradoxes enumerated. Bataille himself indicates that inner experience is akin to science in that the attempt to observe or record the experience changes what is observed: "La science, la connaissance scientifique, peuvent il est vrai se donner l'expérience comme objet, mais il arrive au cours de savantes études que les conditons de l'observation changent la nature du phénomène observé. C'est le cas, s'il en est, de l' « expérience intérieure »" ["Science and scientific knowledge can, it is true, give themselves experience as an objective, but it happens in the course of studies that the conditions of observation change the nature of the phenomenon observed. That is the case with 'inner experience'"] (5: 428). Where inner experience differs from both science and mysticism, as they are portrayed in this note, is in its refusal of knowledge as its goal. If mysticism arrives at pre-established knowledge and science aims, like systematic philosophy, at well-established conclusions supported by its evidence, inner experience remains goal-less and result-less:

> La fin de l' « expérience » est l' « expérience » elle-même et non telle connaissance acquise après coup sans passer par elle. [...] La science appréhende des objets pour les distinguer les uns des autres et saisir entre eux des rapports constants. L' « expérience » fuit des connaissances de cet ordre : elle se distingue plus nettement de la pensée discursive [...]. (5: 430)

[The goal of "experience" is "experience" itself and not any knowledge acquired after the fact without passing through it. [...] Science apprehends objects in order to distinguish them from each other and to capture constant relations between them. 'Experience' flees knowledge of that kind: it distinguishes itself more clearly from discursive thought [...].]

Bataille's definitional impulse is an important part of his project precisely because it demonstrates the impossibility of definitive definition of concepts such as inner experience, which appeal to equally unstable concepts such as mysticism, with which it aligns itself at the same time as it establishes a definitive difference from it. Following Bataille into the labyrinth of definition leads the reader to precisely the kind of experience he is attempting to characterize, one that we could now also consider as the cognate word experiment, a performative thought experiment that engages with the concept in order to lead us away from the concept but keep us within the realm of thought understood differently, as the endless process that resists conclusion because any definitive conclusion could only lead us to the false, or the static, or the facile.

Experience in general is for Bataille a concern with the human limit: "J'appelle expérience un voyage au bout du possible de l'homme. Chacun peut ne pas faire ce voyage, mais, s'il le fait, cela suppose niées les autorités, les valeurs existantes, qui limitent le possible" (5: 19) ["I call experience a journey to the end of the possible of man. Not everyone can take this journey, but, if one does, this supposes the negation of authorities, of existing values, that limit the possible" (14)]. A tension remains between intellectual experience and practices of violence or eroticism which would also test human limits and contest authority. But as we have seen, those experiences inevitably lead back to questions of interpretation, of thinking, in order for them to have any meaning in terms of modes of exploring the limits of the human. Once again, Adorno's characterization of dialectical thinking might be said to be a theoretical articulation of the kind of intellectual experience that Bataille performs in his own text. For Adorno, dialectical thought measures itself against lived experience, but he does not claim that experience surpasses thought; rather, they are mutually constitutive and depend on the conceptual categories of subject and object:

Thinking which genuinely comprehends things, in contrast with one that merely orders and classifies them, is a kind of thinking that measures itself against the living experience which we have with objects. It is a thinking which acknowledges the moment of conceptual order which it must naturally retain— for I cannot indeed think without concepts—but continually confronts that moment of conceptual ordering with the living experience that I actually have. And out of the tension between both these moments—between conceptual order and that pre-conceptual experience from which concepts themselves have also nonetheless always sprung—such thinking, in a process of constant reflection on both the matter and thought itself, eventually leads us out beyond a thinking which simply subsumes things beneath its grasp in a merely external fashion. (*Introduction* 136)

And it is at that reflective moment that thought joins experience, becomes part of it, becomes itself an experience, in ways that tear down the semantic and conceptual distinction between action and thought. It is important to note that Bataille immediately associates the negation of prevailing authorities and values, thus underscoring the political implications of the kind of experience he is describing. I will address these political consequences further below; they are important in terms of addressing the critique of Bataille that some leveled in terms of publishing *L'Expérience intérieure*, a book that at first glance seems consumed with an isolated model of the self engaged in what might be dismissed as frivolous thought experiments, in wartime.

While what we have is not an engaged political text in the conventional sense, it would be an absurd and simplistic reading of the text to propose that it is somehow devoid of political implications or complicit with fascism. It is important to note that Bataille is not calling for an anarchical removal of authority when he supposes the negation of existing authority, as he writes in the passage quoted above, but rather the potential reimagining of authority, its redefiniton and realignment in ways akin to the emptying out and reconceptualizing of categories such as experience, mysticism, and the like. In fact, experience does not oppose authority but is itself authority as Bataille understands it here, an insight that Bataille credits Maurice Blanchot with enumerating in conversation with him when he tells him that "l'expérience elle-même est l'autorité (mais que l'autorité s'expie)" (5: 19) ["experience itself is the authority (but that authority expiates itself)" (14)]. Experience comes to be identified with the function of negation, so any reconceptualizing will involve a dialectical interplay between destruction and construction, the negation of current relations to authority and the setting in place of a temporary and provisional new relation that is aware of its position in the ongoing process of negation that thought entails. This is the sense in which experience as Bataille understands it as "une contestation sans limite" ["a contestation without limit"] leading him to define inner experience as "l'incessante mise en question de l'existence par elle-même" ["the incessant putting into question of experience by itself"] (6: 289). This process of continual contestation and negation installs experience itself as the new, very different, kind of authority: "Du fait qu'elle est négation d'autres valeurs, d'autres autorités, l'expérience ayant l'existence positive deviant elle-même positivement la valeur *et l'autorité*" (5: 19) ["From the fact that it is the negation of other values, of other authorities, experience having positive existence itself becomes value *and authority* positively" (14)].

It is becoming clear that the work of the mind is not in opposition to more direct or conventional forms of "action" but rather something like their fuller form or their completion, insofar as action depends on the work of the mind in order to be conceived as experience at all. Rather than maintaining a thought-action dichotomy, what Bataille is working out in these first pages of the book is a reimagining of what we understand thought to be, by wresting it from orientation toward a goal that we would then label knowledge. The real opposition, then, is not between thinking and acting but between thinking and knowing, whereby knowing is one of the most important limits to be questioned:

> Ce qui préserve en apparence la philosophie est le peu d'acuité des expériences dont partent les phénoménologues. Cette absence d'équilibre ne survit pas à la mise en jeu de l'expérience allant au bout du possible. Quand aller au bout signifie tout au moins ceci : que la limite qu'est la connaissance comme fin soit franchie.
>
> (5: 20)

[What preserves the appearance of philosophy is the lack of acuity of the experiences from which the phenomenologists set out. This absence of equilibrium does not survive the play of experience going to the end of the possible. When going to the end means at least this: that the limit that is knowledge as a goal to be crossed.][14]

To reinvest thinking as experience and as authority is to orient thought away from knowledge, since such an orientation is precisely what has limited thought's potential according to Bataille:

"l'avancée de l'intelligence eut pour effet secondaire de diminuer le possible en un domaine qui parut à l'intelligence étranger: *celui de l'experience intérieure*" (5: 20) ["the advance of that intelligence has had the secondary effect of diminishing the possible into a realm that appears foreign to intelligence: *that of inner experience*" (15)]. The affective dimension of such an approach to thought is an integral part of the experience as Bataille frames it and cannot be separated from it: "cette expérience née du non-savoir y demeure décidément" (5: 15) ["this experience, born of nonknowledge, remains there decidedly" (9)]. This is accomplished in a state of fever and anguish: "l'expérience est la mise en question (à l'épreuve), dans la fièvre et l'angoisse, de ce qu'un homme sait du fait d'être" (5: 16) ["experience is the questioning (testing), in fever and anguish, what man knows of the facts of being" (9)]. Part of the fever and anguish stems, no doubt, from the necessary impossibility of the very ideas about inner experience that Bataille seeks to put in place. In an annex to the text, Bataille complicates yet again the relation between experience and knowledge by claiming that experience needs to be communicable, but that such communication would draw it closer to precisely the realm of knowledge from which he seeks to distinguish it:

> Je propose d'élaborer un ensemble de données scolastiques concernant l'expérience intérieure. Je crois qu'une expérience intérieure n'est possible que si elle peut être communiquée et qu'elle ne pourrait être communiquée en dernier ressort sans atteindre l'objectivité de la scolastique. La communication poétique ou même simplement littéraire n'est sans doute ni vaine ni évitable mais elle engage à la fuite de la conscience et à sa dissipation en fumée. (6: 283)
>
> [I propose to elaborate an ensemble of scholastic data concerning inner experience. I think that an inner experience is only possible if it can be communicated and it could not be communicated in the end without attaining the objectivity of scholasticism. Poetic or even simply literary communication is no doubt neither vain nor avoidable but it entails the flight of consciousness and its dissipation in smoke.]

Like observation, communication is necessary for a phenomenon's existence but at the same time alters the phenomenon, or even dissipates it completely, leaving us again with a split between a (perhaps fictional) thing-in-itself distinct from our representation of it, the latter being all we can claim and work with conceptually. Yet even this is not graspable in the sense of our having definitive knowledge about it; such knowledge can only exist under the sign of negation, transformed into a knowledge of the impossibility of definitive knowledge. Such a realization causes Bataille to fall back on notions of living as opposed to thinking the experience: "Ce qu'on peut nommer l'expérience intérieure existe sans aucun doute et si nous pouvons craindre à la rigueur de ne pas atteindre une extacte connaissance de ce qu'elle est, du moins pouvons-nous tenter de la vivre : dans ce sens, même les erreurs sont valables" ["What we can call inner experience exists without any doubt and if we can possibly fear not attaining an exact knowledge of what it is, at least we can try to live it: in that sense, even errors are valuable"] (6: 287). But what does it mean to "live" an experience, especially in light of what we have already established about the necessity of thought for completing a lived experience, without which one could be said in a real sense not to have had the experience at all? And on what grounds can Bataille affirm that inner experience exists "without any doubt?"

Bataille describes an attempt at knowing that leads only to the knowledge that he knows nothing; a related desire is that of wanting to be all, to be the totality, and the falling into anguish because of the impossibility of knowing and of making sense: "l'occasion de cette angoisse est mon non-savoir, le non-sens sans remède" (5: 67) ["the occasion of this anguish is my nonknowledge, nonsense without remedy" (58)]. Bataille links totality to knowledge as a regulatory ideal but recognizes its impossibility, so that the desire for totality becomes a motor of thought as inner experience only under the sign of negation, as thought can only advance the impossibility of becoming the totality and the self-identical, which Bataille calls the *ipse*. This impossibility is further underscored when Bataille frames it as the desire to communicate while remaining the totality, which is a logical impossibility: "L'angoissse est donnée dans le theme du savoir lui-même : *ipse*, par le savoir, je voudrais être tout, donc communiquer, me perdre, cependant demeurer *ipse*" (5: 67) ["Anguish is given in the theme of nonknowledge itself: as *ipse*, I would like to be everything through knowledge, therefore to communicate, lose myself, yet to remain *ipse*" (58)]. In the process of seeking the *ipse* the subject risks self-loss but without gaining the object in the process, even though one needs the other in order to attain ipseity.[15] The process leads to what Bataille calls *le ravissement*, but this state ultimately leads back to the subject:

> Dans le ravissement, mon existence retrouve un sens, mais le sens se réfère aussitôt à l'*ipse*, devient *mon* ravissement, un ravissement que je *ipse*, possède, donnant satisfaction à ma volonté d'être tout. Dès que j'en reviens là cesse la communication, la perte de moi-même, j'ai cessé de m'abandonner, je reste là, mais avec un savoir nouveau.
>
> Le mouvement recommence à partir de là. (5: 68)

> [In rapture, my existence recovers a meaning, but the meaning immediately refers to the *ipse*, becomes *my* rapture, a rapture that I *ipse* possess, giving satisfaction to my will to be everything. As soon as I return there, communication, the loss of my self ceases, I have ceased to abandon myself, I remain there, but with a new knowledge.
>
> The movement starts again from there. (58)]

The process by which the self is unable to sustain itself as totality but recognizes, through knowledge gained, the impossibility of dwelling in the totality has political stakes in that it allows the subject to resist the stasis of the myth of totality. By recognizing it only under the sign of the impossible, the subject is safeguarded from action that attempts to stop the movement of the dialectic by imposing a kind of necessarily false totality on the self or allowing it to subsume the other in a nondialectical identity that suppresses difference.

Bataille's descriptions of the adventures of these experiences, from ravishment to anguish and joy and back after a period of exhaustion, are of an ambiguous status: are they reports on experience or an evocation of an experience conjured by the writing itself and constituted as such by the interpretive comments Bataille intersperses with the description of the experience? See, for instance, a passage such as this:

> Au début de cette nuit, l'image précise en moi de l'harmonie monacale me communiquait l'extase : sans doute par la sottise à laquelle je m'abandonnais de cette façon. L'inviabilité, l'impossible ! dans la disharmonie à laquelle *je dois* honnêtement me tenir, l'harmonie seule, en raison du *je dois*, représente une possibilité de disharmonie : malhonnêteté nécessaire, mais on ne peut devenir malhonnête par un souci d'honnêteté. (5: 73)

> [At the beginning of this night, the precise image of myself in monastic harmony communicated ecstasy to me: undoubtedly through the foolishness to which I abandoned myself in this way. Nonviability, the impossible! In the disharmony to which *I must* honestly adhere, harmony alone, because of the *I must*, represents a possibility of disharmony; necessary dishonesty, but one cannot become dishonest through a concern for honesty. (63)]

The experience goes hand in hand with its interpretation, to the point where the interpretation becomes woven in as an integral part of the experience in ways that don't allow for a separation between the two or a privileging of the immediacy of the experience over its conceptualization, despite what Bataille might sometimes indicate about the primacy of immediate experience. The immediacy of experience, like the desire for totality, can exist only as conceptualized under the sign of its impossibility, a negation that provides the motor of the experience, different from the one that Bataille explicitly affirms but to which he arrives through the discourse of the book itself.

This conception of thought as experience is performed in *L'Expérience intérieure* in ways that are best revealed when engaging with it actively in a way that goes beyond the surface of what some of the claims seem to be saying. When, for instance, Bataille states that "il faut *vivre* l'expérience" (5: 21) ["one must *live* the experience" (15)], it is only in the context of puzzling out the complex relationship between thought and experience, the one that leads necessarily to a conception of thought *as* experience, that a reader is able to see that the simple affirmation that seems to be operating in that statement cannot, on Bataille's own view, be possible. The very linguistic imperative that it announces about living experience gives the lie to the possibility of separating supposedly direct lived experience from the act of thought that would purportedly be its opposite or a pale copy or representation of the lived experience. Bataille himself indicates as much in a note composed in 1953: "Dans ces livres déjà [including *L'Expérience intérieure*], l'expérience se composait avec la réflexion sur elle. Il est vrai que j'ai fait la part belle à l'*expérience* ..., que la réflexion, *sans laquelle l'expérience ne serait pas*, y est balbutiante, incertaine" ["In those books already [including *Inner Experience*], experience was composed with reflection on it. It is true that I accorded the greater share to *experience* ..., that reflection, *without which experience would not be*, is stammering, uncertain"] (5: 492). Far from limiting experience or opposing itself to it, reason, newly understood as independent of the system or the totality, can, by thinking against itself, both construct and, crucially, tear down what it has built, which is something that madness, for all that Bataille may sometimes seem to embrace extreme nonrational states, simply cannot do: "La raison seule a le pouvoir de défaire son ouvrage, de jeter bas ce qu'elle édifiait. La folie n'a pas d'effet, laissant subsister les débris, dérangeant avec la raison la faculté de commniquer (peut-être est-elle avant tout rupture de la communication intérieure)" (5: 60) ["Reason alone has the power to undo its work, to throw down what it as built up. Madness has no effect, leaving debris to subsist, deranging the faculty of communication with reason (perhaps it is before every rupture of inner communication)" (52)].[16] It is this approach to reason that makes *L'Expérience intérieure* impossible to write as any kind of systematic approach to defining inner experience; the resistance to a clearly delineated and realized project is inscribed in the very introduction that Bataille includes under the sign of the impossibility of his writing it: "L'opposition à l'idée de projet [...] est si nécessaire en moi qu'ayant écrit de cette introduction en plan détaillé, je ne puis m'y tenir" (5: 18) ["Opposition to the idea of project [...] is so necessary for me that, having written a detailed outline of this introduction, I cannot hold myself to it" (13)]. He then lists his abandoned chapter titles and a kind of draft of what they would have contained.

The introduction, like the totality, remains in the text under the sign of its negation and impossibility or, rather, its reinscription within a new kind of possibility, as the reimagining of the possibilities of thought necessarily leads to a new kind of writing. That writing is interrupted by the series of corrections or commentaries that Bataille offers in the book in such a way that the interruptions are not a tangential or temporary deviation from the smooth progression of the book but rather become the essential constituent aspect of it. The interruption, as disruption of the smooth flow of an ultimately false reasoned totality, is the moment when thought opens itself to a larger set of possibilities, an inner conversation which is signaled visually by the interplay of italicized and non-italicized font. That visual interplay serves in turn to make readers attentive to similar moments of dialectical interplay in the text that are not explicitly marked as such. The italics thus serve as a sort of training in how to read the text, so that readers become hermeneutically alert to phrases such as the one quoted above where Bataille seems to be unproblematically asserting the primacy of lived, non-conceptual experience when in fact the whole of the project of inner experience as he works it out in the book stands against such simple affirmations. To take Bataille at face value about the immediacy of direct experience that temporarily annihilates the subject is to embrace the kind of simplification which his writing consistently refuses. It is, one might say, to refuse to read him.

Once we as readers then start asking about the consequences of this kind of reading and writing, we enter into the interplay of reading and writing that constitutes the act of attempting to interpret the book and engaging with the necessary failure of all attempts to propose a totalizing or definitive interpretation, even one that ends in aporia or anguish.[17] The text enters into relation with the self by a similar kind of process of attempts at reading and interpreting, a process which identifies both writing and the self as similar inasmuch as they are both projects but opposed to each other on account of the impossibility of their fusion: "dans ce qui m'importe [le projet] m'apparaît vite ce qu'il est : contraire à moi-même étant projet" (5: 18) ["in what is important to me, [the project] quickly appears to be what it is: contrary to myself being project" (13)]. And this constitutes one of the many fundamental paradoxes of inner experience: "Principe de l'expérience intérieure: sortir par un projet du domaine du projet" (60) ["Principle of inner experience: to get out, through a project, of the realm of the project" (52)].[18] The project is a necessarily constituting element of experience at the same time that it serves as an obstacle to it, that which must be present in order to be negated and to remain under the sign of that negation: "Personne ne peut avoir lucidement d'expérience sans en avoir eu le projet. Cette maladie moins grave n'est pas évitable : le projet doit même être maintenu. Or l'expérience est le contraire du projet : j'atteins l'expérience à l'encontre du projet que j'avais de l'avoir" (5: 69) ["No one can lucidly have experience without having had the project for it. This less serious malady is unavoidable: the project must even be maintained. Now experience is the contrary of the project: I attain experience contrary to the project I have of having it" (59)]. The project, newly understood outside the bounds of a linear goal-oriented model, becomes like thought in that both participate in their own destruction, which is how inner experience can both be a project and be opposed to project at the same time, precisely because the project stands in opposition to itself:

> Néanmoins l'expérience intérieure est projet, quoi qu'on veuille.
> Elle l'est, l'homme l'étant en entier par le langage qui par essence, exception faite de sa perversion poétique, est projet. Mais le projet n'est plus dans ce cas celui, positif, du salut, mais celui, négatif, d'abolir le pouvoir des mots, donc du projet. (5: 35)

> [Nonetheless inner experience is project, no matter what.
> It is project, man being entirely project through language that in essence, with the exception of its poetic perversion, is project. But the project is no longer in this case that, positive, of salvation, but that, negative, of abolishing the power of words, therefore of project. (29)]

Sometimes inner experience presents itself quite apart from a feeling of anguish. Bataille gives this quasi-Proustian description of one such experience that yields happiness rather than anguish:

> Avant de me lever pour aller dormir, je sentis à quel point la douceur des choses m'avait pénétré. Je venais d'avoir le désir d'un mouvement d'esprit violent et, dans ce sens, j'aperçus que l'état de félicité où j'étais tombé ne différait pas entièrement des états « mystiques ». Tout au moins, comme j'étais passé brusquement de l'inattention à la surprise, je ressentis cet état avec plus d'intensité qu'on en fait d'habitude et comme si un autre et non moi l'éprouvait. Je ne pouvais nier qu'à l'attention près, qui ne lui manqua que d'abord, cette félicité banale ne fût pas une expérience intérieure authentique, distincte évidemment du projet, du discours. (5: 131)

> [Before getting up to go to bed, I felt the extent to which the sweetness of things had penetrated me. I had just had the desire for a violent movement of the spirit

and, in this sense, I perceived that the felicitous state into which I had fallen did not differ entirely from the "mystical" states. At the very least, as I had passed quickly from inattention to surprise, I felt this state with more intensity than one normally does and as if another and not me had experienced it. I could not deny that, with the exception of attention, which was lacking only at first, this banal felicity was an authentic inner experience, obviously distinct from project, from discourse.]

But this affirmation of simple happiness is short-lived, as he comes to see experiences such as these as dependent on anguish inasmuch as they take on their value as a moment of respite from that anguish: "c'est d'avoir échappé un instant, à la faveur d'une solitude précaire, à tant de pauvreté, que j'avais perçu la tendresse des arbres mouillés, la déchirante étrangeté de leur passage" (5: 131) ["it is from having escaped for a moment, by means of a precarious solitude, from so much poverty, that I perceived the tenderness of the damp trees, the lacerating strangeness of their passing" (114)]. The immediate experience is thus not the authentic experience he had claimed it to be, because it is based on a misunderstanding or at least a partial understanding, one that can only be completed in retrospect; thus, the experience of happiness and the accompanying feeling that the experience is an authentic one are shown not to be authentic in that the feeling of authenticity was part of what led Bataille to mischaracterize the experience in the immediacy of the moment. Experience thus becomes an epistemological issue in that reflection on the experience, which alters the nature of the experience itself, is not separate from, but rather partly constitutive of, the experience.

Moreover, the interpretation of the experience is mediated not only by further reflection upon the initial moment of immediacy but also by literary texts which form a kind of interpretive filter. The experience Bataille describes is not unlike many moments in Marcel Proust's *A la recherchedu temps perdu*, where the narrator has an experience that he comes to understand quite differently than he had at the moment of the perception, "correcting" his earlier view through a series of hypotheses and transforming the experience through giving it written form. Bataille himself notes this similarity:

Je me rappelle d'avoir fait le rapprochement de ma jouissance et de celles que décrivent les premiers volumes de la *Recherche du temps perdu*. Mais je n'avais alors de Marcel Proust qu'une idée incomplète, superficielle (le *Temps retrouvé* n'était pas encore paru) et jeune, ne songeais qu'à de naïves possibilités de triomphe. (5: 132)

[I recall having made a comparison of my enjoyment with that described in the first volumes of *In Search of Lost Time*. But I then had only an incomplete, superficial idea of Marcel Proust (*Time Regained* had not yet appeared) and young, I dreamed only of naïve possibilities of triumph. (114)]

Literary experience and lived experience intertwine here, so that while Bataille had access to earlier volumes where the narrator reconsiders earlier experiences in light of experience gained afterward, he had not yet seen the way the *Recherche* then ultimately aims at a view where true life is art itself, as the narrator claims in the last volume:

La vraie vie, la vie enfin découverte et éclaircie, la seule vie par conséquent réellement vécue, c'est la littérature ; cette vie qui, en un sens, habite à chaque instant chez tous les hommes aussi bien que chez l'artiste. Mais ils ne la voient pas, parce qu'ils ne cherchent pas à l'éclaircir. Et ainsi leur passé est encombré d'innombrables clichés qui restent inutiles parce que l'intelligence ne les a pas « développés ». (Proust *Recherche* 4: 474)

[Real life, life at last laid bare and illuminated—the only life in consequence which can be said to be really lived—is literature, and life thus defined is in a sense all the time immanent in ordinary men no less than in the artist. But most men do not see it because they do not seek to shed light upon it. And therefore their past is like a photographic darkroom encumbered with innumerable negatives which remain useless because the intellect has not developed them. (Proust *Time* 298–9)

By inscribing the *Recherche* into *L'Expérience intérieure* but also indicating that his understanding of it was incomplete because he had not yet been able to encounter its conclusion, Bataille invites the reader to supply that conclusion and to use that insight further to undermine his own initial claim that his immediate experience of happiness was an authentic inner experience. It shows that the experience is completed not just with conceptual reflection in light of subsequent experience but also via its transformation into writing, which retrospectively both alters the initial experience and shows that it is in an important sense simply the raw material for the process of writing which transforms it into an experience. This insight is only available retrospectively and encourages readers to be suspicious of any other claims in *L'Expérience intérieure* about the immediacy of authentic inner experience as wholly opposed to and separate from either conceptual or esthetic experience.

It is important to add, however, that transferring experience to the esthetic by means of transposing it into language does not cancel the unknown or bring it unproblematically within the realm of the known. Once again Proust is Bataille's interlocutor when he addresses the epistemological consequences of known and unknown objects of experience:

> L'inconnu qu'en définitive la vie révèle, que le monde est, à tout instant s'incarne en quelque objet nouveau. [...] Mais l'inconnu (la séduction) se dérobe si je veux posséder, si je tente de connaître l'objet : quand Proust jamais ne se lassa de vouloir user, abuser de l'objet que la vie propose. Si bien que de l'amour il ne connut guère que la jalousie impossible et non la communication où mollit le sentiment de soi, où dans l'excès du désir nous nous donnons. Si la vérité qu'une femme propose à qui l'aime est l'inconnu (l'inaccessible), il ne peut la connaitre ni l'atteindre, mais elle peut le briser : s'il est brisé, que devient-il lui-même, sinon ce qui dormait en lui d'inconnu, d'inaccessible ? Mais d'un tel jeu, ni l'amant, ni l'amante jamais ne pourront rien saisir, ni fixer, ni rendre à volonté durable. (5: 160–1)
>
> [The unknown that life reveals definitively, what the world is, at every instant is embodied in some new object. [...] But the unknown (seduction) slips away if I want to possess, if I attempt to know an object: while Proust never tired of wanting to see, to take advantage of objects that life proposes. Such that he hardly knew anything of love but impossible jealousy and not the communication in which the feeling of the self softens, when we offer ourselves in an excess of desire. If the truth that a woman proposes to one who loves her is the unknown (the inaccessible), her lover can neither know her nor reach her, but she can shatter him: if he is shattered what does he become, if not that which lay dormant in him, the unknown, the inaccessible? But from such a game neither the lover nor the beloved could ever grasp anything, nor immobilize it, nor make it last. (139, translation modified)]

What Bataille proposes is not a pure descent into absolute unknowing but rather a transfer of the object of knowledge from knowledge of an object to the incomplete and provisional character of knowledge as itself the object of knowledge. In that process, the object of knowledge risks dissolving entirely as it is shown to be the product of a temporary perception, a fact which has important consequences for not only the object but also the subject of knowledge to the extent that the subject constitutes itself as a knower. If the subject had defined itself in a relation of knowledge vis-à-vis the object, that kind of self is dissolved as the subject comes to lucidity about its own ignorance.

Bataille notes that perhaps the linear nature of Proust's novel which, at least at a surface level reading, encourages readers to see it as a progression from delusion to lucidity, smooths over a more skeptical approach whereby the dialectic of knowing and ignorance would not and could not be brought to an end by the narrator's musings about art in the last volume, which on this reading would be taken to yet another part of the fiction rather than a statement of Proust the author's esthetics: "L'absence de satisfaction n'est-elle pas plus profonde que le sentiment de triomphe de la fin de l'œuvre ? [...] Je crois même que l'absence dernière de satisfaction fut, plus qu'une satisfaction momentanée, ressort et raison d'être de l'œuvre" (5: 168) ["Isn't the absence of satisfaction more profound than the feeling of triumph at the end of the work? [...] I even believe that the final absence of satisfaction was, more than a momentary satisfaction, the motivation and purpose of the work" (146)]. Bataille ultimately relates this transformation of knowing to his logic of sacrifice, whereby what is left after the process of dismantling knowledge or experience are the ruins of what had been, which is by no means the same as the oblivion of the former object of knowledge:

> L'image poétique, si elle mène du connu à l'inconnu, s'attache cependant au connu qui lui donne corps, et bien qu'elle le déchire et déchire la vie dans ce déchirement, se maintient à lui. D'où il s'ensuit que la poésie est presque en entier poésie déchue, jouissance d'images il est vrai retirées du domaine servile [...], mais refusée à la ruine intérieure qu'est l'accès à l'inconnu. Même les images profondément ruinées sont domaine de possession. Il est malheureux de ne plus posséder que des ruines, mais ce n'est pas ne plus rien posséder, c'est retenir d'une main ce que l'autre donne. (5: 170)

> [The poetic image, if it leads from the known to the unknown, attaches itself however to the known that gives it body, and even though it lacerates it and lacerates life in this laceration, maintains itself in it Hence it follows that poetry is almost entirely poetry in decline, the enjoyment of images that are, it's true, drawn from the servile realm (poetic as well as noble, formal) but denied the inner ruin that is access to the unknown. Even profoundly ruined images are in the realm of possession. It is unfortunate to no longer possess anything but ruin, but this is not to no longer possess anything, it is to retain with one hand what the other gives. (148)]

It is important to underscore that Bataillean sacrifice does not obliterate the subject, precisely because it is incapable of doing so. The impossibility of accomplishing sacrifice in the fullest sense is what gives the logic of sacrifice its power in Bataille; it exists as an impossible ideal that has all the more impact on the subject on account of its existence as an unfulfillable desire that nonetheless effects change in the subject.

To say that Bataille deals in impossible ideals is not to criticize or reject Bataille but to take his own logic seriously and to extend it to the realm of paradox. In the domain of sacrifice, this means the sacrifice of sacrifice itself. This crucial point for my argument has been made by Leslie Hill:

> But if sacrifice has been sacrificed to the logic of appropriation, perhaps what thus suggests is that sacrifice should be sacrificed again: but to itself as a remnant or a shadow. This possibility is of course *also* inscribed within the economy of sacrifice in Bataille, notably as a kind of profligate overbidding of the historical dialectic of Hegel or Kojève, buy which, impossibly, as far as philosophy itself is concerned, the mediateness or mediation of thought itself is disrupted by the immediacy of an experience of return that, for all its instantaneousness, belongs neither to presence not to the present. Here, to think sacrifice, for Bataille, is to confront a demand for the sacrifice of thought itself. This is the lesson to be drawn from paradoxes, aporias, contradictions, ambiguities and sheer inconsistencies that dog his discussion of unproductive excess, of the general and the restricted economy, and of sacrifice. [...]
>
> As thought reaches the limit of its own certainty, and is exposed to the threat of its own eclipse, it is necessary still to think. A decision must be taken. The demand of writing, like the falling due of an unanswerable debt, cannot be eluded. (61–2)

A pattern of simultaneous necessity and impossibility appears across many of Bataille's frequently recurring notions. What is true of sacrifice is also true of his notion of sovereignty, which also comes to name an ideal whose value inheres precisely in the fact that it cannot be realized, and thus the desired obliteration of subjectivity becomes transmuted into a subjectivity defined by that awareness of the impossibility of its obliteration.[19] As Benjamin Noys argues, "It is this impossibility of sovereignty that forces us to seek it, but while sovereignty is NOTHING it is also a 'nothing' that displaces the philosophical model of the subject. Sovereignty is detached from an ontological interpretation, including that of Bataille" (74–5). The desire to be rid of the subject is of a piece with the desire to reduce words to silence: the very existence of Bataille's texts continues to testify to the impossibility of such a definitive elimination of the subject, but at the same time it requires us to read subjectivity differently by accounting for the simultaneous desire for and necessity of its elimination as constitutive of the subject.[20] As Nick Mansfield has argued:

> As the key enactment of true subjectivity, [sovereignty] becomes something we glimpse as an interruption of the coherence of the real world, in 'the sleep of reason.' [...] The subject does not 'cease being' the subject and does not lose contact with the domain of its truth, but it must also, like the currents of energy with which it rhymes, feel and live the frustration of its native drive toward death and the invisible mystical world of continuity that beckons us from beyond the real It must also live in the narrower world of objectivity as that world's orientating expression. (24)

Or, to put it another way, "sovereignty depends on the individuality it transcends and spurns" (Mansfield 26). This new constitution of subjectivity is entirely interwoven into the practice of reading, which, like sovereignty and subjectivity, exists in Bataille as a category he wishes to, but cannot, get beyond, as Noys underscores:

> There is a necessity to reading that Bataille recognizes and wants to be rid of, and this is what makes him such an acute reader. He is a reader who wants to have done with reading and so he reads to the very limit of reading. It is possible to read Bataille's claim, "But that one should read me—should arrive at the ultimate degree of conviction—one will not be laid bare for all that" (IE 13), not just as a rejection of reading, which it is, but also as a call for a different type of reading. It implicitly rejects all reading but it can be reread to argue that it rejects a reading that arrives "at the ultimate degree of conviction," a reading that is grounded in truth and the homogeneity of a secure and stable conviction, and thereby identity. (129)

There is no knowledge of the insufficiency of experience without passing first through both the experience and the moment in which the subject perceives the experience to be complete in its immediacy, an essential move in the dialectical process that then tears down the assurance about that immediacy and reshapes not only the relation of subject to object but also the very character of both subject and object themselves. I turn now to a more detailed exploration of the consequences of Bataille's conception of inner experience for notions of subject and object.

In the case of subject-object relations as in the case of his claims about the immediacy of non-conceptual inner experience, readers need to be wary of taking individual assertions in the text at face value. Doing so leads not only to untenable positions but also to a partial reading of the text that fails to take into account its dialectical and performative structure and the way it refuses a model of mere communication of ideas in the context of a system in favor of an invitation to read the text against itself sometimes. One such potentially misleading assertion, offered quite early on in the book, claims that "l'expérience atteint pour finir la fusion de l'objet et du sujet, étant comme sujet non-savoir, comme objet l'inconnu" (5: 21) ["experience attains the fusion of the object and the subject, being as subject nonknowledge, as object the unknown" (16)]. I would argue that, just as experience is incomplete and even inaccessible without conceptual reflection even though Bataille claims to refuse that position, so too his concept of inner experience depends on retaining a notion of subject and object; to abandon the subject would be to nullify the entire project of *L'Expérience intérieure*, even if that project is, as he sometimes claims, self-destructing. What inner experience does effect is a transformation of our understanding of subject and object and their relation, just as inner experience effects a transformed understanding of the relationship of knowledge to nonknowledge. Once again, a comment that appears in the annex to the book rather than the final published version helps clarify and temper the assertion quoted above that the subject and object fuse. If they do so, it can only be momentarily; to be conscious of the fusion still requires a subject of perception. Similarly, to be brought to the limits of experience in no way precludes the existence of the subject, as this passage acknowledges:

> L'expérience est ainsi posée tout d'abord indépendamment du sujet qui la vit et de l'objet qu'elle découvre : c'est la mise en question du sujet comme de l'objet. Mais il est clair qu'il ne s'agit nullement de l'expérience d'un être indéfini ou illimité. L'expérience est même exactement le fait d'un être particulier et limité. Ce que je mets en question en moi-même est sans doute l'être lui-même, mais je ne puis mettre en cause l'être lui-même avant de m'être heurté aux limites de l'être que je suis. L'expérience est donc tout d'abord la mise en question des limites de l'être, essentiellement de l'isolement où se trouve l'être particulier. Ainsi est-elle en quête d'un objet extérieur avec lequel elle tentera de communiquer. (6: 290)
>
> [Experience is thus posited first of all independently of the subject who lives it and of the object that it discovers: it is the questioning both of the subject and the object. But it is clear that it is not at all a question of the experience of an undefined or unlimited being. Experience is even exactly the making of a particular and limited being. What I put into question in myself is no doubt being itself, but I cannot investigate being itself before coming up against the limits of the being that I am. Experience is thus first of all the questioning of the limits of being, essentially of the isolation where the particular being finds itself. Thus is it in search of an exterior object with which it will try to communicate.]

To ask how to reconcile seemingly contradictory statements by Bataille on the maintaining or obliterating of the experiencing subject is not the right question; rather, in the experience that is reading and writing the text, the question is how to address the paradoxes of attempts to capture experience, a conceptual activity which is part and parcel of the experience and which mandates a move past the urge to reconcile the paradoxes in some putative synthesis. This is where it is important to uphold the distinction between philosophy, aligned in this instance with scientific inquiry in its commitment to arrive at a conclusion, and thought, which is premised on the impossibility and undesirability of such a conclusion. As Jean-Louis Baudry indicates:

> As opposed to science, inner experience postulates the subject, but as opposed to philosophy which uses the subject to guarantee being, inner experience postulates the subject as resulting from being (from a certain form of matter), but in postulating the subject it also postulates the moment of its negation.
>
> Through inner experience, both a method and a field are defined, whose intent, in itself contradictory (linked to science, to knowledge, but putting science and knowledge into question, remaining inaccessible to them), is determined to expose the movement of contradiction. (280)

Such a method is "inconceivable outside of a practice of the subject, a practice of limits that allows the subject to put itself in question" (280). Thus the destruction of the subject, which at first glance seems so necessary for the kind of quasi-mystic experience Bataille seems to posit as authentic inner experience, is more an ideal than an attainable state; to suppress the subject is both necessary and impossible: "Suppression du sujet et de l'objet, seul moyen de ne pas aboutir à la possession de l'objet par le sujet, c'est-à-dire d'éviter l'absurde ruée de l'*ipse* voulant devenir le tout" (5: 67) ["Suppression of the subject and of the object, sole means not leading to the possession of the object by the subject, which is to say of avoiding the absurd rush of the *ipse* wanting to become everything" (57)]. Once again Bataille puts himself and the reader on guard against the dangerous appetite for totality and sameness that would be disastrous both within the realm of thought and within the political, canceling as it does the alterity that is the motor of thought and moving toward a totalizing sterility.

The unity that thought sometimes desires is thus shown, by the restlessness of dialectical thought, to be not only unrealizable but undesirable; the anguish of an impossible desire for the kind of knowledge that would subsume the object and fuse it with the subject is in fact the very condition of thought insofar as it opposes itself to knowledge in that sense: "Nulle différence entre savoir et être tout. Savoir suppose à un moment quelconque une intervention arbitraire disant d'autorité : cette question n'existe pas, tu sais tout ce que tu dois savoir" (5: 436). Thought, even in the isolation of the individual thinking subject here, is thus inherently political in that it guards against the kind of power that, through knowing the object, obliterates it in a refusal of the subject-object dialectic.

The impossibility of getting beyond objects is at the root of Bataille's critique of asceticism, which merely substitutes experience for objects of desire and makes of experience itself an object:

> L'ascèse est un moyen sûr de se détacher des objets : c'est tuer le désir qui lie à l'objet. Mais c'est du même coup faire de l'expérience un objet (on n'a tué le désir des objets qu'en proposant au désir un nouvel objet).
> Par l'ascèse, l'expérience se condamne à prendre une valeur d'objet positif. [...] L'expérience à l'extrême du possible demande un renoncement néanmoins : cesser de vouloir être tout. (5: 34)

> [Asceticism is a sure means to detach oneself from objects: it is to kill the desire that links one to the object. But it is at the same time to make experience an object (one has not killed the desire for objects, only proposed a new object for desire).
> Through asceticism, experience is condemned to take on the value of a positive object. [...] Experience at the extremity of the possible nevertheless demands a renunciation: to cease to want to be everything. (28)]

Once again, Bataille does not so much eliminate a category as shift its meaning: by rejecting asceticism as it is usually understood, Bataille substitutes for it another kind of renunciation, this time the renunciation of the (suspect) desire of being all, in the name of preserving the subject-object distinction on which thought depends and which traditional asceticism seeks to obliterate, with the dangerous consequences for both thought and political relation to the other that we have seen.

Thus when Bataille claims, as we saw above, that "il faut *vivre* l'expérience" (5: 21) ["one must *live* the experience" (15)], and that "l'expérience atteint pour finir la fusion de l'objet et du sujet, étant comme sujet non-savoir, comme objet l'inconnu" (5: 21) ["experience attains the fusion of the subject and the object, being as subject nonknowledge, as object the unknown" (16)], this may well mean that at that point "la philosophie proprement dite est absorbée, [...] elle se dissout" (5:21) ["philosophy properly speaking is absorbed, [...] it dissolves" (16)], but it is impossible to say the same of thought, given the role the latter plays in experience, as part of the experience by which we recognize the experience as such. The final sentence of this section highlights the tensions involved in this mapping of experience and subjectivity and belies any facile affirmation of the absorption of the subject: "'Soi-même', ce n'est pas le sujet s'isolant du monde, mais un lieu de communication, de fusion du sujet et de l'objet" (5: 21) ["'Oneself' is not the subject isolating itself from the world, but a place of communication, of fusion of subject and object" (16)]. Here Bataille posits fusion as itself a relation, a refusal of (or affirmation of the impossibility of) isolation, but the very syntax of the sentence highlights the tension between two incompatible views of the subject-object relation that Bataille makes live together: a space of communication is by no means synonymous with, or even compatible with, a fusion. To make the sentence comprehensible, we would have to reinterpret fusion, as we have done with some of Bataille's other terms, so that it means the opposite of what it is usually taken to mean, a fusion that does not subsume the object or create a hybrid entity from what had been distinct as subject and object. Puzzling out how "oneself" could be the fusion of subject and object posits that fusion itself as an object of thought, thus maintaining the subject while displacing the object from some element of the perceptual world to the larger domain of the object of thought itself, of thought as object. If philosophy dissolves in this process, thought necessarily remains, reshaping the subject and being reshaped by it, creating a "world" by aligning itself with that which is not the subject but which clearly, as thought, emanates from the subject and, in turn, acts upon it by providing the impetus for experience, now defined as thought. The experience hovers in the syntax of that sentence, where self is defined as "un lieu de communication, de fusion." The section ends here, but the non-sense of the formulation pushes thought onward in light of the impossibility of defining the self as the fusion of subject and object which remains only under the sign of its impossibility.

The obliterated self, which has existence only as the perception of an individuated subject undergoing thought as experience, comes to have some other ontological status that transcends simpler questions of existence or non-existence. It is a necessary posited term in the non system that Bataille is elaborating, even in its impossibility, or perhaps on account of its impossibility. This self is, we might say, a fiction: a product of the imagination independent of its relation to the empirical world but forcefully present in the world of thought as experience. One of the consequences of recognizing the fused self as a fiction is its malleability as a product of the conceptual imagination; another is the way in which seeing the obliterated self as a fiction enables us to see all notions of the self, similarly, as fictional constructs, a move in which a thinking self takes itself as object, not in a fusion of subject and object but in a reinforcing of the subject-object dialectic, inescapable even in those moments when the self reflects on itself, an action which never means, as Bataille has underscored, an isolation from the world. Julia Kristeva notes that Bataille establishes the truth of the subject as fiction: "Pour Bataille la vérité du sujet ne consiste pas à dire qu'il est présent, encore moins de dire qu'il est toujours disséminé. La vérité du sujet consiste dans la fiction (au sens d'une présentation doublement contradictoire [...])" ["For Bataille the truth of the subject does not consist in saying that it is present, even less so in saying that it is always disseminated. The truth of the subject consists in the fiction (in the sense of a doubly contradictory presentation [...])"] (292). She highlights the role of sexual transgression in exploring the limits of the self but underscores that language is always present in this constant doing and undoing of the self and that Bataille's dialectics are constituted by his preservation of a contested but sovereign self:

> C'est donc par la *pluralisation* de la parole et par la *transgression* des interdits, mais toujours dans la parole et en maintenant ces interdits, que le sujet peut abandonner son lieu de Maître spéculaire et en toucher l'engendrement « inconnu » : l'érotisme dans le discours et à forteriori dans le discours du savoir ou dans le discours philosophique : voilà la condition d'une attitude matérialiste et dialectique à l'égard du sujet. [...] Attitude *dialectique* parce qu'elle préserve au sujet la position de « souveraineté contestataire », qui ne se fixe ni dans une maîtrise ni dans une absence, mais refuse, nie, transforme le dispositif du réel et, par là, la réalité.
>
> Ainsi, [...] c'est dans la *fiction*, et non pas dans le *savoir* et son *concept*, que l'expérience trouve son adéquation. (292–3)

[Thus it is by the *pluralization* of speech and by the *transgression* of the forbidden, but always in speech and by maintaining the forbidden, that the subject can abandon its space of specular Master and attain the "unknown" engenderment: eroticism in discourse and *a forteriori* in the discourse of knowledge or philosophical discourse: there is the condition of a materialist and dialectical attitude toward the subject. [...] *Dialectical* attitude because it preserves for the subject the position of "contestatory sovereignty," which is established neither in mastery nor in its absence, but refuses, negates, transforms the mechanism of the real and, through it, reality.

Thus, [...] it is in *fiction*, and not in *knowledge* and its *concept*, that experience finds its adequation.]

Thus Bataille's project, if we can assimilate it in some ways to fiction in the sense of an imaginative construction by a narrator-subject that invites interpretation, distinguishes itself from one such as Blanchot's that would, following Mallarmé, cede initiative to the words themselves in a kind of disappearance of the self into language or discourse.

To say that language speaks is not necessarily to deny the existence of the subject but rather to alter what we mean by a Cartesian, unified subject standing in an undialectical position of potential mastery of a wholly other object. Transforming our understanding of the subject does involve an emptying out of the concept of the subject, a dwelling on it as a void, but to see subjectivity in those terms requires a subject capable of maintaining the paradox of a subject constituted as a void yet conscious of itself as both subject and object of that void. Bataille's concern with limits allows us to identify the subject as a limit point, beyond which we cannot think and which we cannot overcome in non-conceptual experience precisely because that experience needs to be conceptualized in order to be completed as experience, which requires a subject of the experience even as the experience attempts to rethink the subject-object relation. Bataille's attempt to redefine subject-object relations also moves him beyond what we might consider some of the precursors of his approach, in mysticism or negative theology. Bataille neither performs the dissolution of the subject nor restores the subject to the fullness of being that it may have had before the inner experience. Rather, the subject-object relation that constitutes the self is reconfigured in ways that challenge interpreters of the experience to reimagine what an adequate subject-object relationship would look like at the limits of a subjectivity that persists beyond efforts to meld it into discourse or to allow it to envelop the object and cancel a relation altogether. The void cannot be conceived as an endpoint without altering its function as void, and it is the persistence of the subject which guards against such instrumentalization of the void or essentialized definitions of either literature or philosophy.

The experience of thought as Bataille portrays it in *L'Expérience intérieure* is perhaps best understood, as I suggested above, as a kind of drama, a characterization which accommodates the fictive aspect I have been describing as well as the necessarily affective dimension of thought as an experience of anguish in light of the realization of its paradoxical and necessarily impossible goals.[21] These goals nonetheless serve as the motor of its continuation in the unfolding of experience and a reflection on that experience that both changes it and itself constitutes part of it. On this view, states such as ecstasy are nothing more than a dramatized heightening of ordinary experience, as Bataille indicates: "on n'atteint des états d'extase ou de ravissement qu'en *dramatisant* l'existence en général" (5: 22) ["one attained states of ecstasy or ravishment only by *dramatizing* existence in general"] (17).[22] He makes a distinction between this kind of dramatization and the eternal drama of religions and of actions taken to suppress pain, since drama has to maintain pain as part of experience. He later claims as a model for this interior dramatization of pain the spiritual exercises of saint Ignatius, itself a kind of drama of abandoning or projecting the self while maintaining the self in that practitioners put themselves mentally in the place of the suffering Christ. For Bataille, inner experience takes one beyond the banal insignificance of anxiety and into the more penetrating experience of anguish, accessible not by learning but by practice:

> L'angoisse, évidemment, ne s'apprend pas. [...] Si quelqu'un avoue de l'angoisse il faut montrer le néant de ses raisons. Il imagine l'issue de ses tourments : s'il avait plus d'argent, une femme, une autre vie ... La niaiserie de l'angoisse est infinie. Au lieu d'aller à la profondeur de son angoisse, l'anxieux babille, se dégrade et fuit. [...] L'angoisse éludée fait d'un homme un jésuite, agité, mais à vide. (5: 47)
>
> [Anguish, obviously, is not learned. [...] If someone admits anguish, it is necessary to show the nothingness of his reasons. He imagines an escape from his torments: if he had more money, a wife, another life ... The foolishness of anguish is infinite. In place of going to the depths of his anguish, the anxious one babbles, degrades himself, and flees. [...] Evaded anguish makes a man an agitated Jesuit, but empty. (40-1)]

Immediately after the condemnation of mere anxiety that I have just cited, Bataille describes the affective experience of anguish in a paragraph that shifts from generalized commentary to the record of a personal one:

> Tremblant. Rester immobile, debout, dans une obscurité solitaire, dans une attitude sans geste de suppliant : supplication, mais sans geste et surtout sans espoir. Perdu et suppliant, aveugle, demi mort. Comme Job sur le fumier, mais n'imaginant rien, la nuit tombée, désarmé, sachant que c'est perdu. (5: 47)
>
> [Trembling. Remaining immobile, standing, in a solitary darkness, in an attitude without the gesture of the supplicant supplication, but without gesture and certainly without hope. Lost and supplicating, blind, half dead. Like Job on the dung heap, but imagining nothing, night fallen, defenseless, knowing that all is lost. (41, translation modified)]

This is the kind of state that distinguishes the anguished, dramatized experience of thought from philosophy:

> La philosophie n'est jamais supplication, mais sans supplication, il n'est pas de réponse concevable : aucune réponse jamais ne précédera la question : et que signifie la question sans angoisse, sans supplice. Au moment de devenir fou, la réponse survient : comment l'entendrait-on sans cela ? (5: 48)

> [Philosophy is never supplication, but without supplication, there is no conceivable answer: no answer ever preceded the question: and what does the question mean without anguish, without torture. At the moment of going mad, the answer suddenly appears: how would one hear it without that? (42)]

We should be careful here to distinguish this preference for anguish and the refusal of a peaceful static approach to intellectual contemplation from some kind of vitalist affirmation of violence and war, especially given the historical context of the years in which Bataille was writing and then published the book. The violence that Bataille endorses in the book remains a movement of thought, a thinking against one's own thought that necessarily leads to anguish on account of the way it disrupts the smooth functioning of affirmative thought, a move similar to one we shall see in Emil Cioran in the next chapter. In yet another paradox, Bataille ultimately rejects war's approach to violence on grounds similar to those on which he rejects goal-oriented science and philosophy: the goal of war is to win or, at least, to overcome horror by passing into action.

Since Bataille's aim is to maintain a state of anguish as the necessary correlate of authentic inner experience, he cannot affirm the action of war, precisely because war is an exemplary form of action, and "l'expérence intérieure est le contraire de l'action. Rien de plus" (5: 59) ["inner experience is the opposite of action. Nothing more"] (51). War amplifies but ultimately negates the kind of horror that inner experience cultivates, and Bataille must reject it on those grounds:

> L'horreur de la guerre est plus grande que celle de l'expérience intérieure. La désolation d'un champ de bataille, en principe, a quelque chose de plus lourd que la « nuit obscure ». Mais dans la bataille on aborde l'horreur avec un mouvement qui la surmonte : l'action, le projet lié à l'action permettent de *dépasser* l'horreur. Ce dépassement donne à l'action, au projet, une grandeur captivante, mais l'horreur en elle-même est niée. (5: 58)

> [The horror of war is greater than that of inner experience. The desolation of a battlefield, in principle, has something more grave than the "dark night." But in

battle, one approaches horror with a movement that overcomes it: the action and the project linked to action permit the *surpassing* of horror. This surpassing gives action and project, a captivating grandeur, but horror in itself is negated. (50, translation modified)]

Bataille can thus be accused of neither quietism nor vitalism. He does not withdraw from the horrors of the war being waged as he writes in order to embrace some solipsistic contemplation; as I have already suggested, there are political dimensions inherent in the subject-object relation that inner experience implies. Nor does he glorify the violence of war as some kind of externalization of inner experience; rather, he posits it as opposed to inner experience. More than a metaphor, the kind of violence involved in inner experience is lived but at a conceptual level. Rather than purifying violence of its bite, the violence of inner experience transfers the intensity of physical violence to the mental plane while implying a condemnation, despite all Bataille may otherwise claim about violence and sacrifice as limit experiences, of violence precisely because it cancels what is for him the essential experience of anguish and thus represents an untenable stasis as a goal rather than the dialectical movement that animates thought as inner experience.

Bataille borrows from the imagery of war to represent inner experience as combat:

> En premier lieu [...] l'homme doit combattre, devant répondre à la volonté qu'il a d'être seul et lui-même tout. Tant qu'il combat, l'homme n'est encore ni comique ni tragique et tout demeure en lui suspendu : il subordonne tout à l'action par laquelle il lui faut traduire sa volonté. [...]
>
> L'objet du combat est une composition de plus en plus vaste et dans ce sens, il est difficile d'accéder pleinement à l'universel. [...] Pour peu que le combat se relâche [...] l'homme accède à sa solitude dernière : à ce moment la volonté d'être tout le met en pièces.
>
> Il est alors en lutte non plus avec un ensemble égal à celui qu'il représente, mais avec le néant. (5: 108)

[In the first place [...] man must fight before responding to his will to be alone and to be everything himself. As long as he fights, he is still neither comic nor tragic and everything remains suspended in him: he subordinates everything to the action by which he must translate his will. [...]

The object of the fight is a composition, more and more vast, and, in this sense, it is difficult to fully access the universal. [...] If the fight is lessened a little [...] man gains access to his final solitude: at this moment the will to be everything pulls him to pieces.

He is then no longer struggling with an ensemble equal to what he represents but with nothingness. (94)]

This text is included in the book as having been composed in February 1936, an inscription of a kind of combat that predates any fighting from the war that would erupt not long after. Italicized commentary on the passage immediately follows, in which Bataille indicates that "la guerre mit fin à mon « activité » et ma vie se trouva d'autant moins séparé de l'objet de sa recherche" (5: 109) ["the war put an end to my 'activity' and my life became all the less separated from the objects of its search" (95)]. He had just described that activity as an effort to reach others: "la communication profonde des êtres à l'exclusion des liens nécessaires aux projets, que forme le discours" (5: 109) ["the profound communication of beings to the exclusion of the bonds necessary for projects, which discourse forms" (95)]. This desire for communication led Bataille to the paradox of its impossibility given his conclusion that communication often relies on discourse whereas "la communication profonde veut le silence" (5: 109) ["profound communication requires silence" (95)]. Thus, "action" for him meant "fermer sa porte afin d'arrêter le discours (le bruit, la mécanique du dehors)" (5: 109) ["closing one's door so as to stop discourse (noise, the mechanisms of the outside)" (95)]. To accomplish communication along these lines, "la porte en même temps doit demeurer ouverte et fermée" (5: 109) ["the door must remain open and closed" (95)].

The text thus suggests that Bataille was already engaged in combat well before the war, and that the war made it impossible to pursue that combat. Once again, however, it is crucial to remember that the combat was against the desire or inclination to be the totality, a unity that would suppress the other in a way that shuts down thought and assimilates it to mere totalizing domination, an act that is an undesirable perversion of thought and one that finds its analogue in the actual combat of war whose goal is to dominate and obliterate the other. War forces the door open, we might say following Bataille's metaphor, and forecloses the possibility of maintaining it simultaneously open and closed, or rather, forecloses the possibility of reflection on the consequences of the necessary but impossible practice of maintaining a closed and open door. By forcing the door open, so to speak, to both the discourse of the world and to the noise that makes thought impossible, war forecloses the possibility of communication and impedes the combat against a subject's desire to be the totality. Rather, it shoves the subject further along those lines, encouraging the subject to identify with a collective that mindlessly seeks to be totality and, in order to do so, to obliterate the object so as to eliminate the subject-object relation. To maintain the anguish of the impossibility of the simultaneously open and closed door, the relation to the world that is a non-relation, is to maintain the centrality of the subject-object relation as a political act of resistance even through what looks at first glance like a refusal of engagement.

The subject of inner experience, then, when withdrawing from the chatter of discourse, takes others into that experience, complicating our usual senses of what constitutes solitude and community. We can see the play of solitude and community in the way Bataille engages the notion of laughter as part of inner experience. Like experiences such as eroticism and poetry, laughter is one of the possible non-conceptual reactions of the subject to inner experience.[23] At the conclusion of the text from 1936 included in the book which I have been discussing, the subject passes into laughter once he has confronted the void in what becomes a spirit of play that, once again paradoxically, is not opposed to the anguish the void had inspired but an integral part of it: "l'homme n'est plus comme la bête le jouet du néant, mais le néant est lui-même son jouet—il s'y abîme, mais en éclaire l'obscurité de son *rire*, auquel il n'atteint qu'*enivré* du vide même qui le tue" (5: 109) ["man is no longer like the beast, a plaything of nothingness, but nothingness is itself his plaything—he ruins himself in it, but lights the darkness with this *laughter*, which he reaches only *intoxicated* by the very void that kills him" (94)].

His stance on laughter has not changed between that text from 1936 and the more recent writing featured in the book, where he speaks of laughter as stemming not from an individual but from a collective sense of the instability of existence: "d'un bout à l'autre de cette vie humaine, qui est notre lot, la conscience du peu de stabilité, même du profond manqué de toute véritable stabilité, libère les enchantements du rire" (5: 112) ["from one end to the other of this human life that is our lot, consciousness of the lack of stability, even of the profound lack of all real stability, liberates the enchantment of laughter" (98)]. Communal laughter bears a complex relationship to anguish: "le rire commun suppose l'absence d'une véritable angoisse et pourtant n'a pas d'autre source que l'angoisse" (5: 113) ["shared laughter assumes the absence of a true anguish, and yet it as no other source than anguish" (98)]. But laughter cannot be an endpoint, nor can it cancel anguish; in that sense, it is not opposed to thought but complicit in the same kind of never-ending movement away from the temporary resolution, either in something akin to drunkenness or the assurance of established knowledge, back toward the unknown that is the perpetual motor of thought:

> Mais le désir, la poésie, le rire, font incessamment glisser la vie dans le sens contraire, allant du connu à l'inconnu. L'existence à la fin décèle la tache aveugle de l'entendement et s'y absorbe aussitôt tout entière. Il ne pourrait en aller autrement que si une possibilité de repos s'offrait en un point quelconque. Mais il n'en est rien : ce qui demeure est l'agitation circulaire—qui ne s'épuise pas dans l'extase et recommence à partir d'elle. (5: 129–30)

> [But desire, poetry, laughter, unceasingly cause life to slip in the opposite way, going from the known to the unknown. Existence, in the end, discovers the blind spot of understanding and right away absorbs it completely. It could go otherwise only if the possibility of rest offered itself at some point. But nothing like that happens: what alone remains is the circular agitation—which does not exhaust itself in ecstasy and begins again from it. (112)]

Whatever encourages inner experience does so by reanimating the instability and motion that is characteristic of it; the radical lack of endpoint is described by Maurice Blanchot, in his characterization of Bataille's inner experience, as the state of being only question, and he identifies war, along with science and religious conviction, as one of the many antitheses of inner experience in that all of them substitute goal-oriented endpoints for the eternal being-as-question of inner experience:

> L'expérience intérieure est la réponse qui attend l'homme, lorsqu'il a décidé de n'être que question. Cette décision exprime l'impossibilité d'être satisfait. Dans le monde, les croyances religieuses lui ont appris à mettre en cause les intérêts immédiats, les consolations de l'instant aussi bien que les certitudes d'un savoir inachevé. S'il sait quelque chose, il sait que l'apaisement n'apaise pas et qu'il y a en lui une exigence à la mesure de laquelle rien ne s'offre en cette vie. Aller au-delà, au-delà de ce qu'il désire, de ce qu'il connaît, de ce qu'il est, c'est ce qu'il trouve au fond de tout désir, de toute connaissance et de son être. S'il s'arrête, c'est dans le malaise du mensonge et pour avoir fait de sa fatigue une vérité. Il a choisi de dormir, mais il appelle son sommeil science ou bonheur—parfois guerre. Il peut aussi l'appeler l'au-delà. (*Faux pas* 47–8)

> [Inner experience is the answer that awaits a man, when he has decided to be nothing but question. This decision expresses the impossibility of being satisfied. In the world religious beliefs have taught him to call into question immediate

interests, consolations of the moment as well as the certainties of an imperfect knowledge. If he knows something, he knows that appeasement does not appease and that there is a demand in him that nothing in this life answers. To go beyond, beyond what he desires, what he knows, what he is—that is what he finds at the bottom of every desire, of every knowing, and of his own being. If he stops, it is in the disquiet of the lie, and because he has made his exhaustion into truth. He has chosen to sleep, but he calls his sleep "science" or "happiness"—sometimes "war." He can also call it the beyond. (*Faux pas* (English) 37)]

While this could at first glance seem solipsistic, Bataille adamantly affirms that inner experience demands community, a community of those caught up in the unsurpassable link between laughter and anguish; one consequence of inner experience is that it turns constantly back to the world from which it needed to take its distance in order to activate laughter and anguish. The other path is death, itself the same kind of stasis as science or war:

> Ce qui rejette les hommes de leur isolement vide et les mêle aux mouvements illimités—par quoi ils communiquent entre eux, précipités avec bruit l'un vers l'autre comme les flots—ne pourrait être que la mort si l'horreur de ce *moi* qui s'est replié sur lui-même était poussé à des conséquences logiques. La conscience d'une réalité extérieure—tumultueuse et déchirante—qui naît dans les replis de la conscience de soi—demande à l'homme d'apercevoir la vanité de ces replis—de les « savoir » dans un pressentiment, déjà détruits—*mais elle demande aussi qu'ils durent.* […] Cette agonie, comme figée, de tout ce qui est, qu'est l'existence humaine au sein des cieux—suppose la multitude spectatrice de ceux qui survivent un peu. […] Le rire ne demande pas seulement les personnages risibles que nous sommes, il veut la foule inconséquente des rieurs … (5: 114–15)

> [What throws men out of their empty isolation and mingles them with unlimited movements—by which they communicate among themselves, rushing with a great noise one toward the other like waves—could only be death if the horror of this *self* that has folded back on itself was pushed to logical consequences. The consciousness of an external reality—tumultuous and lacerating—which is born in the recesses of self- consciousness—demands that man perceive the vanity of these recesses—to "know" them in a presentiment, already destroyed—*but it also demands that they endure.* […] The agony, as if immutable, of all that is, which is human existence in the heart of the skies—assumes the multitude of spectators for those who survive a little. […] Laughter demands not only the laughable persons that we are, but it demands the inconsequential crowd of those who laugh … (99–100)]

When Bataille adds italicized commentary on this passage, it is not, as is so often the case, to question it or affirm the opposite, but rather to confirm and reinforce it: "l'existence est *communication*—[…] toute représentation de la vie, de l'être, et généralement de « quelque chose » est à revoir à partir de là" (5: 115) ["existence is *communication*—[…] every representation of life, of being, and generally of 'something' must be reconsidered in this light" (100)]. He affirms the primordial importance of anguish as well, indicating that "la voie de la *communication* (lien profond des peuples) est dans l'angoisse" (5: 115) ["the path of *communication* (the profound bond between peoples) is in anguish" (100)]. What exactly communication means here remains undeveloped, but Bataille's affirmation guards against a view of inner experience as a removal from others; it maintains the presence of the other so that the subject-object relation can function, while also allowing for a shared connection to others based on the anguish that is available to the subject in inner experience.[24]

As the text develops, it becomes easier to see that it presents not a report on experience but rather an experience in itself. As I have argued, experience is at best incomplete apart from its conceptual and textual construction; if it is in part ineffable, that ineffability, and the meaning we make of it, itself becomes part of the experience. The undoing and remapping of conceptual categories such as totality, community, anguish, and so on are an integral part of inner experience as it presents itself in the text, as those concepts come together and reconfigure themselves in relation to other words and concepts as the text goes on. Bataille indicates that ecstasy, for instance, is ineffable, but no more so than any other experience:

> De l'extase, il est facile de dire qu'on ne peut parler. Il est en elle un élément qu'on ne peut réduire, qui demeure « ineffable », mais l'extase, en cela, ne diffère pas d'autres formes : d'elle autant—ou plus—que du rire, de l'amour physique—*ou des choses*—je puis avoir, communiquer la connaissance précise ; la difficulté, toutefois, est qu'étant moins communément éprouvée que le rire ou les choses, ce que j'en dis ne peut être familier, aisément reconnaissable.
>
> (5: 143–4)

> [It is easy to say that one cannot speak of ecstasy. There is in it an element that one cannot reduce, that remains "ineffable," but in this ecstasy does not differ from other forms: I can have, can communicate precise knowledge of ecstasy as much—or more—than of laughter, of physical love, *or of things*; the difficulty, however, is that being less commonly experienced than laughter or things, what I can say about ecstasy cannot be familiar, easily recognizable. (124)]

If the experience remains to any extent ineffable, it is changed, as we have seen, by its transposition into language and concept, so that inner experience, despite what Bataille might affirm about its non-conceptuality that resists intellection, returns to that domain once we see the text not as a record of the experience, since such a thing would be impossible, as itself constitutive of an experience in the act of attempting to make meaning from experience and maintaining thought in a dialectical movement that refuses coming to rest in definitive knowledge.

It is this dramatization of thought that forms the affective dimension of the text of *L'Expérience intérieure*. To demonstrate this I would like to examine in some detail the rest of the three-page section from which the passage quoted immediately above is taken, entitled "Seconde digression sur l'extase dans le vide" ["Second Digression on Ecstasy in the Void"]. The passage dramatizes the transformations and relations of many of the categories that have been at play throughout the book, including ecstasy and anguish, subject and object, and totality and nothingness. Bataille begins with what seems like a familiar and straightforward move: "le non-savoir communique l'extase" (5: 144) ["nonknowledge communicates ecstasy" (124)]. Here we are on the well-trodden ground of the quasi-mystical ecstasy of non-knowing that removes us from the plane of the conceptual and eliminates the subject-object relation that structures the conceptual. But Bataille immediately qualifies the statement and takes us a step closer to the complexity he is about to unfold. The sentence continues: "—mais seulement si la possibilité (le mouvement) de l'extase appartenait déjà [...] à celui qui se déshabille du savoir" (5: 144) ["—but only if the possibility (the movement) of ecstasy already belonged. To some degree, to someone who disrobes himself of knowledge" (124)]. This anterior movement is defined as "l'extase devant un objet" (5: 144) ["ecstasy before an object" (124)]; the movement thus requires the suppression of the object by the subject, which induces an anguish which signals the coming of ecstasy:

> si je supprime, après coup, l'objet—comme la 'contestation' fatalement le fait—si pour cette raison j'entre dans l'angoisse—dans l'horreur, dans la nuit du non-savoir—l'extase est proche et, quand elle survient, m'abîme plus loin que rien d'imaginable. [...] Dès lors la nuit, le non-savoir, sera chaque fois le chemin de l'extase où je me perdrai. (5: 144)
>
> [if I suppress, after the fact, the object—as 'contestation' inevitably does—if for this reason I enter into anguish—into horror, into the night of nonknowledge—ecstasy is near and, when it arises, ruins me further than anything imaginable.

[…] From then on the night, nonknowledge, will each time be the path of ecstasy along which I will lose myself" (124–5)].

Once again, this seems straightforward: the object disappears, and then with the object the subject, into the night of non-knowing.

Experience does not stop here, however, since the night then becomes *itself* an object of desire, which is also an object of knowledge. Bataille does not portray this as an interruption or cancelation of the experience but as its next phase:

> Mais le désir de l'existence ainsi dissipée dans la nuit porte sur un objet d'extase. […] Cet objet s'efface et la nuit est là : l'angoisse me lie, elle me dessèche, mais cette nuit qui se substitue à l'objet et maintenant répond seule à mon attente ? Tout à coup, je le sais, le devine sans cri, ce n'est pas un objet, c'est ELLE que j'attendais ! […] Si je n'étais pas allé vers ELLE come les yeux vont à l'objet de leur amour, si l'attente d'une passion ne l'avait pas cherchée, ELLE ne serait que l'absence de la lumière. (5: 144–5)

> [But the desire for existence thus dissipated in the night bears on an object of ecstasy. […] This object effaces itself and the night is there: anguish binds me, it withers me, but this night substitutes itself for the object and now alone responds to my expectation? Suddenly I know it, discover it without a cry, it is not an object, it is THAT which I was awaiting! […] If I had not gone toward IT as eyes go to the object they love, if the anticipation of a passion had not sought it, IT would only be the absence of light. (125)]

This is a crucial passage for understanding the relation of subject-object relation in inner experience and the way that the nothingness of nonknowledge remains impossible of access. We note how quickly the night itself does not substitute itself for a canceled object but rather becomes itself an object of experience and desire, a fact underscored by the capitalized feminine pronoun Bataille repeatedly uses to refer to it. Thus what had at first seemed like a cancelation of the subject-object relation in the ecstasy of unknowing manifests itself as another manifestation of that same relation; what has changed is not the relation but the character of the object. What prevents the night from being mere absence of light is the subject's relation to it, and thus his conceptual construction of it. He figures the original object of knowledge as a stepping stone on the way to the night which the vehicle by which he is able to "découvrir la nuit" ["discover the night"] and affirms that "à contempler la nuit, je ne vois rien, n'aime rien. Je demeure immobile, figé, absorbé en ELLE" (5: 145) ["contemplating night, I see nothing, love nothing. I remain immobile, frozen, absorbed in IT" (125)].

What Bataille does not say, what he cannot say, is that he disappears as a subject or that he forms a new entity together with the night. Even though he may be absorbed in it, the subject-object relation necessarily remains, but transfigured so that experience is no longer associated with vision. Rather, it carves out a new epistemological status for the object by which, paradoxically, it is nothing (in the sense of having no sensory qualities) but not exactly synonymous with nothing, because it is not the nothing of darkness, which means that the night, unusually, is something other than darkness: "Pour belle et bouleversante qu'elle soit, la nuit surpasse ce possible limité et pourtant ELLE n'est rien, il n'est rien de sensible en ELLE, pas même à la fin l'obscurité" (5: 145) ["as beautiful and upsetting as it may be, the night surpasses this limited possible and yet IT is nothing, it is nothing tangible, not even in the end darkness" (125–6)]. Night is thus emptied of its qualities, that is, of darkness, but also of emptiness. It is a nothing which is not nothing since it becomes, like the object it replaced, an object of desire and of knowing, as it challenges us to identify what it might mean to have a night that is not dark.

Bataille affirms that in this night all is erased, but immediately qualifies that assertion with a "but":

> En ELLE tout s'efface, mais, exorbité, je traverse une profondeur vide et la profondeur vide me traverse, moi. En ELLE, je communique avec l' « inconnu » opposé à l'*ipse* que je suis ; je deviens *ipse*, à moi-même inconnu, deux termes se confondent en un même déchirement, différant à peine d'un vide—ne pouvant par rien que je puisse saisir s'en distinguer—en différant néanmoins plus que le monde aux mille couleurs. (5: 145)

> [In IT everything is effaced, but, exorbitant, I traverse an empty depth and the empty depth traverses me. In IT, I communicate with the "unknown" opposed to the *ipse* that I am; I become *ipse*, unknown to myself, two terms merge into the same laceration, hardly differing from a void—distinguished from it by nothing that I can grasp—nevertheless differing from it more than the world of a thousand colors. (126)]

The qualification that Bataille makes actually cancels the assertion that all is erased and substitutes for it an enhanced subject-object relation whereby the empty depth takes on both object and subject status as it acts on the I. Likewise, the speaking subject claims to be a total whole, the *ipse*, in terms that announce the impossibility of that very assertion because the subject is divided against itself in order to become an object for itself. The two terms "se confondent" in what looks like a move similar to the one by which "tout s'efface," but, like that erasure, the mixing of previously distinct entities is shown not to be a mixing at all. What emerges differs "à peine" from a void, but everything rests on this "barely," which completely negates the void, as the end of the passage affirms. At the heart of the night, then, the subject realizes there is no night at all, nor is there a self as totality. The subject-object relation is canceled neither by an all-consuming night-void nor by the self that consumes the object. What inner experience generates is a realignment of words and concepts so that they are not canceled but transformed by the act of thinking as an unstoppable, resultless process where the affective remains alongside the conceptual, an ecstasy that is anguish, which is generated by the subject but somehow communal and communicable. This act of communicating alters what we attempt to communicate, and this too is a vital part of inner experience. It is one which never allows for a static written record of it that would not also be an invitation to transform those words by interpreting them, producing the conditions of a night that then negates itself as night by taking on new qualities.

To see how much Bataille's approach to thinking differs from more commonly accepted and less dialectical approaches, we can turn both to Gabriel Marcel and to Jean-Paul Sartre. Marcel's review of *L'Expérience intérieure* affirms, as I have as well, that Bataille's book "est de ceux dont il est très difficile de parler avec exactitude et équité" ["is among those of which it is diffcult to speak with exactitude and equity"] (Marcel 59). Intriguingly, Marcel claims this is so because "la pensée y est très souvent explicitement dressée contre elle-même: elle est même perpétuellement encline à se contester, à se mettre en accusation" ["thought is very often explicitly set against itself in this book: it is even perpetually inclined to contest itself and to accuse itself"] (59). Marcel's description here prefigures Emil Cioran's notion of "penser contre soi" ["thinking against oneself"], which will play an important role in my analysis in the next chapter. To think against oneself is also to deploy thought as a form of self-critique, that is, a critique both of the thought itself and of the thinker. Here, despite himself, Marcel affirms what I have been identifying as a dialectical aspect of thought whereby the shifting content reveals the importance of the anti-methodological *method* whereby thought resists being conceived as unified or static. For thought to accuse itself in that way is to perpetuate a process of perpetual self-negation and to reshape both the thought and the thinker in ways that can ultimately illustrate the artificiality of any system of thought that claims to be fixed and unified. It is through such contradictions, and not despite them, that Bataille's approach has value.

Marcel goes on to question Bataille's claims about the disappearance of the subject, again in ways that echo my observations about subjectivity in Bataille. Marcel notes that "ce non-savoir ne conserve une réalité, une valeur de non-savoir qu'à condition d'être encore malgré tout appréhendé comme tel—ce qui suppose un minimum de survivance du sujet, ou [...] un minimum de savoir du non-savoir" ["this nonknowledge only retains a reality and a value of non-knowing provided that it is, despite everything, apprehended as such—which supposes a minimum of survival of the subject, or [...] a minimum of knowledge of nonknowledge"] (263).[25] To affirm the disappearance of the self is, in fact, to reaffirm the reshaping of the understanding of the self as defined by negation, by one who remains at a vantage point of declaring the non-existence of the self as it had formerly been perceived. Marcel takes issue with the way Bataille characterizes his inner experience as a kind of mystical experience, implicitly accusing him of blasphemy and narcissism by proposing that what looks at first like an emptying of self is in fact an arrogantly prideful stance:

> Il convient ici, je crois, de dénoncer ce qui est proprement une imposture, je veux dire l'espèce de brevet de supériorité qu'on entend s'octroyer à soi-même lorsqu'on déclare que la vie spirituelle ne peut se fonder que sur l'absence de salut, etc. [...] Non, on ne s'installe pas ainsi dans un au-delà authentique ; on se borne à jouer un jeu inspiré par un orgueil sans mesure. (278)

> [It is appropriate here, I think, to denounce what is properly an imposture, I mean the sort of certificate of superiority that one means to accord oneself when one declares that spiritual life can only be founded on the absence of salvation, etc. [...] No, one does not install oneself that way in an authentic beyond; one limits oneself to playing a game inspired by an enormous arrogance.]

It is only when judged against the standard of a unified truth and the ideal of Christian humility, to which Marcel is committed, that these accusations can be validated. Bataille would likely not deny that a certain obsession with the self remains, and is perhaps even intensified, in the project of attempting to negate the self. The contradiction that emerges from Bataille's attempted obliteration of self is what emerges as a new experience of thought itself, a simultaneous reordering of thought and subjectivity that Marcel comes close to identifying but which his strong rejection of some of Bataille's presuppositions leads him to refuse.

Jean-Paul Sartre, likewise, and perhaps despite himself, allows us to gain perspective on Bataille's approach through his very criticisms, to which Bataille later responds. In Sartre's review of *L'Expérience intérieure*, entitled "Un nouveau mystique" ["A New Mystic"] and later included in *Situations I*, a sort of *dialogue de sourds* emerges as Sartre's review gives the impression that he is judging Bataille's text by criteria entirely foreign to the book's intellectual project. Sartre begins by establishing a distinction between the form and content of the book, approving the former as a way of giving life to the essay form and responding to the "crise de l'essai" ["crisis of the essay"] (143) that Sartre identifies in his time, and he gives an accurate account of the style of the book:

> La prédication orgueilleuse et dramatique d'un homme plus qu'à demi engagé dans le silence, qui parle à regret une langue fiévreuse, amère, souvent incorrecte, pour aller au plus vite, et qui nous exhorte sans nous regarder à le rejoindre fièrement dans sa honte et dans sa nuit : telle apparait d'abord *L'Expérience intérieure*. (152)

> [The prideful and dramatic preaching of a man more than halfway engaged in silence, who speaks regretfully a feverish, bitter, often incorrect language, to go as fast as possible, and which exhorts us without looking at us to join him proudly in his shame and his night: that is how *Inner Experience* appears at first.]

Sartre establishes a firm distinction, however, between the form and the content, and the rest of the review is a scathing attack on the latter. Sartre's comments begin to reveal how different his criteria for judging thought are from Bataille's conception of it. Sartre does not simply identify his approach and Bataille's as separate enterprises but rather sees the latter's approach to thought as utterly lacking: "Mais la philosophie se venge : ce matériel technique, employé sans discernement, roulé par une passion polémique ou dramatique, asservi à rendre les halètements et les spasmes de notre auteur, se retourne contre lui" ["But philosophy takes its revenge: that technical material, used without discernment, rolled by a polemical or dramatic passion, pressed into service in order to give voice to the panting and spasms of our author, turns against him"] (156). He claims that Bataille's writing hints at rigorous thought, "mais dès qu'on cherche à la saisir, la pensée fond comme de la neige. L'émotion seule demeure, c'est-à-dire un puissant trouble intérieur en face d'objets vagues" ["but as soon as one seeks to capture it, thought melts like snow. Only emotion remains, that is, a powerful interior unease in the face of vague objects"] (156). As I have attempted to show, part of Bataille's project is to show that engagement with concepts destabilizes and alters them; Sartre's assertion suggests a rather fixed approach to thought that implies a lack of rigor on Bataille's part because Sartre fails to recognize that thinking is an essentially destructive activity for Bataille. If thought melts away, it is not that it disappears but rather thinks against itself in order to maintain its dialectical movement. What remains is hardly an emotion devoid of thought in the face of vague objects, but rather an affective dimension of thought that stems from it rather than coming to replace it, as the process of inner experience is driven by the anguish that is the vehicle of thought rather than opposing itself to it.

One could argue that what Sartre identifies as the weakness of Bataille's approach in fact constitutes its strength. He identifies that an important aspect of inner experience is the establishing of a self through thought: "d'une part [Bataille] se cherche et s'atteint par une démarche analogue à celle du *cogito*, qui lui découvre son individualité irremplaçable ; d'autre part il sort soudain de soi pour considérer cette individualité avec les yeux et les instrumets du savant, comme si elle était une chose dans le monde" ["on one hand [Bataille] seeks himself and attains himself by a process analogous to that of the *cogito*, which reveals to him his irreplaceable individuality; on the other hand he leaves himself suddenly in order to consider that individuality with the eyes and instruments of the learned, as if it were a thing in the world"] (162). Sartre perspicaciously observes the way in which Bataille complicates the relation of subject and object by breaking down the Cartesian division between the self and the external world to which it stands in a relation of opposition and power in terms of knowing. And he recognizes that the emerging self "paraît un être étrange et contradictoire, [...] une unité qui s'effondre en multiplicité" ["seems to be a strange and contradictory being, [...] a unity which melts away in multiplicity"] (162-3). He adds immediately, however, that "il n'y a pas lieu d'admirer ces contradictions: si M. Bataille les a trouvées en lui-même, c'est qu'il les y a mises, en introduisant de force le transcendant dans l'immanent" ["there is no grounds for admiring these contradictions: if Mr. Bataille found them in himself, it is because he put them there, by introducing the transcendent into the immanent by force"] (163). Later in the review, Sartre elaborates this critique of what he sees as a false transcendence:

> Et s'il est un « supplice » de l'homme, c'est de ne pouvoir sortir de l'humain pour se juger, de ne pouvoir contempler les dessous des cartes. Non parce qu'on les lui dérobe, mais parce que, les vît-il même, c'est à sa lumière qu'il les verrait. De ce point de vue l'expérience mystique doit être considérée comme une expérience humaine parmi d'autres, elle n'est pas privilégiée. (185)

[And if there is a "torture" of man, it is that of not being able to leave the human in order to judge himself, to not be able to contemplate the other side of the cards. Not because he is deprived of them, but because, even if he were to see them, it is by his own light that he would see them. From that point of view, mystical experience needs to be considered as a human experience among others; it is not privileged.]

Sartre's critique is puzzling in part because it is not clear that Bataille would disagree with Sartre here. By calling into question such categories as immanence and transcendence along with the many other opposed pairs he considers, Bataille could hardly be said to be reintroducing transcendence. As I have argued, Bataille indeed shows that there is no privileged position from which he could be the observer of inner experience, of his own or anyone else's, in anything like an objective scientific sense, precisely because the act of observation changes the nature of the experience and to that extent becomes inseparable from it and partially constitutive of it. To realize this is part of the experience of thought itself, and thus to the extent that inner experience becomes self-reflexive in the way in which it reconfigures the subject-object relation, it is indeed privileged on account of the insight it generates about the destructive nature of thought. If there is transcendence here, it is of an immanent kind, not a going beyond the human but providing the occasion for a redefining of what the human experience of thought is as it manifests itself in Bataille's inner experience.

In his reply to Sartre, Bataille indicates that the critique had helped him to "mettre l'essentiel en relief" (6: 196), and he specifically indicates that naming a phenomenon alters it:

Cette expérience particulière qu'ont les hommes et qu'ils nomment expérience de Dieu, j'imagine qu'on l'altère en la nommant. Il suffit qu'on ait à son sujet une représentation de quelque objet, les précautions n'y changent rien. Au contraire le nom éludé, la théologie se dissout et n'est plus là que pour mémoire : l'expérience est rendue au désespoir. (6: 196)

[That particular experience which men have and which they name the experience of God, I imagine that we alter it in naming it. It suffices that we have a representation of some object, the precautions don't change anything. On the contrary, once the name is eluded, theology dissolves and is only still there for memory: the experience is given over to despair.]

Any talk of God thus necessarily brings the subject back to the immanent experience of the effects of that reflection, an affair of the subject himself rather than a move to transcendence. In fact, Bataille objects to Sartre's assertion that Bataille's inner experience leads him either to God or to the void: "ces reproches contradictoires appuient mon affirmation : *je n'aboutis jamais !*" ["these contradictory reproaches support my affirmation: *I never arrive or conclude!*"] (6: 199). Sartre's critique thus becomes the impetus for Bataille's explicit affirmation of what we have been tracing in *L'Expérience intérieure*, its commitment to a form of thought that refuses any notion of synthesis or endpoint and contains within itself the motor of perpetual continuation that is a crucial element of Bataille's construction of thought as experience and not mere reflection on it. And just as we cannot observe any phenomenon without that observation changing it, the experience of reading itself is not the transparent absorption of content but a dynamic process hiding behind the apparent stability of the words on the page: "l'apparente immobilité d'un livre nous leurre : chaque livre est aussi la somme des malentendus dont il est l'occasion" ["the apparent immobility of a book traps us: every book is also the sum total of the misunderstandings of which it is the occasion"] (6: 199–200). We may, in other words, have to pass through the kind of misunderstanding that Sartre exposes by his accusation of mysticism on Bataille's part in order to arrive at a provisional understanding of thought and experience that alters both Bataille's text and our initial experience of it. To aim for a stable understanding would be to assume the stability of the thinking subject that Bataille consistently calls into question: "en un instant donné, ma pensée atteint une appréciable rigueur. Mais comment la lier à ma pensée d'hier ? Hier, j'étais en quelque sens un autre, je répondais à d'autres soucis. L'adaptation des deux demeure possible mais …." ["in a given instant, my thought attains an appreciable rigor. But how can I link it to yesterday's thought? Yesterday, I was in some sense another, I was answering other concerns. The adaptation of the two remains possible but … "] (6: 200). While we have seen that it cannot be a question of dissolving the subject entirely so long as there is in fact a subject of inner experience, the subject has to find its ground, paradoxically, in its lack of fixed self-identity, a shifting ground on which and from which inner experience is realized.

So where does this leave us in terms of the political stakes of a project such as *L'Expérience intérieure*? Many have noted that 1943 did not seem especially right for a book by and about a subject removed from the outside world of action in pursuit of a form of contemplation in a book written in Saint-Germain-en-Laye. Michel Surya summarizes some of the criticism at the time of publication:

> Bataille seems to have been wrong to publish *Inner Experience* in 1943, during the war. Jules Monnerot reproached him for it in a friendly, discreet and, moreover, justified, way. Patrick Waldberg did so too, but publicly (in the journal *VVV*, published in the United States) and in a far more aggressive way. Souvarine later saw it as a heinous sign at least of its author's acceptance of the Occupation, if not of collusion with the occupier. There were others in Paris itself who at the time responded negatively to the publication of *Inner Experience* for quite different reasons: if this book merited being denounced, it was not because it was published during the war, but because it was itself, in a *morbid* way, war. (329)

Alexander Irwin succinctly poses the question at the heart of any discussion of the political valence of the work in the context of what came to be formed as Bataille's projected *Somme athéologique* of which *L'Expérience intérieure* was to be the first installment: "Was Bataille's atheistic 'religion' a liberation from ossified political forms or a rejection of a real responsibility in favor of self-indulgent textual transgression?" (Irwin xxv). To what extent is it valid, as Irwin goes on to ask, to see these writings as "marking an abrupt break with the political concerns that absorbed him during the 1930s?" (30).[26] I follow Irwin in his argument that these writings by Bataille are best understood as "a provocative response to war's political, psychological, and philosophical challenges in a context in which standard modes of political reflection had been rendered largely inoperative [...]. Bataille rejects war not in the name of pacifism, but in the name of a purified and heightened violence: that of sacrifice internalized in mysticism and writing" (126).[27] What could have been a reactionary project translatable into enthusiasm for war in its antirationalist evocation of violence is ultimately not that at all, on account of the unalterable openness of Bataille's text. The impossibility of concluding, on the part of him who says "je n'aboutis jamais," precludes any dogmatic assertion of the kind that would be necessary to see these writings as implicit or explicit endorsement of, or in complicity with, reactionary politics. To claim the opposite is to have no understanding of the project of inner experience as it emerges in the dynamism of the writing and reading of the text. The self that remains, despite efforts to dissolve it in mysticism or eroticism, serves, in its very existence as a self that never "arrives," as a guard against fascism and war insofar as war is a definitive and goal-oriented action and thus incompatible with inner experience. The absolutization of violence as an instrumental means puts a definitive end to a process and installs a totalizing and permanent answer to the questions that inner experience poses but about which it insists that definitive answers are unacceptable and even impossible.[28]

By refusing the comfort of a goal and especially of a goal attained, Bataille enacts a form of thought that is necessarily imbricated with anguish, a consequence of the divided self as subject and object, of a self whose subjectivity is established in its own observation as a self mediating and mediated by the object world. This is an approach that depends on the persistence of the aspiration toward a unified self but only under the sign of its own impossibility; thought produces and is then conscious of those conditions of impossibility by virtue of the movement of thought itself. The experience of thought does not, cannot abolish the self or effect the passing over of the self into writing. As Patrick ffrench indicates, "The exposure pursued in Bataille's thought and writing remain fundamentally the exposure of the human, of the person, [...] an exposure which is not assumed into the impersonal neutrality of a language" (113). The thinking self thus lends itself neither to closure nor to foreclosure; it establishes itself as in a relation with the external world and with its own self as a mediated and mediated actor in that world and thus realizes what Adorno calls "the essentially relational character" of dialectical concepts which leads us to the realization that "there is no such thing as a partial individual truth," but rather that "here is truth only in the constellation which the quite specific individual instances of knowledge come to make up" (*Introduction* 208). Bataille performs this relationality through the creation and portrayal of a subject in perpetual unity and opposition to itself and to the external world of which it figures itself a part while at the same time standing outside. To work through what a notion of dialectical subjectivity would look like is, I hope to have shown, what is at stake in *L'Expérience intérieure*, an attempt to work on the self in a way that reconfigures conceptions of unity, certainty, and knowability of the external world in and through and as the mediated and mediating self. To come to a stable endpoint in our articulation of such a process could only mean admitting we have understood nothing of where a dialectical subjectivity leads. To think with Bataille is to recognize the non-identity of the concept with the thing it attempts to represent and to sustain that contradiction. When the object of thought is the self which the thinking subject attempts to seize, then that subject-object split within the self leads to what we could call thinking against oneself, a central guiding concept for essayist and aphorist Emil Cioran, to whom I now turn.

2

Emil Cioran: Thinking against Oneself

Emil Cioran emerged on the French literary scene in 1949 with *Précis de décomposition* [*A Short History of Decay*] after having published several books in Romanian. His writing does not sit comfortably within any one genre. Most of the short sections of the *Précis* are longer than aphorisms (which he would practice more recognizably in his next book, *Syllogismes de l'amertume* [*Syllogisms of Bitterness*]) and shorter than essays. They are written in a sort of uncanny voice from nowhere in particular, a mix of the oracular and the personal, floating between a *je* and a *nous*, contemplation and engagement, a universal and a particular.[1] That writing voice consistently refuses systems, summoning the history of philosophy or thought more broadly while establishing distance from it, evoking rather than citing most of the authors he does occasionally mention. One could say that he engages with the history and legacy of thought by not engaging with it, or, rather, by performing a kind of non-engagement with it that transforms our understanding of thinking in ways that are to some degree consistent with Bataille's approach.[2] Cioran's thought operates by paradox and contradiction, by situated moments that seem to announce what appears to be a universal idea, only to call that idea into question elsewhere in the text implicitly, performatively, or explicitly. Like Bataille, he engages the reader through a writing that poses a challenge to one who wishes to establish a coherent point of view from the text; that can only be done by an approach that makes room for the possibility that totalizing meanings will not emerge from the writing. As in Bataille, to impose a systematic approach that would generate such closed and totalizing meanings would do violence to the text. Beyond the literary and open-ended quality of the writing, both authors share an affective investment in thought, an anguish that is one of the motors of thinking and which is inseparable from its processes.

Cioran could be said to be the thinker of the "à quoi bon?," the "what's the use?," often espousing quietism as a refusal of the vanity of thought or action, or of thought as a kind of action.³ But as I will show, the very impossibility of maintaining full skepticism or quietism constantly relaunches Cioran into thought, to attempt to draw the full consequences, through thought, of the impossibility of abandoning thought.⁴ He is led, in other words, to think the refusal of thought; this is one way of thinking "against himself," a phrase that is central to Cioran's writing project more generally. I will elaborate what is at stake in thinking against oneself below; for now it is enough to note both that that approach both conditions a thought that refuses resolution and also that it contains the violence against a split self implied in the evocation of thinking as an action undertaken "against" oneself, which gives rise to the attacks, suffering, and accusations that are part and parcel of a thought against thought that places the thinker against himself at the same time. I shall begin below with a reading of the lead section of *La Tentation d'exister* (1956) entitled "Penser contre soi," seeing it as an implicit program of the project he elaborates seven years before in the *Précis*.

What was to become one of the constants of Cioran's writing over the years is the nature of thought as combative or as provoking the opposite of tranquil reflection. He writes in *De l'inconvénient d'être né* (1975): "en paix avec lui-même et le monde, l'esprit s'étiole. Il s'épanouit à la moindre contrariété. La pensée n'est en somme que l'exploitation éhontée de nos gênes et de nos disgrâces" (1375) ["at peace with itself and the world, the mind atrophies. It flourishes at the slightest contrariety. Thought is really no more than the shameless exploitation of our embarrassments and our disgraces" (*Trouble* 171)]. He characterizes resignation as what turns out to be an impossible ideal, suggesting a certain degree of hostility for himself for failing to uphold it nonetheless: "toutes mes pensées sont tournées vers la résignation, et cependant il ne se passe pas de jour que je ne concocte quelque ultimatum à l'adresse de Dieu ou de n'importe qui" (1381) ["all my thoughts are turned toward resignation, and yet not a day passes when I fail to concoct some ultimatum to God or to anyone" (181)]. I will address below some of the consequences of that impossibility as I trace why thought necessarily leads both to the desire for resignation and to the realization of its impossibility for Cioran. It springs, I will argue, from a sense of duality that ultimately relates back to a certain form of dialectical thinking, consistent with his assertion that the mind languishes when it is at peace, and which necessitates the refusal of any definitive conclusion that would bring thought to a tranquil halt.

A passage from Cioran's posthumously published *Cahiers* provides a revealing glimpse both into his compositional process and into the complex relation between affirmations in the first-person singular and more generalized assertions about people in general, referred to by the moralist's general pronoun "on."

> Je n'éprouve une sensation de bien-être que lorsque aucune pensée n'effleure mon esprit.
>
> Ou
>
> On n'éprouve une sensation de bien-être que dans l'absence de pensée.
>
> (Il n'y a de bien-être qu'en deçà de la pensée.)
>
> <div align="right">(<i>Cahiers</i> 237)</div>
>
> [I only have a sense of well-being when no thought touches my mind.
>
> Or
>
> We only have a sense of well-being in the absence of thought.
>
> (There is only well-being outside of thought.)]

Cioran reshapes the sentence for brevity and concision as he moves from one version to the next, while also gradually depersonalizing the assertion as it moves from a situated and specific comment by a first-person subject to the more generalized statement about people in general. He then moves on through the third iteration that fully depersonalizes the assertion in such a way as to make it seem like not a generalized maxim about people's behavior and feelings but an ontological statement. It becomes a universal statement about thought and well-being rather than about a single or collective subject. Cioran's compositional process also accomplishes an erasure of the subject, but the thought's origin in personal experience encourages us to read all of Cioran's writings both engaging and hiding the personal experience of thought, the fruit of a kind of mental exercise whose origins cannot be so simply erased. The process actually accomplishes a complex back-and-forth movement between thought and the experience of the thinking subject, since we move from experience to thought but then, in the final iteration, are implicitly invited to draw the consequences of the universal statement about well-being found only beyond thought.

We are implicitly invited, through the act of thought itself, to evaluate the maxim by comparing it to our own experience, thus bringing the process back full circle to the first person and engaging in the very act that is already described as disturbing our well-being. By leading us to evaluate the statement, the maxim invites personal intervention in the thought and unleashes the conceptual movement that the statement affirms will disturb well-being, thus making the statement self-fulfilling and providing evidence for this assertion that Cioran makes years later in the *Cahiers*: "penser, c'est ne pas laisser les choses en place—c'est un travail de dislocation. La pensée est la forme la plus subtile de l'agressivité" ["to think is to not leave things in place—it is a work of dislocation. Thought is the most subtle form of aggressivity"] (707). To read Cioran is to be drawn into the process of thought as an active creation with an experiential conceptual dimension that emerges by and through the thought itself. His texts defy simple categorization because of the way they float between a literary quality and a philosophical aspect. As Patrice Bollon has claimed: "On lit Cioran comme un écrivain. Certes, il en est un, et des plus grands. [...] Mais l'on oublie, ce faisant, qu'il fut aussi, *d'abord et avant tout*, un penseur, et même l'un des plus actuels" ["We read Cioran as a writer. Certainly he is one, and one of the greatest. [...] But we forget, when doing that, that he was also, *first and before all else*, a thinker, and even one of the most contemporary"] (29).

Cioran seeks, we might say, a relation of non-relation to other thinkers. As Sylvain David has argued, the idea of thinking against oneself also implies thinking against one's contemporaries or those who have had a role in forming one's thought: "il aspire moins à se détruire physiquement qu'à démolir systématiquement en lui la moindre idée, image ou illusion qu'il pourrait avoir en commun avec ses contemporains" ["he aspires less to destroy himself physically than to demolish systematically in himself the least idea, image, or illusion that he could have in common with his contemporaries"] (15). The general lack of references to other thinkers reinforces the dialogical aspect of Cioran's own thought, a thinking against himself that animates the potential contradictions and dialectical relationships of the ideas in his own writing and the relationship they imply to experience. Cioran's style features an approach to thought that plays itself out through the echoes and resonances at work in the writing, so that the dynamic complexity of the ideas are captured in those resonances rather than being revealed in any one particular local moment.[5]

I turn now to the section of *La Tentation d'exister* (1956) entitled "Penser contre soi," to see in it a sort of nonprogrammatic program for thought and writing, before using that approach as a lens through which we can approach Cioran's first book in French, *Précis de décomposition* (1949). Cioran situates thought, not just for himself but for his frequently unspecified general "we," in a lineage that sees action on the self as a kind of violence, which he opposes to the supposed calm of Taoism: "le virus chrétien nous travaille : légataires des flagellants, c'est en raffinant nos supplices que nous prenons conscience de nous-mêmes. La religion décline-t-elle ? Nous en perpétuons les extravagances" (822) ["the Christian virus torments us: heirs of the flagellants, it is by refining our excruciations that we become conscious of ourselves. Is religion declining? We perpetuate its extravagances" (*Temptation* 34)]. To think against oneself is not so much to inflict division so much as to reveal the division that was already there in the constitution of the self and to give the lie to a notion of a unified self. What can seem a perversion at first is in fact a methodological move by which we might both make manifest and draw the consequences of the notion of the divided self. Cioran identifies Nietzsche, Baudelaire, and Dostoyevsky as those who have taught us to "miser sur nos périls, à élargir la sphère de nos maux, à acquérir de l'existence par la division d'avec notre être" ["side with our dangers, to broaden the sphere of our diseases, to require existence by division from our being" (35)]; thus the act of conceptual violence by which we think against ourselves is for Cioran "l'unique modalité de nous posséder, d'entrer en conatct avec nous-mêmes" (822) ["the sole mode of possessing, of making contact with ourselves" (35)]. Cioran thus advances a point of view that goes against the kind of passivity he often expresses the desire to achieve, and which is embodied in Asian thinkers such as Lao-Tse whom he cites in this section. Cioran highlights the paradox of the impossibility of achieving quietude on account of quietude's participation in a tension of which it is one of the poles and which cannot be resolved despite any potential longing for such a state of calm, which means that apathy is also, like the self, divided against itself: "L'apogée de l'indifférence, comment y atteindre, quand notre apathie même est tension, conflit, agressivité ?" (822) ["the apogee of indifference—how attain it, when our very apathy is tension, conflict, aggression?" (35)]. What begins to emerge here is the fact that both thought and the self are divided against themselves, which implies an important connection between thought and self-identity, since it is dialectical thought that both produces and reflects a dialectical self which constitutes itself through the act of thinking itself as divided.

To consider Taoism as a foil to the active, suffering-inducing conception of the self advanced by Nietzsche and company serves only to deepen the divide in the self rather than posing a viable alternative to it.[6] Taoism does this by reminding us of a potential ideal which serves as a kind of temptation to the restless and divided self while at the same time establishing its own impossibility as a viable model precisely because it participates in that relation of tension. To resolve the tension in favor of passivity would mean to cancel thought, and with it to cancel the self altogether. What Cioran sometimes calls our "nature" or our "instinct" against the kind of passivity that we sometimes claim to want to attain is more like a recognition of the self in thought, as present to itself as subject and object and thus inherently divided, making "salvation" through passivity impossible:

> L'apprentissage de la passivité, je ne vois rien de plus contraire à nos habitudes. [...] Le taoïsme m'apparaît comme le premier et le dernier mot de la sagesse : j'y suis pourtant réfractaire, mes instincts le refusent, l'hérédité de la rébellion. [...] Il est des formes de sagesse et de délivrance que nous ne pouvons ni saisir du dedans, ni transformer en notre substance quotidienne, ni même enserrer dans une théorie. La délivrance, si l'on y tient en effet, doit procéder de nous : point ne faut la chercher ailleurs dans un système tout fait ou quelque doctrine orientale. C'est pourtant ce qui arrive souvent chez maint esprit avide, comme on dit, d'absolu. Mais sa sagesse est contrefaçon, sa délivrance duperie. [...] Quel pullulement de faux « délivrés » qui nous regardent du haut de leur salut ! (823)[7]

> [The apprenticeship to passivity—I know nothing more contrary to our habits. [...] Taoism seems to me wisdom's first and last word: yet I resist it, my instincts rejects it, as they refuse to *endure* anything—the heredity of revolt is too much for us. [...] There are certain forms of wisdom and deliverance which we can neither grasp from within nor transform into a daily substance, nor even frame in a theory. Deliverance, if we insist upon it, must proceed from ourselves: no use seeking it elsewhere, in a ready-made system or in some Oriental doctrine. Yet this is often what happens in many a mind avid as we say, for an absolute. But such wisdom is fraudulent, such deliverance mere dupery. [...] What a swarm of the pseudo-"delivered" stares down at us from the pinnacle of their salvation! (35–6)]

By reading across various moments in Cioran, we can see that he sometimes affirms passivity as an aspirational ideal and sometimes a fiction that would be impossible even to strive for. What is significant here is not simply that he contradicts himself but rather that he works out, across his writings, the way in which the desire for passivity is not the end of a process but rather one term in it; passivity depends on its own cancelation in order to continue playing a role at all for the thinking subject. Once we place emphasis on the process rather than on the content of any one particular thought, the fragmentary and aphoristic style that characterizes most of Cioran's writings emerges as a way of facilitating our putting those moments of thought and writing in dialogue with each other and to avoid taking any one situated thought as a definitive pronouncement, even though the aphoristic style seems at first to encourage to apply the thought as a general maxim rather than as one term in a more complex textual dynamic.

In that sense, the aphoristic style is a writing against itself. The "suffering" implied by thinking against oneself is not simply a reaction to it but a manifestation of it, an experience that is a part of the thought itself.[8] And even suffering is not simple in its meaning for Cioran, since there can be a kind of happiness generated from the experience of recognizing doubleness and not attempting to cancel or overcome it in something akin to salvation:

> C'est par nos œuvres, ce n'est pas par nos silences, que nous avons choisi de disparaître : notre avenir se lit dans le ricanement de nos figures, dans nos traits de prophètes meurtris et affairés. [...] A la limite, nous concevons le bonheur ; jamais la félicité, apanage de civilisations fondées sur l'idée de salut, sur le refus de savourer ses maux, de s'y délecter ; mais, sybarites de la douleur, rejetons d'une tradition masochiste, qui de nous balancerait entre le sermon de Bénarès et l'*Héautontimorouménos* ? « Je suis la plaie et le couteau », voilà notre absolu, notre éternité.(826)

> [It is by our works, not by our silences, that we have chosen to disappear: our future may be read in our features, in the grimaces of agonized and busy prophets. [...] At best, we conceive happiness, never felicity, prerogative of civilizations based on the idea of salvation, on the refusal to savor one's sufferings, to revel in them; but, sybarites of suffering, scions of a masochistic tradition, which of us would hesitate between the Benares sermon and Baudelaire's *Heautotimoroumenos*? "I am both wound and knife"—that is our absolute, our eternity. (39–40)]

Cioran identifies this condition as a "degraded" form of wisdom, which is not to say that we can simply revert to the kind of wisdom that seeks the annihilation of the self as an active potential alternative. For all of the apparently universalizing use of the "we" in these texts and the general lack of historical reference, there is a strong implication that the move toward the realization of degraded wisdom as our only current alternative is historically generated, an effect of working out what was always the impossibility of the quietistic ideal removed from any relationship with its own impossibility:

> voués à des formes dégradées de sagesse, maladies de la durée, en lutte avec cette infirmité qui nous rebute autant qu'elle nous séduit, en lutte avec le temps, nous sommes constitués d'éléments qui tous concourent à faire de nous des rebelles partagés entre un appel mystique qui n'a aucun lien avec l'histoire et un rêve sanguinaire qui en est le symbole et le nimbe.
>
> (827)

[doomed to corrupted forms of wisdom, invalids of duration, victims of time, that weakness which appalls as much as it appeals to us, we are constituted of elements that all unite to make us rebels divided between a mystic summons which has no link with history and a bloodthirsty dream which is history's symbol and nimbus. (41)]

For Cioran, both passivity and action are equal and opposite temptations, to be resisted by the subject lucid enough to realize their status as temptations. In a passage that echoes Georges Bataille's affirmation, in defending himself against Sartre: "*je n'aboutis jamais!*" ["I never arrive or conclude!"] (Bataille 6: 199), Cioran too guards against the notion that ideas should be goal-oriented and directed: "contaminés par la superstition de l'acte, nous croyons que nos idées doivent *aboutir*. Quoi de plus contraire à la considération passive du monde ? Mais c'est là notre destin : être des incurables qui *protestent*, des pamphlétaires sur un grabat" (827) ["contaminated by the superstition of action, we believe that our ideas must *come to something*. What could be more contrary to the passive consideration of the world? But such is our fate: to be incurables who *protest*, pamphleteers on a pallet" (41)]. The dialectical state of affairs exists against what should according to Cioran be the way of the world that would lead us to a desirable paralysis: "nos connaissances, comme nos expériences, devraient nous paralyser, et nous rendre indulgents à l'égard de la tyrannie elle-même, du moment qu'elle représente une constante. […] Bien que nous puissions faire des stoïciens accomplis, l'anarchiste veille en nous et s'oppose à nos résignations" (827–8) ["our knowledge, like our experience, should paralyze us and make us indignant to tyranny itself, once it represents a constant. […] Though we might have made accomplished Stoics, the anarchist keeps watch within us and opposes our resignations" (41–2)]. While the stoic ideal remains impossible, it is equally impossible to abandon it, for it is only through its persistence under the sign of negation or impossibility that we can activate the dialectical relationship of passivity and action and maintain the conceptual tension between them that allows us to articulate subjectivity as divided. Awareness of the dissonance between the two conceptions is an important motor of the process of thinking against oneself, which means that eliminating one pole or the other would shut down that very process. Such a shutdown would bring us to the realm of non-thought, but that sort of ideal is something that Cioran considers dangerous because it comes to rest in a false sense of conviction that leads to horror historically, a kind of violence turned toward the other when one senses, falsely, that one is unified with oneself, as Bataille also indicates in his exploration of the *ipse*.

By conceiving subjectivity as a sort of violence that reveals the necessarily divided nature of the self, Cioran, paradoxically perhaps, eliminates a hard and fast distinction between thought and action, which come to have a similar structure in that both reveal duality and attempt to function within the consequences of that duality, making of the subject the one who thinks and acts in the face of the necessarily impossible (and ultimately undesirable) mitigation of duality:

> Tout acte institue et réhabilite la pluralité, et, conférant à la personne réalité et autonomie, reconnaît implicitement la dégradation, le morcellement de l'absolu. Et c'est de lui, de l'acte, et du culte qui s'y attache, que procèdent la tension de notre esprit, et ce besoin d'éclater et de nous détruire *au cœur de la durée*. La philosophie moderne, en instaurant la superstition du Moi, en a fait le ressort de nos drames et le pivot de nos inquiétudes. Regretter le repos dans l'indistinction, le rêve neutre de l'existence sans qualités, ne sert de rien ; nous nous sommes voulus *sujets*, et tout sujet est rupture avec la quiétude de l'Unité. Quiconque s'avise d'atténuer notre solitude ou nos déchirements agit à l'encontre de nos intérêts et de notre vocation. Nous mesurons la valeur de l'individu à la somme de ses désaccords avec les choses, à son incapacité d'être indifférent, à son refus de tendre vers l'objet. D'où le déclassement de l'idée de Bien, d'où la vogue du Diable.(828–9)

[Every act institutes and rehabilitates plurality, and, conferring reality and autonomy upon *the person*, implicitly recognizes the degradation, the parceling-out of *the absolute*. And it is from the act, and from the cult attached to it, that the tension of our mind proceeds, the need to explode and to destroy ourselves *at the heart of duration*. Modern philosophy, by establishing the superstition of the Ego, has made it the mainspring of our dramas and the pivot of our anxieties. To regret the repose of indistinction, the neutral dream of an existence without qualities, is pointless; we have chosen to be *subjects*, and every subject is a break with the quietude of Unity. Whoever takes it upon himself to attenuate our solitude or our lacerations acts against our interests, against our vocation. We measure an individual's value by the sum of his disagreements with things, by his incapacity to be indifferent, by his refusal as a subject to tend toward the object. Whence the obsolescence of the idea of Good; whence the vogue of the Devil. (42–3)]

On this view, the unitary self cannot serve as a corrective to the divisiveness of action but rather is shown to be a fiction when in fact the self participates in the same duality that characterizes action. What is meant to be a point of distinction ends up revealing similarity and the way in which the self can only be constituted as in rupture with a purportedly desired unity.

Like Baudelaire before him, Cioran considers this duality as a diabolical attribute, thus assimilating the diabolical to the fundamentally human aspect of being simultaneously subject and object and, more specifically, to the specific aspect of thinking, the two-in-one of dialogue that gives rise to skepticism.

In this way, humans and the devil are assimilated to one another. Cioran writes about the devil that:

> ses protestations, ses violences ne manquent pas d'équivoque : ce « grand Triste » est une rebelle qui doute. S'il était simple, tout d'une pièce, il ne nous toucherait guère ; mais ses paradoxes, ses contradictions sont nôtres : il cumule nos impossibilités, il sert de modèle à nos révoltes contre nous-mêmes, à la haine de nous-mêmes. (829)
>
> [his protests, his violences have their own ambiguity: this "Great Melancholic" is a *rebel who doubts*. If he were simple, all of a piece, he would not touch us at all; but his paradoxes, his contradictions are our own: he is the sum of our impossibilities, serves as a model for our rebellions against ourselves, our self-hatred. (43)]

Cioran goes on to characterize history as an "*aggression de l'homme contre lui-même* [...] de sorte que se vouer à l'histoire, c'est apprendre à s'insurger, à imiter le Diable" (829) ["*man's aggression against himself* [...] so that to dedicate oneself to history if to learn to rebel, to imitate the Devil" (44)]. Paradoxically, by insisting on duality, Cioran ends up establishing a series of equivalences here. If the self is divided against itself, as in the model of Baudelaire's self-torturer that Cioran evokes above, then the aggression of man against man is a kind of mirror of that internal split, whether that means the actual armed conflicts that many take to be the key moments of "history" or the more abstract, quasi-Hegelian sense of the unfolding of a series of characterizations of humanity that are in rupture with previous conceptions. These new characterizations force a redefinition of what we understand humanity to be.

Beyond assimilating the individual and humanity writ large, Cioran also, by assimilating humanity to the devil on account of this (real and/or conceptual) aggression, erases a fundamental distinction between the devil and humanity. So by insisting on duality and division, Cioran implicitly sets up a division within this notion of division itself by demonstrating the similarity that the difference puts in place. And it is through the notion of what he labels a diabolical orientation toward division that he establishes what I have been calling the drama of thought, an installation of an irreconcilable tension that identifies any attempt to go beyond that tension as either impossible or undesirable. Thus Cioran concludes that "sagesse et rébellion" ["Wisdom and Revolt"] are "deux poisons" ["two poisons"]: "inaptes à les assimiler naïvement, nous ne trouvons dans l'une ni dans l'autre une formule de salut. Il reste que dans l'aventure luciférienne nous avons acquis une maîtrise que nous ne posséderons jamais dans la sagesse" (830) ["unfit to assimilate them naively, we find neither one a formula for salvation. The fact remains that in the Satanic adventure we have acquired a mastery we shall never possess in wisdom" (44–5)]. Wisdom, aligned here with the resignation and passivity that Cioran himself sometimes identifies as his goal, is nonetheless rejected, a stance that resonates with his rejection of remedies and salvation in the *Précis de décomposition* in the context of the waning years of classical Athens: "l'obsession des remèdes marque la fin d'une civilisation ; la quête du salut, celle d'une philosphie" (610–11) ["the obsession with remedies marks the end of a civilization; the search for salvation, that of a philosophy" (*Short* 34)]. That is not to say that those in the opposed lineage of the self-torturing self represent any less of a temptation or seduction: "Rimbaud et Nietzsche, acrobates se démènent à l'extrême d'eux-mêmes, nous invitent à leurs dangers. Seuls nous séduisent les esprits qui se sont détruits pour avoir voulu donner un sens à leur vie" (830) ["Rimbaud and Nietzsche, acrobats straining at the extreme limits of themselves, engage us in their dangers. The only minds which seduce us are the minds which have destroyed themselves trying to give their lives a meaning" (45)]. But the divided and suffering selves of Rimbaud or Nietzsche are necessarily more than simply a temptation or an option to elect in opposition to the Tao with which Cioran explicitly contrasts them here. The very fact that we are torn between the two models suggests that the model of suffering duality necessarily wins the day as the only viable one, since to conceive of the self at all is, as we have seen, to conceive of it as divided; liquidating its multiplicity would liquidate the self and its conceptualizing functions altogether. To affirm the unity of the Tao would necessitate a conceptualization of its opposite, which is precisely the subject-object division on which thought depends and which precludes an affirmation of that unity.

With this framework of what it would mean to "think against oneself" as the fundamental motor of thinking and writing in Cioran, let us turn to the *Précis de decomposition*, the work in which he emerged on the post-Second World War literary scene in France. As I have already suggested, the voice that speaks in this writing is curiously both personal and generalized, engaged in the lived world and abstracted from it. Nicolas Cavaillès identifies this as a shift from what he calls the "voix suicidaire" ["suicidal voice"] of the earlier texts to the "voix décomposée" ["decomposed voice"] of the first French works:

> si les thèmes qui la préoccupent sont semblables, c'est avec scepticisme, finesse et érudition, qu'ils sont abordés. La vanité du monde, des espoirs et des idéologies, est exposée sans étonnement. [...] Un cynisme froid y croise une sentimentalité douloureuse, tournée vers ses erreurs et vers sa naïveté d'antan ; Cioran s'isole, à distance des autres, de son siècle et de lui-même, dans une hyper-conscience de soi qui n'exclut pas, *in fine*, de douces larmes mélancoliques ni un fin sourire moqueur. (97)

> [if the themes that preoccupy him are similar, he approaches them with skepticism, finesse, and erudition. The vanity of the world, of hopes, and of ideologies is exposed without astonishment. A cold cynicism encounters a painful sentimentality, turned toward his errors and naiveté of his former years. Cioran isolates himself, at a distance from others, from his century, and from himself, in a hyper-consciousness of himself that does not exclude, *in fine*, tender melancholic tears or a thin mocking smile.]

The lack of specifically personal remarks reinforces the power of the more generalized "I" which implicates readers in that it implicitly invites them to construct a relation of identification or opposition with the textual "I." The first self encountered is an epigraph to the work taken from *Richard III*: "I'll join with black despair against my soul, / And to myself become an enemy" (581). The implication is that the speaking subject in Cioran's text assimilates itself to the speaker in the play, joining itself with another subject in order to announce the project of thinking against oneself. The rest of the text could be seen as an attempt to work out the implications of that split in the writing subject, the diabolical consequences of the experience of thinking against oneself.[9] The active nature of the speaking subject comes through in the provisional title Cioran had chosen for the book, "Exercices négatifs," explicitly evoking the spiritual exercises of Ignatius of Loyola, a guided mental exercise by which one seeks to conquer the self in favor of greater union with the divinity. By taking up and negating the exercises, Cioran calls into question the notion of unity but suggests the necessary perpetuation of the self through its impossible unity. This self is formed by and through thought, the process that becomes inseparable from the subject-object relations of the thinker.

His opening move in the first of the very short sections that comprise the book, "Généalogie du fanatisme," evokes, in order to reject, the notion that ideas reside beyond an individual consciousness and, especially, beyond history. This is the first and, arguably, one of the most important negations that this paradoxical singular-collective "je-nous" voice will effect:

> En elle-même, toute idée est neutre, ou devrait l'être ; mais l'homme l'anime, y projette ses flammes et ses démences ; impure, transformée en croyance, elle s'insère dans le temps, prend figure d'événement : le passage de la logique à l'épilepsie est consommé ... Ainsi naissent les idéologies, les doctrines, et les farces sanglantes. (581)[10]

> [In itself, every idea is neutral, or should be; but man animates ideas, projects his flames and flaws into them; impure, transformed into beliefs, ideas take their place in time, take shape as *events*: the trajectory is complete, from logic to epilepsy ... whence the birth of ideologies, doctrines, bloody farces. (*Short* 3, translation modified)]

There is all the difference in the world between the casually phrased options that ideas either are neutral or should be. There is ambiguity in the "should": this implies either that ideas would in fact be neutral if it were not for inappropriate human action that transforms them, or that while in theory ideas should be neutral, they never can be, because it is impossible to divorce an idea from human conception and from the history and culture within which ideas move. Our interpretation of the "should" determines whether humanity's interaction with these ideas is inappropriate (according to the first model) or inevitable (according to the second).

Given that it is impossible to determine what a "pure" idea would be, detached from the history in which it emerges and changes, it seems that the second option is the only viable one, and that the regret that ideas become "impure" reflects a nostalgia for a model of ideas that was never actually borne out in thought. Supposedly pure and immobile logic is set into motion in the opening move of the *Précis*, a text whose own ideas would be simply unintelligible outside its own immediate context of the disaster of the rise of fascism and the Shoah, the historical events from whose ruins the *Précis* emerges both historically and in terms of Cioran's endorsement of the extreme right in Germany and Romania in the 1930s, and to which the reference to "ideologies, doctrines, and bloody farces" makes direct if unnamed reference.[11] In this passage we see in another form the regret or nostalgia for the passivity or quietism of renunciation that

Cioran addresses in his reflections on "penser contre soi" that we have just analyzed. But given that such quietism is impossible, the incipit of the *Précis* implicitly questions whether the emergence of doctrines and their bloody farces are the only and inevitable consequence of the impossibility of neutral ideas and their necessary insertion into time and thus into history. Put in the terms that both Bataille and Cioran have evoked, is it possible for ideas to emerge in history in a way that is not goal-oriented, that staunchly refuse to "aboutir," to calcify in a set of doctrines that would put an end the movement of thought? In other words, in order for Cioran's own thought to remain dynamic, his own ideas must seek to keep open the dialectical nature of thought that resists their becoming ideology.[12]

Cioran continues to speak in a generalized and oracular tone about humanity's secular idolatry and the catastrophe that a history generated from such idolatry generates:

> Idolâtres par instinct, nous convertissons en inconditionné les objets de nos songes et de nos intérêts. L'histoire n'est qu'un défilé de faux Absolus, une succession de temples élevés à des prétextes, un avilissement de l'esprit devant l'Improbable. Lors même qu'il s'éloigne de la religion, l'homme y demeure assujetti ; s'épuisant à forger des simulacres de dieux, il les adopte ensuite fiévreusement : son besoin de fiction, de mythologie triomphe de l'évidence et du ridicule. Sa puissance d'adorer est responsable de tous ses crimes : celui qui aime indûment un dieu, contraint les autres à l'aimer, en attendant de les exterminer s'ils s'y refusent. Point d'intolérance, d'intransigeance idéologique y de prosélytisme qui ne révèlent le fond bestial de l'enthousiasme. Que l'homme perde sa *faculté* d'indifférence : il devient assassin virtuel ; qu'il transforme son idée en dieu : es conséquences en sont incalculables. (581)

> [Idolaters by instinct, we convert the objects of our dreams and our interests into the Unconditional. History is nothing but a procession of false Absolutes, a series of temples raised to pretexts, a degradation of the mind before the Improbable. Even when he turns from religion, man remains subject to it; depleting himself to create fake gods, he then feverishly adopts them: his need for fiction, for mythology triumphs over evidence and absurdity alike. His power to adore is responsible for all his crimes: a man who loves a god unduly forces other men to love his god, eager to exterminate them if they refuse. There is no form of intolerance, of proselytism or ideological intransigence which fails to reveal the bestial substratum of enthusiasm. Once man loses his *faculty of indifference*

he becomes a potential murderer; once he transforms *his* idea into a god the consequences are incalculable. (3)]

At first glance this appears to be a simplistic and fatalistic view of history, anchored in precisely the kind of dogmatic assertion that Cioran condemns in his opening volley. But to be aware of the way recent history can and in fact did manifest itself as secularized idolatrous carnage is already to have gained a critical perspective on it that implies that the cause may not be the inevitability of history manifesting itself that way, but rather of the way that undialectical thinking is what leads to the formation of rigid doctrine that unleashes that kind of catastrophe. What Cioran provides in the passage just quoted is a catalogue of mental attitudes hostile to thought: idolatry, intransigence, proselytism, and so on. Contrary to what the text seems to imply, the problem perhaps lies not in the fact that ideas actualize themselves in history but rather that goal-oriented or overly systematic approaches to ideas glide effortlessly into dogma by not insisting thoroughly enough on their distance from a religiously oriented approach to thought as teleologically oriented toward truth, which forecloses thought by asserting that it can have an endpoint once its instrumental function of identifying truth has been achieved:

> Le principe du mal réside dans la tension de la volonté, dans l'inaptitude au quiétisme, dans la mégalomanie prométhéenne d'une race qui crève d'idéal, qui éclate sous ses convictions. [...] Qu'est-ce que la Chute sinon la poursuite d'une vérité et l'assurance de l'avoir trouvée ? Le fanatisme en résulte,—tare capitale qui donne à l'homme le goût de l'efficacité, de la prophétie, de la terreur,—lèpre lyrique par laquelle il contamine les âmes, les soumet, les broie ou les exalte … N'y échappent que les sceptiques (ou les fainéants et les esthètes), parce qu'ils ne *proposent* rien, parce que—vrais bienfaiteurs de l'humanité—ils en détruisent les partis pris et en analysent le délire. (582)

[The principle of evil lies in the will's tension, in the incapacity for quietism, in the Promethean megalomania of a race that bursts with ideals, that explodes with its convictions. [...] What is the Fall but the pursuit of a truth and the assurance you have found it, the passion for a dogma, domicile within a dogma? The result is fanaticism—fundamental defect which gives man the craving for effectiveness, for prophecy, for terror—a lyrical leprosy by which he contaminates souls, subdues them, crushes or exalts them … Only the skeptics (or idlers or esthetes) escape, because they *propose* nothing, because they—humanity's true benefactors—undermine fanaticism's purposes, analyze its frenzy. (4)]

Here Cioran nuances what had seemed to be his initial position about ideas always falling into dogma and generating bloody farces. He identifies fanaticism as "la poursuite d'une verité et l'assurance de l'avoir trouvée" ["the pursuit of a truth and the assurance you have found it"]. The second element is key; it is not simply the search for truth, the emergence from quietism into thinking, but rather the assurance of having found truth, which on the definition of thinking that we have been using would constitute the point at which one is no longer thinking, since thinking is by nature restless and unwilling to come to rest in a purported truth. So what Cioran is identifying is not the danger of thinking but of not thinking, the calcification of ideas into a suspect conclusion that we label truth and are willing to become fanatics to defend. It is to those sorts of thinkers that skeptics stand heroically opposed here, as those who are able to preserve the movement of thought, while not orienting that movement toward a goal, a move that would align thought dangerously with instrumental reason. While it may be as impossible to be a full skeptic as it is to attain full resignation, the experience of thought as a way to attempt to live out the consequences of skepticism reorients thought away from the risk of dogmatism.

Later in the *Précis*, Cioran elaborates the paradoxical relation between history and skepticism:

> L'Histoire confirme le scepticisme ; cependant elle n'*est* et ne *vit* qu'en le piétinant ; aucun événement ne surgit du doute, mais toutes les considérations sur les événements y conduisent et le justifient. C'est dire que la tolérance—bien suprême de la terre—en est en même temps le mal. Admettre tous les points de vue, les croyances les plus disparates, les opinions les plus contradictoires, présuppose un état général de lassitude et de stérilité. On en arrive à ce miracle : les adversaires coexistent, –mais précisément parce qu'ils ne peuvent plus l'être ; les doctrines opposées se reconnaissent des mérites les unes aux autres parce qu'aucune n'a de vigueur pour s'affirmer. [...]
>
> Les époques d'effroi prédominent sur celles de calme ; l'homme s'irrite beaucoup plus de l'ascèse que de la profusion d'événements ; aussi l'Histoire est-elle le produit sanglant de son refus de l'ennui. (729)

[History confirms skepticism; yet it *is* and *lives* only by trampling over it; no event rises out of doubt, but all considerations of events lead to it and justify it. Which is to say that tolerance—supreme good on earth—is at the same time the supreme evil. To admit all points of view, the most disparate beliefs, the most contradictory opinions, presupposes a general state of lassitude and sterility. When we arrive at this miracle: the adversaries coexist—but precisely because they can no longer be adversaries; opposing doctrines recognize each other's merits because none has the vigor to assert itself. [...]

The periods of fear predominate over those of calm; man is much more vexed by the absence than by the profusion of events; thus History is the bloody product of his rejection of boredom. (172)]

Here Cioran suggests the difficulty of adopting skepticism as what we might call a way of life. A risk of deep skepticism is that it could lead to a potential indifference that would have the same result as quietism, an ultimately intolerable state that leads, in Cioran's view, to the violent release that we label historical events. So both dogmatism and skeptical indifference ultimately lead to the same risk of historical violence. The implication seems to be that skepticism can only avoid violent release if it is animated by a tension which allows thought to remain in movement, so that the violence is turned productively against oneself at the conceptual level.

That conception of thought, of Cioran's own formulation as "penser contre soi," is thus essential to preventing historical catastrophe according to Cioran in the passage cited above. That is important context for understanding other moments in the *Précis* where he could otherwise be seen as advocating a kind of radical passivity that is purportedly unconnected to the world politically on account of what can look like autoreferentiality: "Les désoeuvrés saisissent plus de choses et plus profonds que les affairés : aucune besogne ne limite leur horizon ; nés dans un éternel dimanche, ils regardent—et se regardent regarder" (600) ["The idle apprehend more things, are deeper than the industrious: no task limits their horizon; born into an eternal Sunday, they watch—and watch themselves watching" (23)].[13] For Cioran, "la paresse est un scepticisme physiologique, le doute de la chair" (600) ["sloth is a somatic skepticism, the way the flesh doubts" (23)], and laziness has the same potential benefit as skepticism, namely that skeptics and the lazy, collectively "les désoeuvrés [...] seraient les seuls à n'être pas assassins" (600) ["the idle would be the only ones not to be murderers" (23)]. Cioran immediately adds a crucial qualification, however: "Mais, ils ne font pas partie de l'humanité" (600) ["But they do not belong to humanity" (23)]. Once again, a realm of total skepticism would simply be an unlivable reality, and Cioran goes on to admit that "l'exaspération dans le vrai pourrait les induire à imiter les autres et à se plaire à la tentation avilissante des besognes. C'est le danger qui menace la paresse—miraculeuse survivance du paradis" (600) ["Exasperation in the truth might induce them to imitate the others and to indulge in the degrading temptation of tasks. This is the danger which threatens sloth, that miraculous residue of paradise" (23)]. Cioran elevates the practical unlivability of skepticism to a kind of secularized theological status, once again implying that we must pursue the diabolical heritage of doubleness by thinking against ourselves even within the domain of skepticism in order to live what could be called a human life of the mind.

It is important to recognize that the distinctions and relations I have been implying between thought and lived experience in this account of Cioran so far are by no means straightforward. The case of skepticism brings the complexity to the fore, since skepticism hovers between a mode of thought and a way of life. As Brian Ribeiro has indicated:

> [S]kepticism was essentially a view of the good life, a eudaimonistic account, in direct competition with other such accounts. Think for a moment of the claims made on behalf of Stoicism. Stoic writings tell us that the *Sage* is not worried over things beyond his control, that he controls, his emotions and serenely accepts what must be, that he wishes things to be just exactly as they are, and so on. Now ask yourself, did any *actual* Stoic—or better yet, the bulk of them—ever really live that way? Answer: Probably not. The "Sage" is an ideal character type for the Stoics, in very much the same way other ethical traditions have their own ideal types. (55)

Ribeiro's remarks, which he extends as well to Christians in terms of the contrast between what is posited as an ideal form of life and the highly incomplete and imperfect ways in which those lives are lived out, help point to an ambiguity in Cioran that stems from the way his writing participates in several kinds of genre without corresponding cleanly to any given one. Like Bataille, he engages philosophical questions without doing what virtually anyone would label philosophy, working out his thought unsystematically and in a way that not only makes room for the esthetic but depends on it. It is not irrelevant that Cioran's writings feature a character who says "I" and "we" and that his situated unsituatedness lends an esthetic shape to the writings that lead us to conclude, in total agreement with Cioran, that to read his texts as straight-up interventions in thought would be to miss the point. Rather, the drama that animates the process of thinking against oneself is played out in these texts, and in that process the texts give the lie to systematic approaches and reveal the fictive aspect of any attempts to clearly and distinctly delineate the relationship between thought and experience. As Cioran indicates above, no one fully participates in humanity while withdrawing fully from it into skepticism, but nor is it, we can affirm following Ribeiro, that one could truly inhabit a full skepticism. And so we are left to work out the consequences of wanting to affirm what we know to be an impossible state; that is the diabolical aspect of such a "temptation," one that leaves us with the duality that is staged when we desire what we know to be impossible and thus fall into thought which can be labeled self-torture but which can serve to prevent violent catastrophe.

We can thus see the *Précis* as dramatizing and working out the consequences of the impossibility and undesirability of coming to rest in simplistic skepticism (or its counterpart in laziness) that would shut down any metaphysical or ethical questions. Cioran points, in a section entitled "L'animal indirect," to a complexity in the very attempt at defining humanity that both tempts those who seek simple answers even when those are arbitrary or absurd and invites reflection on the impossibility ultimately to be satisfied with those definitions:

> ce que [*l'homme*] est, mille définitions le dénoncent et aucune ne s'impose : plus elles sont arbitraires, plus elles paraissent valables. L'absurdité la plus ailée et la banalité la plus pesante lui conviennent pareillement. [...] Alors que les bêtes vont directement à leur but, il se perd dans des détours ; c'est l'animal indirect par excellence. (601)
>
> [*what [man] is* a thousand definitions expose and none compels recognition: the more arbitrary they are, the more valid they seem. The airiest absurdity and the weightiest banality are equally appropriate. [...] Whereas the animals proceed directly to their goal, man loses himself in detours; he is the indirect animal *par excellence*. (24)]

Here Cioran adds another dimension to the idea of never attaining or arriving at a goal which we have seen operating in both Bataille and Cioran, elevating it to a defining characteristic of humanity, albeit one that makes of a human being "un convalescent qui aspire à la maladie" (601). The drama of thought is described at length as a desirable illness:

> Son sang mal composé a permis l'infiltration d'incertitudes, d'ébauches de problèmes ; sa vitalité mal disposé, l'intrusion de points d'interrogation et de signes d'étonnement. [...] Quel ver s'est emparé de son repos, quel agent primitif de la connaissance l'a obligé au retard des actes, à l'arrêt des envies ? [...] L'homme est invalide—ou il n'est pas. (601-2)
>
> [His poorly constituted blood has allowed the infiltration of uncertainties, approximations, problems; his wavering vitality, the intrusion of question marks and exclamation points. [...] What worm has burrowed into his repose, what primal agent of knowledge has forced him to the backwardness of actions, the arrested development of desires? [...] Man is an invalid—or he is nothing. (25)]

Such a person remains "surpris et confondu" when thinking about himself after thinking about the universe, "mais il continue de préférer à la nature qui échoue éternellement dans la santé son propre échec" (602) ["but he continues to prefer, to the nature which eternally capsizes into health, his own defeat" (25)]. For Cioran there is no escape via thought either from the self or from the external world, and in fact the desire to evade one or the other sends us back into the cycle of failed evasion and itself forms an essential part of the experience of thought, where both words and nonverbal emotive sounds give voice to the experience:

> Au début c'est pour nous évader des choses que nous pensons ; puis, lorsque nous sommes allés trop loin, pour nous perdre dans le regret de notre évasion ....Et c'est ainsi que nos concepts s'enchaînent comme des soupirs dissimulés, que toute réflexion tient lieu d'interjection, qu'une tonalité plaintive submerge la dignité de la logique. (606)

> [At first it is in order to escape things that we think; then, when we have gone too far, in order to lose ourselves in the regret for our escape .... And so our concepts are linked together like dissimulated sighs, every reflection replaces an interjection, a plaintive tonality submerges the dignity of logic. (30)][14]

Such descriptions of the incitement to thought and of its progression as the drama of thinking against oneself offer important insight into how to read the text in which they appear. Once we are aware of the characterization of thought as mobile—as a dialectical process where any one local moment cannot be taken as a definitive pronouncement on account of the fact that thought understood this way never arrives at an endpoint in the usual sense of a logical conclusion—we are confronted with the need to reevaluate the way we read the *Précis* itself. One effect of the quasi-moralist first person voice is that it seems to offer definitive statements, unbounded by context or, given the structure of the text in short independent sections, by the place of the statement in a broader context of linear development.

The work's form encourages us to see the content differently, to see what seem like definitive statements as provisional, passing thoughts in an overarching movement of thought that is always subject to the thinker's act of thinking against himself. They are performative rather than descriptive utterances, elements in a drama rather than propositions in a syllogism. When we encounter passages such as this one, which seemingly advocates a removal from concern about injustice, it is less than clear that we should take this as a conclusion as opposed to one localized moment in the dynamics of thought:

> Dans ce monde rien n'est à sa place, en commençant par ce monde même. Point ne fait s'étonner alors du spectacle de l'injustice humaine. Il est également vain de refuser ou d'accepter l'ordre social : force nous est d'en subir les changements en mieux ou en pire avec un conformisme désespéré, comme nous subissons la naissance, l'amour, le climat et la mort. […]
>
> Personne ne peut corriger l'injustice de Dieu et des hommes ; tout acte n'est qu'un cas spécial, d'apparence organisée, du Chaos originel.
>
> (615–16)

> [In this world nothing is in its place, beginning with this world itself. We must therefore not be surprised by the spectacle of human injustice. It is equally futile to refuse or to accept the social order: we must endure its changes for the better or the worse with a despairing conformism, as we endure birth, love, the weather, and death. […]
>
> No one can correct God's injustice or that of men: every action is merely a special, apparently organized case of the original Chaos. (40)]

To accept this affirmation of the world as it is would go against not only our dual nature that Cioran has underscored but also the principle of thinking against oneself, which he has endorsed. Read in the light of the passage we have considered immediately above, it would be to come to a potentially dangerous point of rest, given that we are ultimately as unable to accept the world as it is given as we are to live the full consequences of a consistent and thoroughgoing skepticism. The reader is thus drawn into the drama of thinking by its very portrayal in the form of the *Précis*; to take any local assertion at face value and affirm what appears to be its universal status for the speaking subject is to fall into the trap of coming to rest in an easily graspable and static idea. Rather, passages such as this one should, by the very logic of the text, incite readers to think against it, to ask how we can in fact react against injustice in a way that is neither goal-oriented and war-inducing in its dogmatism nor quietistic. Affirming defeat in the sense of claiming not to be able to find a viable solution to that problem of thought simply leads to the dangerous and impossible quietism that Cioran had already denounced.

To do anything except act in the domain of the "as if," to continue the self-torturing enterprise of thinking would be something other than human, a status we can only escape in imagination and not in lived reality without putting an end to consciousness altogether. Refusing to draw all the consequences about what we know about the impossibility of satisfaction, the ever-present temptations of dogmatism and quietism, and so forth, is what animates thought and lived experience, and thought *as* lived experience. Cioran writes:

> Toutes les vérités sont contre nous. Mais nous continuons à vivre, parce que nous les acceptons en elles-mêmes, parce que nous nous refusons à en tirer les conséquences. Où et celui qui aurait traduit—dans sa conduite—une seule conclusion de l'enseignement de l'astronomie, de la biologie, et qui aurait décidé de ne plus quitter son lit par révolte ou par humilité en face des distances sidérales ou des phénomènes naturels ? Y eut-il jamais orgueil vaincu par l'évidence de notre irréalité ? Et qui fut assez audacieux pour ne plus rien faire parce que tout acte est ridicule dans l'infini ? (619)

> [All truths are against us. But we go on living, because we accept them in themselves, because we refuse to draw the consequences. Where is the man who has translated—in his behavior—a single conclusion of the lessons of astronomy, of biology, or humility in the face of the sidereal distances or the natural phenomena? Has pride ever been conquered by the evidence of our unreality? And who was ever bold enough to do nothing because every action is senseless in infinity? (43–4)]

There is a tension not only between thought and action in the world but within thought itself, as the rhetorical questions here force reflection on whether it is preferable, or even possible, to live a life that would be consistent with the enlarged perspective that thought reveals and which would call into question the significance of our day-to-day actions in the larger scheme of the meaningless universe. To pose the question is not to shut down reflection on it but rather to open it up, to attempt the impossible task of articulating the right conclusions to draw from the multiple perspectives implied by the back and forth between lived experience and thought and between the scale of an individual life, the perspective of humanity more broadly, and the cosmic scale. To introduce scientific considerations only broadens the questions rather than resolving them; it serves as a further motor of thought.

The problem, according to this section of the work, is not a surfeit but a deficit of thought and of engaging it meaningfully and substantially:

> Seul l'animal rationnel n'a rien su apprendre de sa philosophie : il se situe à l'écart—et persévère néanmoins dans les mêmes erreurs d'apparence efficace et

de réalité nulle. Vue de l'extérieur, de n'importe quel point archimédien, la vie— avec toutes ses croyances—n'est plus possible, ni même concevable. On ne peut *agir* que contre la vérité. L'homme recommence chaque jour, malgré tout ce qu'il sait, contre tout ce qu'il sait. Cette équivoque, il l'a poussée jusqu'au vice. (619)

[Only the rational animal has been able to learn nothing from his philosophy: he locates himself apart—and perseveres nonetheless in the same errors of effective appearance and void reality. Seen from outside, from any Archimedean point, life—with all its beliefs—is no longer possible, nor even conceivable. We can *act* only against the truth. Man starts over every day, in spite of everything he knows, against everything he knows. He has extended this ambiguity to the point of vice. (44)]

Here again, there is a tension between what seems to be an oracular pronouncement from an omniscient, universal point of view and the situated nature of what it expresses, evident in the reference to the Archimedean point from which, as the speaker confidently announces, life is impossible. But what is missing to verify the claim is precisely such an Archimedean point; this absence reduces the claim to speculation and forces us into something more akin to the world of fiction, where verisimilitude rather than verifiability is the criterion.

Given the lack of such an external point from which to verify the claims, the assertions about truth must be reevaluated as a potential perspective based on imaginative speculation about a universal perspective beyond the human. To say as much is not to invalidate the claim but rather to highlight the creative aspect of the thought involved here, one which reinforces the distinction between thought and knowledge by calling into question the basis on which one could establish "truth" as the speaker establishes it here. The implication would seem to be that the proper role for philosophy would be to lead to its own obliteration because we would realize the futility of doing or thinking or believing anything at all once we have reached the conclusions to which philosophy should lead us, thus making of philosophy a self-destructing enterprise. But to do this would revert to a goal-oriented approach to philosophy; part of thinking against oneself is not to withdraw from drawing all the conclusions from thought, but that will to draw those conclusions reveals itself to be in tension with the resistance to coming to rest. It is impossible to stop living and thinking not because we lack the insight or the courage but because to do so would cancel the process of thinking against oneself, even if it were to be in the service of philosophy rather than religious faith or war. Cioran has no way to distinguish the "truth" he announces in the passage quoted above from the kinds of truth he attacks in other sections of the *Précis*: "ceux qui croient à *leur* vérité [...] laissent après eux le sol parsemé de cadavres. [...] Les vérités commencent par un conflit avec la police et finissent par s'appuyer sur elle" (648) ["those who believe in *their* truth [...] leave the earth behind them strewn with corpses. [...] Truths begin by a conflict with the police and end by calling them in" (73–4)]. Passages such as these highlight Cioran's ongoing concern to prevent catastrophes that spring from commitment to ideas or systems no matter the basis on which those ideas may have been generated; his advocacy of shutting down life altogether could be seen as a kind of intellectual defense mechanism against the always present danger of an overly strong commitment to a nondialectical ideal that we are tempted to label truth.

Inherent in the *Précis* is a critique of philosophy, or at least of a certain kind of philosophy that leads away from affective engagement with ideas. "Je me suis détourné de la philosophie au moment où il me devint impossible de découvrir chez Kant aucune faiblesse humaine, aucun accent véritable de tristesse ; chez Kant et chez tous les philosophes. [...] A peu près tous les philosophes ont fini *bien* : c'est l'argument suprême contre la philosophie" (622) ["I turned away from philosophy when it became impossible to discover in Kant any human weakness, any authentic accent of melancholy; in Kant and in all the philosophers. [...] Almost all the philosophers came to a *good end*: that is the supreme argument against philosophy" (47)]. This affirmation of the necessity of an affective dimension or a lived reaction to ideas in order to validate philosophy is perhaps ironic given Cioran's sometimes stated goal of complete retreat from life in the face of lucidity about its nature. Cioran joins Bataille in seeing thought as an affective experience; a section entitled "Non-résistance à la nuit" ["Non-Resistance to Night"] gives an idea of what it would mean to both think and live according to the logic of the fall which, as we have seen, shapes Cioran's conception of thought as one of the main figurative representations of thinking against oneself:

> Et, naguère amoureux des sommets, puis déçus par eux, nous finissons par chérir notre chute, nous nous hâtons de l'accomplir, instruments d'une exécution étrange, fascinés par l'illusion de toucher aux confins des ténèbres, aux frontières de notre destinée nocturne. La peur du vide transformée en volupté. [...]
>
> Et pourtant cette chute [...] est loin d'être solennelle et lyrique. [...] Pour ressentir continuellement cette dilatation où nous rivalisons avec les dieux, où nos fièvres triomphent de nos effrois, il faudrait nous maintenir à une température

tellement élevée qu'elle nous achèverait en quelques jours. Mais nos éclairs sont instantanés ; les chutes sont notre règle. La vie, c'est ce qui se décompose à tout moment ; c'est une perte monotone de lumière, une dissolution insipide dans la nuit, sans sceptres, sans auréoles, sans nimbes.

(627)

[And we, once in love with the peaks, then disappointed by them, we end by cherishing our fall, we hurry to fulfill it, instruments of a strange execution, fascinated by the illusion of reaching the limits of the darkness, the frontiers of our nocturnal fate. Fear of the void transformed into a kind of voluptuous joy. [...]

And yet this fall [...] is far from being solemn and lyric. [...] In order to experience that continual expansion in which we rival the gods, in which our fevers triumph over our fears, we should have to remain at so high a temperature that it would finish us off in a few days. But our illuminations are instantaneous; falls are our rule. Life is what decomposes at every moment; it is a monotonous loss of light, an insipid dissolution in the darkness, without scepters, without halos. (52, translation modified)]

The passage gives an idea of what it would mean to live in a perpetual state of falling, where the moments of intensity are particularly revelatory and sustain the other moments by revealing the potential for that intensity within the otherwise calm monotony. The fall is thus a complex interplay between calm and intensity whereby each element depends on the other; they are mutually constitutive rather than simply opposed, and each one reveals the truth of the other, making it accessible and thinkable.

One of the more surprising characterizations of the ideal role of philosophers and their relation to the social world they inhabit is that of a positively valued prostitute:

Le philosophe, revenu des systèmes et des superstitions, mais persévérant encore sur les chemins du monde, devrait imiter le pyrrhonisme de trottoir dont fait montre la créature la moins dogmatique : la fille publique. Détachée de tout et ouverte à tout ; épousant l'humeur et les idées du client ; changeant de ton et de visage à chaque occasion ; prêt à être triste ou gaie, étant indifférente prodiguant les soupirs par souci commercial ; portant sur les ébats de son voisin superposé et sincère un regard éclairé et faux—elle propose à l'esprit un modèle de comportement qui rivalise avec celui des sages. Etre sans convictions à l'égard des hommes et de soi-même, tel est le haut enseignement de la prostitution, académie ambulante de lucidité, en marge de la société comme la philosophie. « Tout ce que je sais je l'ai appris à l'école des filles », devrait s'écrier le penseur qui accepte tout et refuse tout, quand, à leur exemple, il s'est spécialisé dans le sourire fatigué, quand les hommes ne sont pour lui que des clients, et les trottoirs du monde le marché où il vend son amertume, comme ses compagnes, leur corps. (651–2)

[The philosopher, disappointed with systems and superstitions but still persevering in the ways of the world should imitate the sidewalk Pyrrhonism exhibited by the least dogmatic of creatures: the prostitute. Detached from everything and open to everything; espousing her client's mood and ideas; changing tone and face on each occasion; ready to be sad or gay; being indifferent; lavishing sighs out of commercial concern; casting upon the frolic of her superimposed and sincere neighbor an enlightened and artificial gaze—she proposes to the mind a model of behavior which vies with that of the sages. To be without convictions in regard to men and oneself, such is the high lesson of prostitution, peripatetic academy of lucidity, marginal to society—as is philosophy. "Everything I know I learned in the School of Whores!" should be the exclamation of the thinker who accepts everything and rejects everything, when, following their example, he has specialized in the weary smile, when men are to him merely clients, and the world's sidewalks the marketplace where he sells his bitterness, as his companions sell their bodies. (77–8)]

Cioran's decidedly ambivalent characterization of the work of philosophy highlights a distance from others that allows for a lucid perspective on one's own work and an awareness of the marginal status that thinkers need to do their work and to which they are relegated in a world motivated by other concerns. Cioran highlights the transformation of the philosopher, in the narrow sense of a systematic thinker, into the more desirable roles of the sage or the thinker. Unlike many figural appropriations of prostitution that concentrate, for instance, on the debasement of the artist in a market-driven culture where, in the absence of patronage, the artist needs to conform his taste to those of the ruling bourgeoisie, there is no implication here that the thinker's work is degraded. Rather, the emphasis is on the relative independence of the thinker who maintains only a minimum of contact with clients while cultivating indifference to the views of others not engaged in the drama of thinking.

The essential relationship that a thinker cultivates, then, is not with an audience but with the subject matter itself, an idea that Cioran explores in the section immediately preceding the one we have just considered. He writes in "Hantise de l'essentiel" ["Obsession of the Essential"] about the risk of the futility of thought:

Quand toute interrogation paraît accidentelle et périphérique, quand l'esprit cherche des problèmes toujours plus vastes, il arrive que dans sa démarche il ne se heurte plus à aucun objet sinon à l'obstacle diffus du Vide. Dès lors, l'élan philosophique, exclusivement tourné vers l'inaccessible, s'expose à la faillite. A faire le tour des choses et des prétextes temporels il s'impose des gênes salutaires; mais, s'il s'enquiert d'un principe de plus en plus général, il se perd et s'annule dans le vague de l'Essentiel. (652)

[When every question seems accidental and peripheral, when the mind seeks ever greater problems, it turns out that in its procedure it no longer comes up against any object but the diffuse obstacle of the Void. Thereupon, the philosophic energy, exclusively oriented toward the inaccessible, is exposed to ruin. Scrutinizing things and their temporal pretexts, it imposes salutary embarrassments upon itself; but, if it seeks an increasingly general principle, it is lost and annihilated in the vagueness of the Essential. (78)]

Cioran's description of thinking here begins to resemble Bataille's characterization of inner experience; thought loses its object and confronts that absence of object as a void, an effect that can only be mitigated by stopping short of drawing the full consequences of the process of thought. As "Hantise de l'essentiel" continues, it takes as its own object of analysis a reflective thought and its effect on the thinker:

Ne prospèrent dans la philosophie que ceux qui s'arrêtent à propos, qui acceptent la limitation et le confort d'un stade raisonnable de l'inquiétude. Tout problème, si on en touche le fond, mène à la banqueroute et laisse l'intellect à découvert : plus de questions et plus de réponses dans un espace sans horizon. Les interrogations se tournent contre l'esprit qui les a conçues : il devient leur victime. Tout lui est hostile : sa propre solitude, sa propre audace, l'absolu opaque, les dieux invérifiables, et le néant manifeste. (652)

[Only those who stop apropos in philosophy flourish, those who accept the limitation and the comfort of a reasonable stage of anxiety. Every problem, if we get to the bottom of it, leads to bankruptcy and leaves the intellect exposed: no more questions and no more answers in a space without horizon. The interrogations turn against the mind which has conceived them: it becomes their victim. Everything is hostile to it: its own solitude, its own audacity, the opaque absolute, the unverifiable gods, and the manifest nothingness. (78)]

Cioran once again draws an implicit distinction between philosophy and thought in order to imply that philosophy falsifies the objects of its thought by failing to push its inquiries far enough; to acknowledge this is to be prepared to confront the lack of answers to the questions put in motion by thought, to be suspicious of tidy answers. As Cioran characterizes it here, thought instigates a drama whereby the questions, which had at first been the product of thinking, take on character and agency by in turn having an effect on the thinker who had conceived them. There is thus a risk in attempting to draw all conclusions from thought, one which has an effect on the thinker as well as on the "product" of the thought, which Cioran labels sterility, stemming from the inability to conclude in the usual sense:

> Malheur à celui qui, parvenu à un certain moment de l'essentiel, n'a point fait halte ! L'histoire montre que les penseurs qui gravirent jusqu'à la limite l'échelle des questions, qui posèrent le pied sur le dernier échelon, sur celui de l'absurde, n'ont légué à la postérité qu'un exemple de stérilité, tandis que leurs confrères, arrêtés à mi-chemin, ont fécondé le cours de l'esprit ; ils ont *servi* leurs semblables, ils leur ont transmis quelque idole bien façonnée, quelques superstitions polies, quelques erreurs camouflées en principes, et un système d'espoirs. (652)
>
> [Woe to the man who, having arrived at a certain moment of the essential, has not drawn up short! History shows that the thinkers who mounted to the top of the ladder of questions, who set their foot on the last rung, that of the absurd, have bequeathed to posterity only an example of sterility, whereas their confreres, stopping hallway up, have fertilized the mind's growth; they have *served* their kind, they have transmitted some well-turned idol, some polished superstitions, some errors disguised as principles, and a system of hopes. (78–9)]

There is a general ambivalence in the tone of this section, and its irony complicates our reading of the passage. Given Cioran's critique of philosophy and its resistance to draw all the consequences of the inquiries it initiates, the endorsement of philosophy's having served others is a mere condemnation in ironic disguise, but the critique raises the question of whether thought as Cioran endorses it is livable.

If there is to be a connection between thought and lived experience, or if we are to perceive thought, as I have been arguing, *as* experience, and if drawing the full and right conclusions from thought is of crucial importance to Cioran, what would be the right conclusions to draw from the fact that philosophy as it is commonly practiced yields only "polite superstitions" and "errors disguised as principles?" Cioran's model of thought advocates not for a different set of principles but rather for the absence of principle in the void, the impossibility of drawing any conclusions at all. It endorses an approach that is not afraid of its own conclusions and that labels all reassuring conclusions as false, and then affirms that any definitive conclusions can lead only to that horizonless conceptual space where ideas turn against the thinker. This is a point even beyond the practice of thinking against oneself, since in this case the self loses agency and it is the thoughts themselves that think against the thinker. Not even the void can serve as an appropriate end point, precisely because it is in the nature of thought not to come to a conclusion, an implication of which is that potential conclusions can only end up being shown to be overly simplistic or false. To abandon thought is not to be left in peace, however, since the distress caused by thoughts turning against their thinker precludes the kind of resignation and embrace of nothingness that one might be tempted to identify as a release from the torment of thinking.[15] But to appeal to that is to give in to temptation of a simple and false conclusion, given the impossibility of resignation.[16] So to remain alive is to be engaged with the eternal fall into thought as a resultless and endless process which, while it may never arrive at truth, at least has the potential to avoid certain kinds of untruth, thus reinforcing thought's status as a form of negation.

Despite the irony in the affirmation quoted above about how philosophers have "served" others by not going as far as they should have, we can perceive a certain ambivalence as the section continues:

> Eussent-ils [les philosophes] embrassé les dangers d'une progression excessive, ce dédain des méprises charitables les eût rendus nocifs aux autres et à eux-mêmes; ils eussent inscrit leur nom aux confins de l'univers et de la pensée—chercheurs malsains et réprouvés arides, amateurs de vertiges infructueux, quêteurs de songes dont il n'est pas loisible de rêver ... (652)

> [Had [philosophers] embraced the dangers of an excessive progression, this scorn of charitable mistakes would have rendered them disastrous to others and to themselves; they would have inscribed their names on the confines of the universe and of thought—unhealthy seekers and arid reprobates, amateurs of fruitless dizziness, hunters of dreams it is not permitted to dream ... (79)]

It becomes increasingly difficult to say for certain whether the vocabulary of illness is applied sincerely or ironically. Are we to understand that these adventures in thought are "unhealthy" by the standard criteria of those who either live unreflective lives or by those philosophers committed to a logically verifiable conclusion? If so, is the speaker here proposing a revaluation of our notions of sickness and health such that what others might label "sickness" is in fact the appropriate route for the thinker, despite the real danger of self-destruction inherent in the enterprise? Such is the nature of the uncharted territory to which a kind of thought which is not afraid of its conclusions may lead:

> Point de respiration dans un domaine étranger aux doutes usuels. Et si certains esprits se situent en dehors des interrogations convenues, c'est qu'un instinct enraciné dans les profondeurs de la matière, ou un vice surgissant d'une maladie cosmique, a pris possession d'eux et les a conduits à un ordre de réflexions si exigeant et si vaste, que la mort elle-même leur paraît sans importance, les éléments du destin, des fadaises et l'appareil de la métaphysique, utilitaire et suspect. Cette obsession d'une dernière frontière, ce progrès dans le vide entrainent la forme la plus dangereuse de stérilité, auprès de laquelle le néant semble une promesse de fécondité. (653)

> [No breathing in a realm alien to the usual doubts. And if certain minds locate themselves outside the agreed upon inquires, it is because an instinct rooted in the depths of matter, or a vice rising out of a cosmic disease, has taken possession of them and has led them to an order of reflections so exigent and so enormous that death itself seems of no importance, the elements of destiny mere nonsense, and the apparatus of metaphysics no more than utilitarian and suspect. This obsession with a last frontier, this progress in the void involve the most dangerous form of sterility, beside which nothingness itself seems a promise of fecundity. (79)]

Along with sickness, Cioran calls into question the valence of sterility here as well. While philosophers are able to avoid sterility by advancing toward conclusions, thinkers are prone to leave behind sterility as their only intellectual inheritance.

In the continuation of the passage, cited immediately above, Cioran distinguishes between types of sterility and asks us to imagine one beyond nothingness, to which nothingness would compare favorably. But such a figure of absolute sterility is impossible to maintain in light of the process of thinking itself, which resists the very kinds of coming to rest that would be necessary to end up with the sterility of the void as a final resting place, independently of whether such a rest is sought after and desirable or feared and avoided. Such a void or sterility, to be conceptualized at all, needs to be brought into language, an act by which its very existence as absolute void is canceled and which incites a response from thinkers, thus pulling the thinker out of the very sterility to which thought had led them.[17] As an act of the creative thinking imagination, this sterility has an esthetic dimension which necessarily mitigates the total absorption of the thinker in the void, which means that this experience of sterility can be conceptualized but never experienced, or rather, experienced *as* a conceptualization. The void is thus fecund in terms of keeping thought in motion. Rather than thoughts shutting down the thinker when they take on subjectivity, if the thinker remains within thought by refusing to stop midway, the thoughts then become not only subject but also object, maintaining the dual status of subject and object that allows for interplay between subject and object of thought by precluding the full identity of a subject or object with itself. In that sense, the void or nothingness is an object like any other in that it is not captured in any attempt to describe or conceive it as identical to its concept.

Cioran goes on to develop the parallel between esthetics and metaphysics by comparing the thinker's abandoning of the conception of being to a poet abandoning a poem:

> L'angoisse métaphysique relève de la condition d'un artisan suprêmement scrupuleux dont l'objet ne serait autre que l'*être*. A force d'analyse, il en arrive à l'impossibilité de composer, de parfaire une miniature de l'univers. L'artiste abandonnant son poème, exaspéré par l'indigence des mots, préfigure le désarroi de l'esprit mécontent dans l'ensemble existant. L'incapacité d'aligner les éléments—aussi dénués de sens et de saveur que les mots qui les expriment—mène à la révélation du vide. C'est ainsi que le rimeur se retire dans le silence ou dans les artifices impénétrables. Devant l'univers, l'esprit trop exigeant essuie une défaite pareille à celle de Mallarmé en face de l'art. C'est la panique devant un objet qui n'est plus objet, qu'on ne peut plus manier, car—idéalement—on en a dépassé les bornes. (653)

> [Metaphysical anguish derives from the condition of a supremely scrupulous artisan whose object would be nothing less than *being*. By dint of analysis, he achieves the impossibility of composing, of perfecting a miniature of the universe. The artist abandoning his poem, exasperated by the indigence of words, prefigures the confusion of the mind discontented within the context of the existent. Incapacity to organize the elements—as stripped of meaning and savor as the words which express them—leads to the revelation of the void. Thus the rhymer withdraws into silence or into impenetrable artifices. In the face of the universe, the over-exigent mind suffers a defeat like Mallarmé's in the face of art. It is panic before an object which is no longer an object, which can no longer be manipulated, for—ideally—its limits have been transcended. (79)]

Mallarmé is a telling example here, because he is the poet who transformed the shipwreck of poetic failure into the very means of poetic creation. Rather than simply retreating into silence, he made of silence and failure the very condition and vehicle of his later poetry, exploring the paradoxes by which silence needs to be given voice in order to be conceived and by which the existence of a perfect language of correspondences between word and the thing or concept they are supposed to represent would spell the death of poetry, which depends for its existence on that unbridgeable gap between word and thing and the power of word to reinvent the world in ways that do not correspond to a mimesis of things "as they are." The poetic and philosophical failure are similar in that sense, as Cioran underscores by the thinker's inability to construct "une miniature de l'univers," precisely because the act of modeling such a thing changes it or, rather, shows that it did not have independent existence that could be captured by thought in the first place. The thinker's failure, like the poet's, is the key to his or her success on other grounds, ones that force us to reevaluate whether the terms of success and failure are the best ways in which to conceive the act of thinking. Unlike the poet, however, the thinker cannot contemplate thought from a point of view outside of it, the way the poet can think about poetic creation outside the domain of creation itself. Reflection about thought necessarily brings the thinker back into the realm of thought, which is the arena in which the thinker needs to operate in order to understand thought's failure, which the thinker cannot do outside the realm of thought itself. We can only get beyond thought by actively resisting the questions to which it leads us; even when thought takes on subjective agency, the thinker does not become a mere object or passive vehicle. The only way out of thought is an active refusal of it, which is the experience that leads to catastrophe that Cioran associates with action. So the void to which we are led, by virtue of the fact that it can never be identical to itself as an object or result of thought, serves to ingrain the thinker in thought, thus challenging any facile distinction between the inside and outside of thought, of thought and referent.

Such a conclusion is at odds with the one Cioran actually arrives at in "Hantise de l'essentiel," which ends with this passage:

> Ceux qui ne restent pas à *l'intérieur* de la réalité qu'ils cultivent, ceux qui transcendent le métier d'exister, doivent, ou composer avec l'inessentiel, faire machine arrière et se ranger dans la farce éternelle, ou accepter toutes les conséquences d'une condition séparée, et qui est superfétation ou tragédie, suivant qu'on la regarde ou que l'on l'éprouve. (653)

[Those who do not remain *inside* the reality they cultivate, those who transcend the task or existing, must either compromise with the inessential, reverse gears and take their places in the eternal farce, or accept all the consequences of a severed condition which is either superfetation or tragedy, depending on whether it is contemplated or endured. (79–80)]

The options presented here are to live life within a sort of lucid illusion, ignoring the full set of consequences of the way that thought leads to the void, or to live out those consequences, in an emplotment that Cioran labels tragic. But as we have seen, living out the consequences cannot simply mean entering nothingness. Such a comforting simplicity is exactly what Cioran seeks to avoid precisely on account of the way it is a false solution, a temptation to a reality that we cannot live out while remaining conscious beings. In lieu of the temptation, we are subject to the eternal fall which leaves us within the realm of thought, able to conceive the void but not to conceptualize it fully, a situation which repeatedly reveals the lack of identity between the void and its concept, which is precisely the place where thinking arises.

Like Bataille's text, Cioran's is a sort of record of the experience of thought but also the process of thought as it unfolds dynamically; the ideas presented in the text thus cannot be taken as definitive pronouncements but rather as moments in a process, presented in constellation with other moments with which the reader needs to put them in dialogue, working with the contradictions rather than attempting to reconcile them. The speaker's statements that seem to make universal claims take on interest precisely because they are situated in a particular process of thought that defies the very universalizing perspective the speaker sometimes seems to be adopting. It is that interplay between the situated and the attempt to speak universally that animates the text by illustrating the way it invites malleability, as we have seen with the impossibility of the resignation that the speaker sometimes claims to endorse as a solution to the anguish of thought. If in "Hantise de l'essentiel" the speaking voice was a third person universalizing one, a counterpart is the section "Le penseur d'occasion" ["The Second-Hand Thinker"] in the first person. I turn now to that section, which portrays from the outset a first-person thinker at work on what emerges as a futile task:

Je vis dans l'attente de l'Idée ; je la pressens, la cerne, m'en saisis—et ne puis la formuler, elle m'échappe, elle ne m'appartient pas encore : l'aurais-je conçue dans mon absence? Et comment, d'imminente et confuse, la rendre présente et lumineuse dans l'agonie intelligible de l'expression? Quel état dois-je espérer pour qu'elle éclose—et dépérisse?

Anti-philosophe, j'abhorre toute idée *indifférente* : je ne suis pas toujours triste, donc je ne pense pas toujours. Quand je *regarde* les idées, elles me paraissent plus inutiles encore que les choses; aussi n'ai-je aimé que les élucubrations des grands malades, les ruminations de l'insomnie, les éclairs d'une frayeur incurable et les doutes traversés de soupirs. (666)

[I live in expectation of the Idea; I foresee it, close in upon it, get a grip—and cannot formulate it, it escapes me, does not yet belong to me: might I have conceived it in my absence? And how, once imminent and vague, to make it present and luminous in their intelligible agony of expression? What conditions should I hope for if it is to bloom—and decay?

Anti-philosopher, I abhor every *indifferent* idea: I am not always despondent, hence I do not always think. When I *consider* ideas, they seem even more useless than things; hence I have loved only the elucubrations of the great invalids, the ruminations of insomnia, the flashes of an incurable fear and the doubts intersected by sighs. (95)]

The affective element of thought here is not a reaction to it but rather its condition; the personal engagement lends thought its vitality but also is the condition from which it springs and by which it is evaluated.

He cautions against unfounded optimism by privileging the stark, and dark, mode of thought revealed through insomnia, a particularly privileged state or condition of lucid thought in Cioran because it reveals the contrasts and contradictions that daytime thought risks smoothing over or not perceiving at all:

La somme de clair-obscur qu'une idée recèle est le seul indice de sa profondeur, comme l'accent désespéré de son enjouement est l'indice de sa fascination. Combien de nuits blanches cache votre passé nocturne ?—C'est ainsi que nous devrons aborder tout penseur. Celui qui pense *quand il veut* n'a rien à nous dire : au-dessus—ou plutôt, *à côté*—de sa pensée, il n'en est pas responsable, il n'y est guère engagé, ne gagne ni ne perd à se risquer dans un combat où lui-même n'est pas son propre ennemi. Ren ne lui coûte de croire à la Vérité. (666)

[The amount of chiaroscuro an idea harbors is the only index of its profundity, as the despairing accent of its playfulness is the index of its fascination. How many sleepless nights does your nocturnal past conceal? That is how we ought to confront every thinker. The man who thinks *when he wants to* has nothing to tell us: above—or rather, *alongside*—his thoughts, he is not *responsible* for them, not committed to them, neither wins nor loses by risking himself in a struggle in which he himself is not his own enemy. It costs him nothing to believe in Truth. (95, translation modified)]

Cioran insists here on the intensity of the experience of thought, continuing his critique of philosophy now on the grounds not of its systematicity but of its detachment. The experience of thought is not to be taken casually; to do so would be to risk the temptation of comforting and simplistic conclusions, the antithesis of dialectical thought which depends on tension and contradiction in order to remain in motion. What Cioran proposes is a full awareness of those tensions and contradictions not only within the thought but within the thinkers themselves; his model of engagement looks not to the world but to thought itself, where the experiences we label "inner" and "outer" are themselves navigated, negotiated, defined, negated, and redefined within the domain of thought as experience rather than between the purportedly interior world of thought and the world "out there" with which it interacts from a position of sovereignty apart from that world.

While "Le penseur d'occasion" begins with an intensely personalized focus on the thinker as subject, it goes on, at the end, to call that subjective autonomy into question by indicating that the first-person singular thinker is shaped both by the conditions that give rise to thought and to the thoughts themselves:

> Les « saisons » de l'esprit sont conditionnées par un rythme organique ; il ne dépend pas de « moi » d'être naïf ou cynique : *mes vérités sont les sophismes de mon enthousiasme ou de ma tristesse*. J'existe, je et je pense au gré de l'instant—et malgré moi. Le Temps me constitue ; je m'y oppose en vain—et *je suis*. Mon présent non souhaité se déroule, me déroule ; ne pouvant le commander, je le commente ; esclave de mes pensées, je joue avec elles, comme un bouffon de la fatalité. ... (667)

[The mind's "seasons" are conditioned by an organic rhythm; it is not up to "me" to be naïve or cynical: *my truths are the sophisms of my enthusiasm or of my dejection*. I exist, I feel, and I think according to the moment—and in spite of myself. Time constitutes me; in vain I oppose myself—and I *am*. My undesired present unfolds, unfolds *me*; unable to command it, I comment upon it; slave of my thoughts, I play with them, fatality's buffoon .... (96)]

This section performs the undoing of the unified and autonomous thinking subject by recognizing the subjective agency of thoughts themselves in a reversal of the creative relationship by which thoughts create the subject rather than the other way around. The subject is compelled into being by the thoughts which are in turn to some extent a product of the circumstances that give rise to them.

The subjective agency of thoughts complicates the subject-object model for the thinking subject and compels the thinker to account for the involuntary nature of thought, bringing that to the fore as a criterion of thought by confirming that thought cannot simply be voluntary or carried out on demand or at one's convenience, but rather is compelled and at least to some extent determined by the circumstances which compel thought to account for them as the thinker and the thoughts are shaped by their interaction with those circumstances. It is by the process described here that the self is emptied or, rather, revealed to be a fiction in terms of an autonomous entity in control of its thoughts. The admission of the agency of thoughts over the subject is what creates the conceptual space for the realization of the thinker as a self-torturer, the conditions by which the speaker can think against himself. Paradoxically, ceding agency is the way that the thinker can reassert himself in the necessarily self-torturing process. It is not that masochistic types are more given to thought or, as the speaker here at first implied, that dark lived experience is the criterion for effective thought, but rather that the thinking process itself produces that split which leads to the affective condition that drives the thought itself.

In a later unnamed section of the *Précis* under the larger section title "Visages de la décadence," Cioran identifies fatigue or exhaustion as a condition that challenges creative action:

> Nous vivons dans un climat d'épuisement : l'acte de créer, de forger, de fabriquer, est moins significatif par lui-même que par le vide, par la chute qui le suit. Pour nos efforts toujours et inévitablement compromis, le fond divin et inépuisable se situe en dehors du champ de nos concepts et de nos sensations. L'homme est né avec la vocation de la fatigue : lorsqu'il adopta la position verticale, et qu'il diminua ainsi ses possibilités d'*appui*, il se condamna à des faiblesses inconnues à l'animal qu'il fut. Porter sur deux jambes tant de matière et tous les dégoûts qui s'y rattachent ! Les générations accumulent la fatigue et la transmettent ; nos pères nous lèguent un patrimoine d'anémie, des réserves de découragement, des ressources de décomposition et une énergie à mourir qui devient plus puissante que nos instincts de vie. Et c'est ainsi que l'accoutumance à disparaître, appuyée sur notre capital de lassitude, nous permettra de réaliser, dans la chair diffuse, la neurasthénie—notre essence .... (685–6)

> [We live in a climate of exhaustion: the act of creation, of making and producing, is less significant in and of itself than in relation to the void, to the fall which

follows .... For our invariably compromised efforts, the divine and inexhaustible depths are situated outside the field of our concepts and our sensations. Man was born with the vocation of fatigue: when he adopted the vertical posture and thereby diminished his possibilities of *support*, he was doomed to weaknesses unknown to the animal he was. To carry on two legs so much substance and all the disgusts related to it! The generations accumulate weariness and transmit it; our fathers bequeath to us a patrimony of anemia, reserves of discouragement, resources of decomposition, and an energy in dying which becomes more powerful than our instincts to live. And it is in this fashion that the habitude of disappearing, propped on our capital of fatigue, will permit us to realize, in the prolix flesh, neurasthenia—our essence .... (118)]

Insofar as thinking resists the inclination to laziness and the tendency to disappear, it actively resists what the speaker claims to be inherent in human nature. While he employs terms that we have seen in other sections of the work such as "vide" and "chute," what he has said about them earlier works to undo the claims in this section, if we attempt to take him at his word that the void necessarily follows creation because we are naturally given over to it. As we have seen, he has shown in other parts of the work that nothingness is in fact impossible to achieve. If the thought of fatigue and exhaustion is, as he had implied in the passage we have examined above, determined and imposed on us by the situations dictating those thoughts, the fact of writing about them immediately invites claims to the contrary and thus the process of thinking against oneself precisely because we should be on the lookout for overly facile generalizations of the type that the speaker seems to be offering here. Falling into neurasthenia is a convenient avoidance of the more complex questions at hand about the relationship of exhaustion to creation; it is the sort of nonthinking that we have seen to be equivalent to commitment to other kinds of facile commitment. The text has, in other words, prepared us to be suspicious of the kinds of claims it makes in sections such as this one.

The perpetually changing landscape that shapes thought and concurrently forms the thinker should not, however, be confused with a narrative of progress. Here too, Cioran sets up a dynamic interplay between the changing and the unchanging, but is careful to take his distance from a notion of improvement over time. He writes in a part of the work called "Le décor du savoir":

> Nos vérités ne valent pas plus que celles de nos ancêtres. Ayant substitué à leurs mythes et à leurs symboles des concepts, nous nous croyons « avancés » ; mais ces mythes et ces symboles n'*expriment* guère moins que nos concepts. L'Arbre

de Vie, le Serpent, Ève et le Paradis, signifient autant que : Vie, Connaissance, Tentation, Inconscience. Les figurations concrètes du mal et du bien dans la mythologie vont aussi loin que le Mal et le Bien de l'éthique. (706)

[Our truths are worth no more than those of our ancestors. Having substituted concepts for their myths and symbols, we consider ourselves "advanced"; but these myths and symbols *expressed* no less than our concepts. The Tree of Life, the Serpent, Eve, and Paradise signify as much as Life, Knowledge, Temptation, Unconsciousness. The concrete figurations of good and evil I mythology go as far as the Good and Evil of ethics. (145)]

He goes on to add that "le savoir—en ce qu'il a de profond—ne change jamais : seul son *décor* varie" (706) ["knowledge—insofar as it is profound, never changes: only its décor varies"] (145, translation modified)]. At first glance, he would seem to be defending an anti-historical and static view, reducing the change from the mythology of Genesis to the Freudian inflected ideas of "inconscience" to mere window-dressing or different labels for the same reality. But it is important to note that he refers to "knowledge," which, as we have already seen, is opposed to thought in that knowledge is goal-oriented and static, whereas thought refuses instrumental directionality and unalterable conclusions. To embrace the view of "knowledge" that he puts forth would, again, be contrary to the spirit of thinking against oneself and would lead to the sedimentation of convictions which we take to be solid because of the systematic and/or scientific nature of the process that generates knowledge. And as we saw him claim at the start of the *Précis*, firm convictions, whether religious, scientific, or political, lead to catastrophe on account of the totalizing vision that they endorse.

Moreover, Cioran's evocation of language in the passage cited above in order to claim that changes in words are merely cosmetic or superficial changes hiding the same reality gives evidence of the kind of identity thinking that shuts down dialectical thought. It in fact multiplies identity thinking by not just assuming that a word is identical to its concept but that a different set of words could be identical to the same concept, thus implying a radically static notion of the "truth" he evokes at the start of the passage. The critique Cioran levels against the concept in other sections of the *Précis* thus works to undermine what he claims about them here, once we are alerted to the necessity of thinking against oneself. What his texts call for, once placed into these sorts of constellations whereby one passage illuminates another by calling it into question, is a shift in our usual categories and sets of oppositions, one that would present change or stasis as the only options with which to categorize the way human thought has conceived its relation to experience. Likewise, the texts challenge us to articulate a notion of time that would be outside the dichotomy of changelessness or linear progression by posing the question of the relation between contemporary thought and ancient models:

> La suffisance moderne n'a pas de bornes : nous nous croyons plus éclairés et plus profonds que tous les siècles passés, oubliant que l'enseignement d'un Bouddha plaça des milliers d'êtres devant le problème du néant, problème que nous imaginons avoir découvert parce que nous en avons changé les termes et y avons introduit un tantinet d'érudition. [...] Si nous voulons conserver une décence intellectuelle, l'enthousiasme pour la civilisation doit être banni de notre esprit, de même que la superstition de l'Histoire. (706)

> [Modern complacency is limitless: we suppose ourselves more enlightened, more profound than all the centuries behind us, forgetting that the teaching of a Buddha confronted thousands of beings with the problem of nothingness, a problem we imagine we have discovered because we have changed its terms and introduced a touch of erudition into it. [...] If we want to keep some intellectual decency, enthusiasm for civilization must be banished from our mind, as well as the superstition of History. (145)]

As with other key concepts such as the "chute," which need to be redefined in a way that questions their common usage, what appears to be a simple dismissal of history is actually calling for a reevaluation of what we mean by it, in this case a view of history that would align it with progress or with movement toward a goal. The negation inherent in the flattening of ancient and contemporary modes of thought has the potential to open up conceptual possibilities rather than shutting them down; the risk is otherwise, as it always is, the stagnation which Cioran critiques both because total resignation is impossible and, in other moments, because resignation ultimately explodes in cataclysmic violence.

There is a fundamental tension in Cioran between the affirmation of the active and dynamic process of thinking against oneself and the divisions it identifies both within subjects and objects and the new configurations it generates of the relations between those subjects and objects, which I have identified as dialectical, and the kind of eternal sameness he evokes in the passages we have just considered and in others where the speaking subject claims to live in total indifference to the problems of the world, as a consequence, we might suppose, of that eternal sameness. He affirms, for instance, that:

Pour ce qui est des grands problèmes, nous n'avons aucun avantage sur nos ancêtres ou sur nos devanciers plus récents : on a toujours *tout* su, au moins en ce qui concerne l'Essentiel ; la philosophie moderne n'ajoute rien à la philosophie chinoise, hindoue ou grecque. D'ailleurs il ne saurait y avoir de *problème nouveau*, malgré notre naïveté ou notre infatuation qui voudrait nous persuader du contraire. (706-7)

[As for the great problems, we have no advantage over our ancestors or our more recent predecessors: men have always known *everything*, art least in what concerns the Essential; modern philosophy adds nothing to Chinese, Hindu, or Greek philosophy. Moreover, there cannot be a *new problem*, despite our naiveté or our infatuation which would like to persuade us to the contrary. (145)]

In a short section entitled "Théorie de la bonté" ["Theory of Goodness"], consisting of a dialogue in the form of a question and answer, the second speaker affirms that in his world weariness, he contributes to no new suffering because he does not act and that he leaves the world the way he found it:

« Puisque pour vous il n'y a point d'ultime critère ni d'irrévocable principe, et aucun dieu, qu'est-ce qui vous empêche de perpétrer tous les forfaits ? »

—« Je découvre en moi autant de mal que chez quiconque, mais, exécrant l'action—mère de tous les vices—je ne suis cause de souffrance pour personne. Inoffensif, sans avidité, et sans assez d'énergie ni d'indécence pour affronter les autres, je laisse le monde tel que je l'ai trouvé. Se venger présuppose une vigilance de chaque instant et un esprit de système, une continuité coûteuse, alors que l'indifférence du pardon et du mépris rend les heures agréablement vides. Toutes les morales représentent un danger pour la bonté ; seule l'incurie la sauve. Ayant choisi le flegme de l'imbécile et l'apathie de l'ange, je me suis exclu des actes et, comme la bonté est incompatible avec la vie, je me suis décomposé pour être bon. » (714)

["Since for you there is no ultimate criterion nor irrevocable principle, and no god, what keeps you from committing any and every crime?"

"I find in myself as much evil as in anyone, but detesting action—mother of all the vices—I am the cause of no one's suffering. Harmless, without greed, and without enough energy or indecency to affront others, I leave the world as I found it. To take revenge presupposes a constant vigilance and a systematic mind, a costly continuity, whereas the indifference of forgiveness and contempt renders the hours pleasantly empty. All ethics represent a danger for goodness; only negligence rescues it. Having chosen the phlegm of the imbecile and the apathy of the angel, I have excluded myself from actions and, since goodness is incompatible with life, I have decomposed myself in order to be good." (156)]

On one hand, Cioran appears to be advocating for a dangerous kind of quietism that involves indifference to suffering and a lack of will to attempt to lessen it, even if we know that the efforts are unlikely to succeed. The fear of the consequences of action seems to lead to a morally questionable paralysis here, even as the speaker attempts to redefine goodness to accommodate extreme withdrawal as the full consequence of the idea that it is an unchanging fact that action causes suffering. On the other hand, however, we need to pay attention to the fact that this section, rather unusually, is presented entirely as dialogue. In other sections where the "je" speaks, it is more tempting, although, as I have indicated, not recommendable, to see that speaker as a universalizing voice rather than a particularized subjectivity. The dialogic form of this section highlights the situatedness of the speaker and of the thoughts expressed, calling more directly for the reader to evaluate the situated claim and to enter the dialogue.

To do so is to give the lie to claim that one can act on the will to total resignation (and to point out that a will to act on an urge to resignation is necessarily itself an act). What Cioran had labeled a diabolical aspect of duality does not cease to be operative in claims to passive acceptance of an unchanging and unchangeable world. If anything, such a rejection of the world serves all the more to unleash the tension and dialogue of thought, which emphasizes the conflict between a will to resign and the impossibility of accomplishing it and thus poses new questions about what it would mean to draw all consequences from that tension. As Cioran says explicitly in *La Tentation d'exister*, in a passage I quoted near the outset of this chapter, "Regretter le repos dans l'indistinction, le rêve neutre de l'existence sans qualités, ne sert de rien ; nous nous sommes voulus *sujets*, et tout sujet est rupture avec la quiétude de l'Unité" (828) ["To regret the repose of indistinction, the neutral dream of an existence without qualities, is pointless; we have chosen to be *subjects*, and every subject is a break with the quietude of Unity" (42)]. Given that it does no good to regret impossible repose outside the domain of being a human subject, the dialogue presented in "Théorie de la bonté" leads us to affirm that the speaker's claim is not tenable; the fact that it is contestable already brings us back to the drama of dialectical thought, which depends on both the desire for resignation and its possibility in order to animate it. The claim to have withdrawn from the world in order to "leave it as it is" always necessarily confronts the idea of not being able to do so, and so the claim to avoid duality always becomes a term in the dialectical opposition of unity and duality, leading back to the imperative to think against oneself, which will always reveal claims such as those expressed by the speaker in "Théorie de la bonté" to be impossible as anything except a situated, localized moment of thought, which in turn undoes the claim of eternal sameness that the speaker is advancing.

By reading the text in this constellated manner and juxtaposing various sections not in order to show inconsistency we can demonstrate that the text performatively establishes or prompts a dialectical model of thinking that is not necessarily evident in any one particular section, because such single moments need to be considered as one localized moment in the implied dialogue of the text more broadly, and in conversation with readers as well. Reading this way also encourages us to pay attention to the ways in which single terms that Cioran uses can cover a multiplicity of meanings, once again giving the lie to his claims about eternal sameness by showing a lack of identity of a term to itself across a variety of contexts, which in turn reflect a variety of uses of them historically on which Cioran is drawing. One such term is "penser" or "penseur." In the section "La part des choses," which immediately follows "Théorie de la bonté," he writes: "Tous les penseurs sont des ratés de l'action et qui se vengent de leur échec par l'entremise des concepts" (715) ["All thinkers are failures with regard to action who take revenge by the intermediary of concepts" (157, translation modified)].[18] It is not immediately apparent how we should read this claim, given the oft-repeated denunciation of action in the *Précis*. If action is not desirable, then it would not necessarily follow that thought is some kind of second-best compensation for the failure of action. The passage goes on:

> Nés *en deçà* de l'acte, ils l'exaltent ou le décrient, selon qu'ils aspirent à la reconnaissance des hommes ou à l'autre forme de gloire : leur haine ; ils élèvent indûment leurs propres déficiences, leurs propres misères au rang des lois, leur futilité au niveau d'un principe. La pensée est un mensonge tout comme l'amour ou la foi. Car les vérités sont de fraudes et les passions des odeurs ; et en fin de compte on n'a d'autre choix qu'entre ce qui ment et ce qui pue. (715)

> [Born *this side* of the deed, they exalt or decry it, depending on whether they aspire to humanity's gratitude or that other form of fame: its hatred; they unduly erect their own deficiencies, their own miseries to the rank of laws, their futility to the level of a principle. Thought is as much of a lie as love or faith. For the truths are frauds and the passions odors; and ultimately there is no choice except the one between what lies and what stinks. (157)]

Such a critique is, of course, a form of thinking against oneself, but one that highlights the impossibility of doing away with thinking altogether. Cioran's definition of "concepts" and "truths" is ambiguous here: the critique seems to hold only if concepts are mistakenly held to have the same kind of certainty as mathematical concepts. To claim that thought is a lie is in fact to affirm a kind of truth about thought, and one that can be considered a laudable attribute rather than a critique if we understand thought to be that which moves beyond certainty and beyond a simplistic affirmation of the identity principle to a view that is suspicious of the kind of certainty that some kinds of systematic philosophy identify as a goal.

The affective tone of the passage registers the disruption in an approach to thought that would claim that it is goal-oriented, and that the goal is the truth. In that sense, there is indeed truth in the lie that would pretend to totality or universality. But thought's difference from itself, the split that results from the process of thinking against oneself, moves away from that kind of conception of the relationship of thought to truth and, once again, shows the value of the passage to lie in the way it illustrates a single frozen moment of thought, one which will go on to be negated, a necessary step along the way to a reconstitution of what we mean by thought and concepts, and a recognition that it is thought's very restlessness that prevents us from affirming that what is labeled "thought" in this passage can ultimately be taken to be what thought is. The lie that is thought, as it is affirmed here, is unseparable from an approach to truth that depends on that lie in order to emerge into conceptuality, and the affirmation of the lie goes on to serve as a guard against other affirmations which we may take to be unquestionable truth.

The following section, "Merveilles du vice" ["Wonders of Vice"] is particularly rich in terms of its elaboration of the condition of the thinker in surprising comparison to a figure that plays a very minimal role in Cioran's writing generally, the homosexual, a figure who is defined first and foremost, like the thinker, by what Cioran labels a "condition séparée" with regard to the majority. He claims that the homosexual has a direct route to a similar position to which the thinker arrives after much effort:

> Alors qu'il faut à un penseur—pour se dissocier du monde—un immense labeur d'interrogations, le privilège d'une tare confère d'emblée une destinée singulière. Le Vice—dispensateur de solitude—offre à celui qui en est marqué l'excellence d'une condition séparée. Regardez l'inverti : il inspire deux sentiments

contradictoires : le dégoût et l'admiration ; sa déchéance le rend à la fois inférieur et supérieur aux autres ; il ne s'accepte pas, se justifie devant lui-même à chaque instant, s'invente des raisons, tiraillé entre la honte et l'orgueil ; cependant— fervents des sottises de la procréation—nous marchons avec le troupeau. (715)

[Whereas a thinker requires—to dissociate himself from the world—an enormous labor of interrogations, the privilege of a flaw confers from the start a singular destiny. Vice—bestower of solitude—offers the man marked out by it the excellence of a separate condition. Consider the invert: he inspires two contradictory sentiments: disgust and admiration; his "failure" makes him at once inferior and superior to the others; he does not accept himself, constantly justifies himself, invents reasons, torn between shame and pride; yet—enthusiasts of the fatuities of procreation—we go with the herd. (157)]

This is a complex and nuanced portrayal of the homosexual as figure, not unproblematic in its generalizations about shame and disgust, but as with other figures in the *Précis*, Cioran is constructing a particular type—a concept, we might say to his horror—without regard necessarily for a resemblance of the stylized figure to people in the lived world. As with other figures to whom Cioran attributes a positive valence even though, or precisely because, society judges them negatively, for Cioran to be a "taré"—he evokes the term more generally before naming the homosexual as a specific example—is admirable because it provides the pariah status of an outcast who has the benefit of a perspective outside the assumptions and illusions according to which the majority live their lives. As he writes later in the section: "l'instinct égaré se situe à l'antipode de la barbarie" (715) ["the distracted instinct is located at the antipodes of barbarism" (158)]. The exception does not deviate from the rule; the exception *exemplifies* the rule, despite appearances to the contrary.

Like the insomniac, those who are actively shunned by upright society hold the key to crucial insights about it, and this is a key source of similarity between the thinker and the homosexual. The latter is portrayed here as double, as self-tormenting subject and object to himself, which is another source of similarity to the thinker, and that status elevates both thinker and homosexual above those caught in the trap of affirming procreation, that is, the continuation of life as it had been, the stagnation of the status quo for which both thinker and homosexual serve as a disruption.[19] To act in a way that society would claim to be "against nature" is to free ourselves from that nature, to imagine other possibilities: "Comment devinerions-nous les avantages fétides des aberrations? Resterons-nous à jamais progénitures de la nature, victmes de ses lois, arbres humains enfin?" (715) ["How could we divine the fetid advantages of aberrations? Shall we remain forever the progeniture of nature, victims of her laws, nothing but human trees?" (157–8)]. To stay within the bounds of a plant-like nature would be easier and more comfortable, yet Cioran, thinking here against what he affirms at other moments, valorizes the step outside of "nature," which could perhaps to see that what had been affirmed as "natural" was a product of a particular and changeable human conception; better to be the victim of the suffering involved in one's own emergence beyond received opinion than to be the "victims" of a nature that never was natural to begin with.

Thus Cioran constructs the thinker as aligning with, and even as envious of, those who are "contre nature" as commonly understood:

> Dans les tréfonds de sa naïveté, le penseur jalouse les possibilités de connaître ouvertes à tout ce qui est contre nature ; il croit—non sans répulsion—aux privilèges des « monstres » … Le vice étant une souffrance, et la seule forme de célébrité qui vaille la peine, le vicieux « doit » être nécessairement plus profond que le commun des hommes, puisque indiciblement séparé de tous ; il commence par où les autres finissent. (716)

> [In the depths of his naïveté, the thinker envies the possibilities of knowledge open to whatever is *contra naturam*; he believes—not without repulsion—in the privileges of "monsters" …. Vice being a suffering and the sole form of celebrity worth the trouble, the "vicious" man has to be deeper than the common run, since unspeakably separated from the rest; he begins where the others leave off …. (158)]

Cioran constructs a narrative of immediacy whereby the person who pursues what is labeled vice has privileged insight that is also available directly to thinkers but only through a conceptual process. The implication of an "unsayability" ("indiciblement séparé de tous") harks back to the kind of ineffable, purportedly "direct" experience we saw operating in Bataille under the label of mysticism, with which conceptual thought enters a play of similarity and difference. The affirmation of the supposedly intuitive arrival of the pariah at the same insight as the thinker faces the same problem that we encounter in the case of mystical experience: in order to be able to bring that experience into the realm of the thinkable, it needs to be conceptualized and translated into words, which immediately introduces the problem of the non-identity of experience and concept, the fact that the experience, to be labeled experience, cannot be identical to what it had been before it was considered an experience. By assimilating the pariah and the thinker, Cioran is in fact articulating an important difference that has to do with the question of process. To assimilate the two experiences by claiming, as he does, that one begins where the other ends is to discount the role the process itself plays and the way in which the very reflection on the similarity and difference between the two, which is his own subject in this section, is part of a dialectical process. To make sense of the similarity and difference he is establishing, in other words, is part of the task and elaborative process of thinking, and cannot be accounted for intuitively through a non-conceptual lived "experience." The comparison does, however, illustrate the way in which thinking is itself an experience, not simply a post facto reflection on experience but rather part of an experience which alters it while assigning it meaning.

I am claiming, then, that what Cioran goes on to say about a "plaisir naturel," namely that it is self-canceling, is also true of the kind of immediacy he claims for the social outsider. He writes in the final paragraph of "Merveilles du vice":

> Un plaisir naturel, puisé dans l'évidence, s'annule en lui-même, se détruit dans ses moyens, expire dans son actualité, alors qu'une sensation insolite est une sensation *pensée*, une réflexion dans les réflexes. Le vice atteint au plus haut degré de *conscience*—sans l'entremise de la philosophie ; mais il faut au penseur toute une vie pour parvenir à cette *lucidité affective* par laquelle débute le perverti. Ils se ressemblent pourtant dans leur propension à s'arracher aux autres, encore que l'un s'y astreigne par la méditation, tandis que l'autre ne suit que les merveilles de son penchant. (716)

> [A natural pleasure, taken in what is obvious, cancels itself out, destroys itself in its own means, expires in its actuality, whereas an unwonted sensation is a *thought out* sensation, a reflection in the reflexes. Vice attains the highest degree of *consciousness*—without the intermediary of philosophy; but the thinker requires a whole lifetime to arrive at this *affective lucidity* by which the pervert begins. Yet they resemble one another in their propensity to wrest themselves from the others, though the one strives to do so by meditation while the other merely follows the wonders of his inclination. (158)]

Once again, in order to make an assertion about the similarities of the arrival point of the thinker and the outcast, it is necessary to participate in the process of thinking, which cancels the total assimilation between the two experiences that Cioran posits here in a way that is only possible if we reflect on those similarities and differences, thus altering them in the process. To say that a "sensation insolite" is a "sensation pensée" itself requires an act of thought separate from the sensation itself. Cioran's description also invites the question of whether "thinking" and "philosophy," which he seems to be assimilating here, are in fact synonymous, given that at other times he, like Bataille, is careful to distinguish philosophy, a systematic and goal-oriented discipline, from thought, a more open-ended, actively anti-systematic activity that can never arrive at a goal. The ambiguity comes to the fore in the comment on vice attaining the highest degree of *conscience*, which is precisely the word Hannah Arendt uses, in her exploration of thinking, to describe the "two-in-one" of dialogue, drawing on the double meaning of the French word *conscience* as both consciousness and conscience and claiming that it is the dialogic nature of thought that defines it and makes itself present to itself, in a move which requires a splitting of the thinking subject. This appeal to the split subject echoes the split he had identified in the outcast as both part of society and separated from it, and if we are to take philosophy as distinct from thought, then it would indeed be possible to attain that consciousness without the mediation of philosophy, but not without thought, understood as I have been understanding it as itself *a form of experience able to form itself by reflection on itself in a destabilizing of the subject-object relationship*.

Considering the similarities and differences between the thinker and the outcast in this way should make us vigilant about any implicit stability or goal-oriented resting point in the characterization of lucidity that Cioran offers here. A full commitment to thinking against oneself requires such questioning as part of the *lucidité affective* that Cioran advocates. If the divided self is a crucial aspect of that lucidity, then it can only be an arrival point, as implied in the word "parvenir" in a qualified sense; the lucidity is a point of departure that will allow the thinker to continue to attempt to draw all the consequences of the divided self and impossibility of either unity or resignation; both the outcast and the thinker are predisposed, above all, to thinking against oneself in a way that would resist the very kind of definitive assertion that the speaker in "Merveilles du vice" makes in this section. This section, we might say, points far beyond itself in ways that it cannot yet fully articulate, and in that sense it is itself a particular moment in a process in which it participates even as it appears to announce a conclusion rather than a departure.

To close, I turn to a section on one of Cioran's most important themes across his work, that of insomnia. In "Invocation à l'insomnie" ["Invocation to Insomnia"] he puts insomnia in relation to philosophy, describing how at seventeen "je croyais à la philosophie. Ce qui ne s'y rapportait pas me semblait péché ou ordure […] Seule l'abstraction me paraissait palpiter : je m'abandonnais à des exploits ancillaires de peur qu'un objet plus noble ne me fît enfreindre mes principes et ne me livrât aux déchéances du cœur" (726) ["I believed in philosophy. What did not relate to philosophy seemed to me either a sin or slops. […] Only abstraction seemed to palpitate with life: I gave myself up to ancillary exploits lest some nobler object might make me infringe my principles and submit to the degradations of the heart" (169)]. Insomnia comes to interrupt that fascination: " … lorsque tu vins, Insomnie, secouer ma chair et mon orgueil, toi qui changes la brute juvénile, en nuances les instincts, en attises les rêves, toi qui, en une seule nuit, dispenses plus de savoir que les jours conclus dans le repos" (726) [" … when you came, Insomnia, to shake my flesh and my pride, you who transform the childish brute, give nuance to the instincts, focus to dreams, you who in a single night grant more knowledge than days spent in repose" (169)]. What is striking to the speaker about the night is its eternal sameness: "chaque nuit était pareille aux autres, chaque nuit était éternelle" (727) ["each night was like the others, each night was eternal" (169)]. Paradoxically, though, the sameness of the night becomes the canvas from which thought emerges; the speaker is unable to assimilate himself to the night and its sameness but is troubled by it in a way that also generates solidarity with others who have undergone the torment of the kind of lucidity that the night brings: "et je me sentais solidaire de tous ceux qi ne peuevnt dormir, de tous ces frères inconnus" (727) ["and I felt one with all those who cannot sleep, with all those unknown brothers" (169)]. What is revealed in the night is not its contrast to the day and its variety of lived experience but rather its similarity, the way in which the night is the truth of the day, which appears to have been false in view of the negation that night facilitates.

This realization prompts fantasies of violence and salvation: "J'eusse voué un culte à un tyran qui—pour se venger de ses nuits—eût défendu le repos, puni l'oubli, légiféré le malheur et la fièvre" (727) ["I would have worshipped a tyrant who—to take revenge on his night—would have forbidden rest, punished oblivion, prescribed disaster and fevers" (170)]. It is at that moment that the speaker turns once again to philosophy, only to find it defenseless and impotent in light of the night's revelations:

> Et c'est alors que je fis appel à la philosophie : mais point d'idée qui console dans le noir, point de système qui résiste aux veilles. Les analyses de l'insomnie défont les certitudes. Las d'une telle destruction, j'en étais à me dire : plus d'hésitation : dormir ou mourir …, reconquérir le sommeil ou disparaître … (727)

[And it was then that I appealed to philosophy; but there is no idea which comforts in the dark, no system which resists those vigils. The analyses of insomnia undo all certainties. Weary of such destruction, I came to the point of telling myself: no more vacillation, sleep or die ... reconquer sleep or disappear ... (170)]

Night, in the sameness of its nothingness, thus serves to be the motor of thought rather than canceling it; the night reveals that the subject is inassimilable into it, just as the subject is inassimilable to the kind of resignation he sometimes seems to desire. In that sense, night as truth shows up the falseness of the possibility of resignation as well as of solutions that one may seek in comforting religious truths. The night likewise serves to disrupt and render impossible the kind of clarity one may have thought to have attained via philosophy, unleashing thought instead in its untamed dynamism:

> Idées cristallines, enchaînement heureux de pensées ? Vous ne penserez plus: ce sera une irruption, une lave de concepts, sans consistance et sans suite, des concepts vomis, agressifs, partis des entrailles, châtiments que la chair s'inflige à elle-même, l'esprit étant victime des humeurs et hors de cause. (726)

> [Crystalline ideas, happy sequence of thoughts? You will not think any more: it will be an explosion, a lava of concepts, without consequence and without order, a vomit of aggressive concepts spewed from your guts, punishments the flesh inflicts upon itself, the mind being a victim of the humors and out of the question. (170)]

Such an experience is transformative and permanently removes the subject from the peace of mind that some may associate with intellectual contemplation:

> C'est que les veilles peuvent cesser ; mais leur lumière survit en vous : on ne voit pas impunément dans les ténèbres, on n'en recueille pas sans danger l'enseignement ; il y a des yeux qui ne pourront plus rien apprendre du soleil, et des âmes malades de nuits dont elles ne guériront jamais ... (727)

> [Waking may come to an end, but its light survives within you; one does not see in the dark with impunity, one does not gather its lessons without danger; there are eyes which can no longer learn anything from the sun, and souls afflicted by nights from which they will never recover .... (170)]

We might say that the night is the negation that refuses to become identical with itself: from the very sameness of the night, the supposedly empty or dark canvas emerges the truth of the separation of philosophy and thought, where any pretention any variants of philosophy may have had to comfort or consolation are shown to be comparable to religious illusions and dependent on the same sort of blind trust that the night reveals to be false.

Night thus reveals an inherent difficulty in living that what we might call "day blindness" leads us to ignore. Early on, writing in Romanian in a work that was translated into French in 2019, Cioran had already articulated the need to respond to the difficulty of being, of living, as it is revealed in the retreat from the busy-ness with which we occupy ourselves. What he calls a revelation serves, like thought as I have been characterizing it, as a stumbling block to the smooth functioning of unconscious existing:

> Le plus dur n'est pas de faire quelque chose, mais de vivre. [...] Nous trouvons tous à nous occuper – car on ne saurait continuer à vivre sans la superstition de l'action – mais *être* en tant que tel est un exercice de tourment, une autodestruction sans issue. La révélation de notre existence entrave nos pas, nous coupe le souffle et nous fige au milieu d'un monde sans horizon. L'inconvénient qu'il y a à exister ne résulte pas de nos années de mûrissement ou de maturation automnale, mais constitue notre déficience originelle, et la source où puise notre manque de fondement. (*Divagations* 80)

> [The hardest thing is not to do something, but to live. We all find something to occupy us—since we would not be able to continue to live without the superstition of action—but *to be* as such is an exercise in torment, an inevitable self-destruction. The revelation of our existence hinders our steps, takes our breath away and fixes us in the middle of a world without horizon. The disadvantage that comes with existing results not from our years of maturing or from autumnal maturity, but constitutes our original deficiency, and the source from which our lack of foundation draws.]

That moment of revelation unleashes the drama of a thought informed by the illusion of identity thinking that is challenged to be faithful to a concept of thought that draws on the negative in order to proceed with a model of thought as destruction of sure principles and to inaugurate a necessarily goalless spirit of doubt into whatever we seek to call thought. As Cioran would later write in *De l'inconvénient d'être né*: "la pensée n'est jamais innocente. C'est parce qu'elle est sans pitié, c'est parce qu'elle est aggression, qu'elle nous aide à faire sauter nos entraves" (1279) ["thought is never *innocent*, for it is pitiless, it is aggressive, it helps us burst our bonds" (15)].[20] In its aggressivity, thought drains the one who experiences it: "penser, c'est saper, c'est se saper. Agir entraîne moins de risques, parce que l'action remplit l'intervalle entre les choses et nous, alors que la réflexion l'élargit dangereusement" (1387) ["to think is to undermine—to undermine *oneself*. Action involves fewer risks, for it fills the interval between things and ourselves, whereas reflection dangerously widens it" (192)]. In that sense, thought is akin to insomnia in terms of its negative effects.

Insomnia is the plot twist that calls for thought to account adequately for the experience of having negated all one might have thought one knew and replacing it with a negative model of knowledge, one that is based in negation, takes account of human suffering, and leaves room for solidarity with others who have come to see the falsity in what they have previously called truth. What such a thought might look like is necessarily left unspecified, for to attempt that would be to be radically unfaithful to its revelations. That infidelity would involve installing a goal or a positive definition of truth as opposed to a commitment, despite oneself perhaps, to the experience of thinking as a way to resist the simplistic and the false, to avoid the catastrophe of acting on false commitments and ends, and to live in the division of the split self while resisting the temptation to attempt the impossible task of resolving it into an impossible and ultimately undesirable unity. Cioran's failure to achieve quietude is thus, paradoxically, his success, a success enacted as a kind of violence on the writing subject that results not in its annihilation but in its perpetuation as a self-undermining, self-negating subjectivity that persists through that very act of self-negation. Thought never lets us forget the presence of the thinking subject even as it works to perpetuate its division; in that way, it necessarily remains similar to insomnia, both of which are states of hyper-consciousness predicated on the impossibility of the thinking self becoming perceptible to itself in any other way.

3

Clément Rosset: Thinking the Real

Eugene Thacker characterizes pessimism by way of what he calls the "three refusals" of crying, laughing, and sleeping:

> The logic of pessimism moves through three refusals: a no-saying to the worst (refusal of the world-for-us, or Schopenhauer's tears); a yes-saying to the worst (refusal of the world-in-itself, or Nietzsche's laughter); and a no-saying to the for-us and the in-itself (a double refusal, or Cioran's sleep).
>
> Crying, laughing, sleeping—what other responses are adequate to a life that is so indifferent? (Thacker 12)

As with any taxonomy, this one both reveals and hides what it attempts to classify. Cioran does value sleep for the temporary unconsciousness of intolerable reality that it provides, and criticizes Nietzsche for his all too affirmative outlook.[1] But there is laughter in Cioran as well, a laughter associated not with affirmation but negation, as Michel Jarrety has indicated:

> La négation est alors aussi bien réappropriation de ce qu'elle conteste, manière de vivre avec ce qu'on refuse, signe enfin d'une vigueur qui est la vie même.
>
> C'est donc à tort qu'on l'interpréterait simplement comme le signe du malheur, la postulation du refus ou de l'affirmation de l'insoumission car une part essentielle de son bénéfice, au contraire, s'affirme dans le bonheur de nier qui seul permet de supporter le réel tel qu'il est : d'où la tonicité si souvent remarquée qui rend parfois étrangement gaie la lecture de Cioran et procède directement de la jubilation sensible, et justement de la *dérision*, qui accompagnent les modalités de la négation que son écriture multiplie. (130)

[Negation is thus also reappropriation of what it contests, a way of living with what one refuses, and the sign of a vigor which is life itself.

It is thus wrong to interpret it simply as a sign of misfortune, the postulation of refusal of the affirmation of insubordination because an essential part of its benefit, on the contrary, is affirmed in the happiness of negating which is the only thing that allows us to tolerate the real as it is: from there we get the tone, so often noticed, that, sometimes strangely, makes reading Cioran a happy experience and proceeds directly from the palpable jubilation, and from the *derision*, that accompanies the modalities of negation that his writing multiplies.]

The philosopher Clément Rosset, who was a friend of Cioran's, takes his distance from him on questions of joy and negation, adopting a more conventionally Nietzschean stance of affirmation despite full lucidity about the intolerable nature of reality and of suffering. Rosset said in an interview that Cioran "jubile en noirceur [...], sa jubilation à écrire le malheur est si grande qu'elle permet justement de surmonter le malheur" ["rejoices in darkness [...], his jubilation at writing about misery is so great that it permits him to overcome misery"] (in Tellez 146). As Jean Tellez indicates:

> ce qui sépare Rosset de Cioran—alors que tout semble aussi les rapprocher—n'est sans doute [...] qu'une simple inversion des termes qui défissent le problème de l'existence. Toute l'horreur d'exister, pour Cioran, est d'être *quelque chose* et de *compter pour rien*. Le secret de la joie est dans une inversion : *on compte pour rien,* mais *on est quelque chose.* L'inversion permet de déplacer l'accent sur « quelque chose ». Etre quelque chose, voilà qui réjouit absolument. (148)

[what separates Rosset from Cioran—whereas everything seems also bring them together—is no doubt only [...] a simple inversion of the terms that define the problem of existence. All the horror of existing, for Cioran, is to be *something* and to *count for nothing.* The secret of joy is in an inversion: *we count for nothing,* but *we are something.* The inversion allows us to displace the accent on "something." To be something, that is what causes absolute rejoicing.]

For Rosset, the unrepresentable nature of the real, in which we are immersed without having philosophical knowledge of it, is the greatest source of that suffering, which conventional philosophy attempts to appease by crafting what it takes, erroneously, to be knowledge of the real. Joy as Rosset conceives it is not a mere palliative measure meant to help us endure life but a reaction that emerges from within the context of that life itself as opposed to a negation of it, an irrational and grace-filled reaction to the fact that there is something rather than nothing, in full and paradoxical acknowledgment of the horror of that something. He advances a strong critique of pessimism, not because he would deny its claims about suffering, but rather because he argues, as we will see, that pessimism, like optimism, draws undemonstrable conclusions about the nature of reality. By conceiving joy within the context of suffering rather than opposed to it, he challenges most conventional definitions of it, and seems nondialectical in that act of affirmation. I will argue, however, that the notion of tragic living that he endorses depends upon the kind of dialectical thinking that he seems to reject.

Rosset himself writes in *Le choix des mots* that all of the questions with which his work has been preoccupied can be summarized in this question:

> Comment concilier l'amour de l'existence avec l'ensemble des arguments plausibles ou raisonnables qui tous contribuent à tailler celui-ci en pièces ? Il y avait là, me semblait-il, un problème crucial encore qu'il n'engageât [...] que la simple question de savoir s'il était possible d'aimer la vie *en conscience*, c'est-à-dire sans être obligé tous les jours d'un peu mentir à soi-même. (*Le choix* 15–16)
>
> [How can we reconcile love of existence with the set of plausible or reasonable arguments which all contribute to break that into pieces? There was, it seemed to me, a crucial problem even though it only engaged [...] the simple question of knowing whether it was possible to love life *consciously*, that is, without being required to lie a bit to oneself each day.]

Rosset's project is thus one of attempted reconciliation between what seem like incompatible situations, as Andrew Goffey notes: "Rosset [...] seeks to reconcile an unconditional love or affirmation of existence with the set of plausible or reasonable arguments which contribute to its demolition" (in Rosset "Despite" 73). Rosset's approach inspires more questions than answers, and in this lies what strength it has, on my reading, precisely because it maintains awareness of philosophy's necessarily failed project to account for the fullness of the real, and infuses that experience of thought with the full weight of the consequences for coming to that realization. The way he understands tragedy is an effective characterization of what I have been calling the experience of thought, manifest in other thinkers, including Adorno, Cioran, and Bataille, in ways much different than in Rosset.[2] Chief among those differences is a rejection of thinking. He claims in *Le principe de cruauté* that the function of philosophy "est moins d'apprendre que de désapprendre à penser" ["is less to learn than to unlearn thinking"] (*Le principe* 41) if we see philosophy's role consisting "plutôt à dénoncer des erreurs qu'à énoncer des vérités" ["moreso of denouncing errors than enunciating truths"] (41). While at one level, this is consistent with thinking's creative destruction function as Arendt identifies it, Rosset's commitment to the belief that philosophy deals only with doubles and thus distances us from the real makes him prefer, not this sort of thinking, but rather a particular variant of what he calls "la bêtise" ["stupidity"] "pusique celle-ci ne consiste pas, contrairement à ce qu'on pense généralement et à tort, en une paresse d'esprit mais bien en une débauche désordonnée d'activité intellectuelle" ["since that does not consist, contrary to what is generally, and wrongly, thought, in a mental laziness but rather in a disordered debauchery of intellectual activity"] (41) for which Flaubert's characters Bouvard and Pécuchet serve as a model.[3]

Rosset's repeated affirmation of the impossibility of making sense of the real, precisely because the real has no meaning, only draws us more deeply into processes by which we might make sense of the negation of sense. This is one of the paradoxes that necessarily arises when thinking about the real, since an affirmation of meaninglessness begs questions about the consequences of that meaninglessness and how we might conceptualize it. Those questions, which spur thought by nature of the paradox they bring to light, bring us, *pace* Rosset, back to the experience of thought rather than allowing us to dismiss thought in light of the possible meaninglessness of the real. As we will see, Rosset claims an absolute identity of the real to itself, so that tautology, A=A, is the richest mode we have for conceiving it: "nothing is as 'rapid,' if I may say so, as the real, which occurs so quickly that for it to be perceived requires, like a complicated musical score, a virtuoso deciphering. And nothing is as close either: it is proximity itself" (Rosset "Despite" 75). To decipher the real, however, is to make an object of it, to give it conceptual reality for a thinking subject, which returns us to the subject-object relations that have been the basis of non-identity thinking as all of the thinkers we have been considering have conceived of it. The impetus of thinking is the non-identity of the thing to itself as an object of thought, its non-tautological nature that emerges once we place anything in the role of object of thought.

For Rosset, this points to the ultimate unknowability of the real through, paradoxically, its very proximity, but it is also possible to conceive the real as different from itself insofar as it constitutes the object of thought. If we can say that the real is both identical and non-identical to itself, we have already moved away from absolute tautology, or shown that the tautology was only apparent, a convenient way to hide the complexity involved in the real. Revealingly, in a discussion of some of the differences between his thought and Cioran's, Rosset even expresses happiness in similarly tautological terms:

> I was very close to [Cioran] and spent many wonderfully amusing and memorable evenings with him. But I did not experience the real as he did because for me the experience of the real is itself what motivates the *joie de vivre*. I do indeed believe that it's possible to marry lucidity—awareness of the fact that life is

absurd, ridiculous—and happiness [*allégresse*]. Despite everything, happiness is still happiness. ("Despite" 78–9)

It is significant that Rosset announces the reconciliation of lucidity and happiness as belief rather than demonstrable fact; it lends a narrative quality to his thought which is otherwise concerned, in a more traditionally philosophical vein, with the nature of reality. This "marriage" could certainly be said not to be easy to bring about; I would argue that it is not desirable either, precisely because it sidesteps the anguish present in Bataille and Cioran's engagement with the nature of thought as experience. At the same time, though, to keep alive a sense of the tragic as Rosset does is to carve out some role for the kind of thinking in which Bataille and Cioran engage; Rosset's very pronouncements can, and even must, serve as the starting point for dialectical engagement rather than an endpoint that would shut down thought once the believed-in reconciliation had been achieved.

Rosset is interested, like Bataille and Cioran, in the experiential aspect of thought and the way thinking entwines with other forms of lived experience and perception; he also, like them, advances a critique of philosophy. As Jean Tellez has observed, for Rosset, "le tragique est essentiellement une expérience. Cette dernière s'explicite difficilement, elle se livre plutôt à l'état brut, donc silencieux. On peut juste dire : « C'est comme ça ». L'insignifiance, la mort n'ont pas d'autre discours possible : « C'est comme ça, ce n'est pas autrement »" ["the tragic is essentially an experience. It is made explicit only with difficulty; it hands itself over in the raw state, and thus silently. We can only say: 'it's like that.' Insignificance and death have no other possible discourse: 'It's like that, it's not any other way'"] (37). Rather than criticizing the systematic nature of the philosophical enterprise, he reproaches many strands of it for its consoling function, which he claims is medicinal in nature, mitigating the unbearable experience of the real, as opposed to concerning itself with truth. David Bell summarizes the way in which most philosophy is, for Rosset, a "betrayal of the real":

> If one gives philosophy and philosophers half a chance, they almost invariably tend toward the worst excesses. More specifically, the probability is very high that they will devise an approach to reality and the world which in fact turns away from the world, occults it, and replaces it with a representation that supplants it and supposedly expresses its higher truth. Faced with this betrayal of the real, Rosset favors idiocy in its etymological sense, that is, *idiotes*, an approach which is simple, particular, unique, and refuses all doubling. ("Introduction", vii)

Rosset's interest in the real is to demonstrate that it is unthinkable, a conception that brings with it the question of what is livable, and the relation of perceived reality to what he does not hesitate to claim as the "true" nature of reality. Those two aspects of his thought, namely, his work on the real and his exposition of the tragic nature of existence, while developed largely in separate works, work together to pose questions about how thought functions as experience and the way to reconcile, if indeed we can reconcile, thought with other kinds of experience or whether living lucidly, aware of the tragic nature of existence, always involves a voluntary rejection of what lucid reflection has revealed. To draw conclusions about the immediacy of the real automatically brings us into the domain of questions about what it would mean to live well in light of the philosophical conclusions we draw about reality, and about whether lived experience can include thought or whether it must transcend it somehow in order to gain access to the kind of joy that Rosset conceives. Even to say that we should at some point abandon thought is to fall back into it because it yields questions about how and why we would want or need to separate thinking from other kinds of lived experience.

In *Logique du pire*, Rosset establishes a fundamental distinction between pessimistic and tragic philosophy, which may appear to have much in common but whose distinction is fundamental for him: "Schopenhauer, Kierkegaard, Unamuno sont, selon cette distinction, des philosophes pessimistes ; Lucrèce, Montaigne, Pascal, des penseurs tragiques" ["Schopenhauer, Kierkegaard, Unamuno are, according to this distinction, pessimist philosophers; Lucretius, Montaigne, and Pascal are tragic thinkers"] (*Logique* 105). The examples are helpful to begin to distinguish between pessimistic and tragic philosophers on Rosset's account, given that his definition of tragic philosophy seems at first to share, and does indeed ultimately share, much common ground with pessimist philosophy:

> Aussi la philosophie tragique est-elle un art de poisons, orienté vers l'inlassable recherche des pires, des plus violents, des plus meurtriers parmi les philtres de mort et de désespérance. Elle en a besoin, à chaque instant, et du pire d'entre eux immédiatement disponible pour elle, pour réussir à penser *quelque chose* de ce qu'elle éprouve : l'approbation. (*Logique* 49)

> [Thus is tragic philosophy an art of poisons, oriented toward the tireless search of the worst, the most violent, the most murderous of the potions of death and despair. It needs them, at every instant, and of the worst among them

immediately available for it, in order to succeed in thinking *something* about what it feels: approbation.]

Tragic philosophy "diverge fondamentalement" [diverges fundamentally] from pessimism according to Rosset (*Logique* 15), even if the vision of the philosophers he has labeled tragic is "plus pessimiste que tout pessimisme" [more pessimistic than any pessimism] (15). He identifies two types of difference between them, having to do with what he claims are pre-given assumptions about the real on the part of pessimists:

> La première [différence] consiste dans le fait même de la "vision du monde" : donnée première du pessimisme, elle est récusée en tant que telle par les philosophes tragiques. Le pessimiste parle *après avoir vu* ; le terroriste tragique parle pour dire l'*impossibilité de voir*. Autrement dit : le pessimisme—en tant que doctrine philosophique, [...] constitue, bien évidemment, une affirmation du pire. Mais précisément : seulement [...] *à partir* d'un certain sens, ou un certain ordre, déjà donnés, dont il sera loisible de montrer—ensuite—le caractère insatisfaisant ou incohérent. (15)

> [The first [difference] consists in the very fact of the "world vision": the first given of pessimism, it is rejected as is by tragic philosophers. The pessimist speaks *after having seen*; the tragic terrorist speaks in order to say the *impossibility of seeing*. Said otherwise: pessimism—as a philosophical doctrine, [...] constitutes, obviously, an affirmation of the worst. But precisely, only *from the starting point* of a certain meaning, or a certain order, already given, from which it would be permissible to show—afterward—the unsatisfactory or incoherent character.]

Pessimists make judgments about the world that could only be made from an Archimedean point from which the world could be understood and interpreted, which is one of the claims Rosset strongly resists concerning the real. Pessimism is:

> la limite à laquelle peut aboutir—et aboutit en effet, si la pensée est sans assises théologiques—la considération du *déjà ordonné*. Mauvaise ordonnance, mais ordonnance: le monde est *assemblé (mal assemblé)*, il constitue une "nature" (mauvaise) ; et c'est précisément dans le mesure où il est un *système* que le philosophe pessimiste pourra le déclarer sombre *in aeterno,* non susceptible de modification ou d'amélioration. Non seulement le pessimiste n'accède-t-il pas au thème du hasard, encore la négation du hasard est-elle la clef de voûte de tout pessimisme, comme l'affirmation du hasard est celle de toute pensée tragique. (15–16)

[the limit at which the consideration of the *already ordered* can arrive—and in fact arrives, if thought is without theological bases. A bad arrangement, but an arrangement: the world is *assembled* (*badly assembled*); it constitutes a "nature" (bad); and it is precisely insofar as it is a *system* that the pessimist philosopher will be to declare it eternally somber, not subject to change or improvement. Not only does the pessimist not arrives at the theme of chance; the negation of chance is the keystone to all pessimism, as the affirmation of chance is that of all tragic thought.]

The constituted versus unconstituted world is what makes for the difference between pessimistic and tragic philosophy for Rosset, and the source of the tragedy for the latter is precisely that it is incapable of establishing the world's logic, despite its desire to do so, not because the world is absurd or meaningless as the pessimists would assert, but because the real is beyond the realm of what could be meaningful or meaningless, so neither category can be applied to it. Affective and intellectual reaction to this fact is just as strong for tragic thinkers as for pessimists, and, as in all of the other approaches I have considered in this study, this conclusion, in its impossibility to *aboutir*, calls on thinkers to elaborate a set of consequences that would not simply shut down further reflection.

The awareness of the potential inability to do that poses a stumbling block for tragic thinkers that they risk not overcoming, which is at the root of the tragedy since it denies a basic impulse to make sense, even negative sense, of lived experience and lend meaning, however bleak, to it: "le pire pessimiste désigne une logique du monde, le pire tragique, une logique de la pensée (se découvrant incapable de penser un monde)" ["the worst pessimist designs a world logic, the worst tragic thinker a logic of thought (finding himself incapable of thinking a world"] (16). So the pessimistic and the tragic share a similar mood for Rosset: "ce n'est pas l'humeur, mais l'objet de l'interrogation, qui sépare penseur tragique et pessimiste. Le pessimisme est la grande *philosophie du donné*. Plus précisément : la philosophie du donné en tant que *déja ordonnée*—c'est-à-dire la *philosophie de l'absurde*" ["it is not the mood, but the object of the investigation, which separates the pessimist and tragic thinkers. Pessimism is the great *philosophy of the given*. More specifically: the philosophy of the given as *already ordained*— that is, the *philosophy of the absurd*"] (16). In terms of the object it takes, there is a fundamental similarity between pessimism and optimism since both make fundamental assumptions and assertions about the knowability of the world: "le 'pire' de Schopenhauer et le 'meilleur' de Leibniz ont finalement la même signification. Dès lors qu'il se donne—sans références théologiques ou téléologiques—une nature à penser, le pessimiste aboutit nécessairement à une philosophie de l'absurde" ["Schopenhauer's 'worst' and Leibniz's 'best' mean the same thing in the end. Once the pessimist gives himself—without theological or teleological references—a nature to think, he ends up necessarily at a philosophy of the absurd"] (16–17). We arrive at the absurd because we realize that nothing legitimates the order we have imposed on the world, a fact which calls pessimism into question while anchoring us ever more firmly in the tragic. He criticizes Schopenhauer for structuring the will as what Rosset calls "an event" which single-handedly permits us to:

> passer du chaos à la pensée de l'ordre. Pour le penseur tragique, « ce qui existe »—qui n'est ni nature, ni être, ni objet adéquat de pensée—ne donne jamais lieu à des événements : "s'y passent" des rencontres, des occasions, qui ne supposent jamais le recours à quelque principe qui transcende les perspectives tragiques de l'inertie et du hasard. (17)[4]

> [pass from chaos to the thinking of order. For the tragic thinker, "what exists"—which is neither nature, nor being, nor adequate object of thought—never leads to events: encounters, occasions "happen," which never suppose the recourse to some principle that transcends the tragic perspectives of inertia and chance.]

I have argued elsewhere that pessimism is best understood in terms of verisimilitude rather than verifiability, that it appeals to aspects of a narrative approach to making meaning from lived experience; the interest in a thinker like Schopenhauer would thus lie in his particular construction of a framework for meaning rather than in the empirical verifiability of his conclusions about the will. Another way of thinking about the distinction that Rosset is making is to conceive of it in terms of the difference that I have been identifying between philosophy and thought. Rosset's writing attempts to undermine nearly the whole of the philosophical enterprise insofar as he defines its domain of inquiry as general understanding of the real, which he then claims we can have no knowledge of precisely because of its immediacy and inherent meaningless as well as its anchoring in chance. Such an approach necessarily leads him to the tragic, which also infuses his thought with questions about how best to conceptualize how a life can be lived in the face of potentially intolerable knowledge about the world, which, as we have seen, he identifies as an explicit goal of his thought insofar as he seeks a compatibility or reconciliation between lucidity and happiness.

Once we move into the domain of the tragic, we necessarily attempt to make meaning from the absurdity and meaninglessness that are implied by Rosset's conclusions about the real. In that sense, tragic and pessimist philosophy come together once more, since both are involved in the active construction of meaning or meaninglessness, and attempt to create order in that sense. Once we recognize that pessimism has its basis, despite its occasional claims to objectively verifiable knowledge of the world, in a narrative construction, the similarities between tragedy and pessimism become far more salient than the differences Rosset identifies when he critiques the unjustifiable system-building of the pessimists. While Rosset's tragic perspective makes room for a variety of thinkers including Lucretius, Montaigne, and Pascal, he identifies a stunningly small range of potential "acts" according to tragic thinking:

> Selon une perspective tragique, seuls donc auront « agi » en leur vie, d'une part les suicidaires, de l'autre les affirmateurs inconditionnels. Si la "morale" avait, aux yeux de la pensée tragique, un sens quelconque, tel en serait l'unique critère de valeur : la « dignité » étant d'approuver globalement ou de nier globalement, de vivre en le voulant ou de mourir en le voulant. (47)

> [According to a tragic perspective, only suicides on one hand, and unconditional affirmers on the other, will have "acted." If "morality" had, in the eyes of tragic thought, some meaning, such would be the only criterion of its value: "dignity" being to approve globally or negate globally, to live wanting it or to die wanting it.]

Once again, to begin to think through the consequences of such a restricted domain of action necessarily sends us back to a view of thinking as an experience; to foreclose the realm of potential actions in this way can only open up the domain of thinking against oneself, a fall into the kind of thought that we saw as inevitable in Cioran, against a fully inert (non)existence that he sometimes seems to valorize. To think against oneself necessarily calls into question the livability not only of Rosset's assertions about the meaninglessness of the real but also, and perhaps especially, the claim that unconditional affirmation is, from a tragic perspective, the only choice available to those who do not kill themselves. To affirm thinking this way, I would argue, is not incompatible with Rosset's notion of the tragic. It is to valorize the situated and dialectical approach to thinking as experience that we have seen in Bataille and Cioran rather than lamenting the impossibility of making meaning on account of the inaccessibility or overly accessible immediate nature of the real. It is, in other words, a viable and preferable alternative to unconditional affirmation precisely because it makes room for the possibility of affirmation without requiring it as the only viable way to craft meaning from experience.

Rosset recognizes the possibility of a dead end if one attempts to draw all conclusions from tragic discourse which, he claims, could and even should end in silence, since "faire parler davantage le silence supposerait qu'on dispose d'un mot magique, qui sache parler sans rien dire, penser sans rien concevoir, dénier toute idéologie sans s'engager lui-même dans une idéologie quelconque" ["to make silence speak more would suppose that we have at our disposal a magic word that can speak without saying anything, think without conceiving anything, deny all ideology without engaging itself in some ideology"] (70). Surprisingly perhaps, he then affirms that "un tel mot existe peut-être : le *hasard*" ["such a word exists perhaps: *chance*"] (70). What he proposes is a sort of end of no end, an endless end that brings all thought about the real back to the notion of chance in order not to end in silence. But again, the very fact that there are a variety of tragic thinkers suggests that adopting a tragic approach to thought does not condemn us to a narrow set of undesirable options that would return constantly to the rather undialectical affirmation of chance. Thought conceived of this way would align itself more closely to literature, as indeed Bataille and Cioran's texts do, and both can, *pace* Rosset, attempt to represent the real within the realm of perception.

Alison James has argued that Rosset's claims about the unrepresentable nature of the real confront literature with "la tâche paradoxale de dire le silence, d' « habiller en parole » une réalité dont la caractéristique essentielle est de ne pas parler, d'être insignifiante. Mais comment habiller le réel sans le doubler d'une fausse apparence, d'une signification ?" ["the paradoxical task of saying silence, to 'dress in words' a reality whose essential characteristic is not to speak, to be insignificant. But how could we dress the real without doubling it with a false appearance or a signification?"] (James 105). She goes on to wonder, in the face of this "aporie apparente" ["apparent aporia"], if it is "nécessaire de souscrire à cette conception du langage comme reflet" ["necessary to subscribe to this conception of language as reflection"] (105). Indeed, a more nuanced view of language as creative of its worlds and not merely reflective of them makes space for a thinking that does not attempt to make unfounded truth claims about reality but that nonetheless allows the building, sometimes paradoxically through destruction, of tentative attempts to articulate meaning as part of the act of thinking itself, taken as an enterprise not entirely identified with the project of representing the world. Rosset could be said to be engaging in this act of meaning-making in his own work, as James goes on to conclude: "l'idée de hasard suppose déjà une interprétation de notre propre rapport à l'événement, et elle dépend précisément d'une notion de sens et de récit" ["the idea of chance already supposes an interpretation of our own relation to the event, and it depends precisely on a notion of meaning and story"] (114). In other words, the subject is not so easily removed from general considerations of the real, and thinking as I have been characterizing it both allows us to realize this and to continue the dynamic process of making sense of thought, via thought.

Thought understood this way resists resolution; that is at the heart of its negative dialectical character and is both a cause and an effect of thinking's inability to attain a goal and its resistance to the idea of goal-directed thought more broadly. Rosset, as we have seen, articulates his project in terms of bringing about the reconciliation of lucidity and happiness, which he claims to accomplish by making room for joy. As with many of the other terms he employs, his characterization of joy is quite far from common understandings, and in fact true joy depends on a full acknowledgment of the meaninglessness and absurdity that tragic and pessimistic philosophy share, rather than a rejection of them. It is what is left to us when, as David Bell puts it:

> [O]ne lays aside all mediation between oneself and the real. But it is also a veritable epistemological necessity and tool. No one who has not known the joyful approbation of the real can ultimately *know* the real. The reason is simple enough. Those who have not experienced that joyful approbation have of necessity turned away from the real, pulled back from it in horror and suffering. (xi)

Joy is thus marked by being "parfaitement absurde et indéfendable" ["perfectly absurd and indefensible"] according to Rosset (*La force* 102).[5] If joy is so paradoxical as not to negate tragedy, we should be led to wonder in what sense we could still be talking about joy. Rosset is, ultimately, performing creative work on language, that is, engaging in precisely the kind of work that allows us to create conceptual worlds through negation of the given. To do that is, however, to affirm meaning as a creative act, which undermines Rosset's claims about the unrepresentability of the real. While it still may be the case that the real is ultimately unrepresentable, thought operates outside that particular conception of the generalizable real in order to make sense of it.

Rosset lays out the paradoxical nature of joy in *La force majeure*, which appears in English translation in *Joyful Cruelty*:

Ou bien la joie consiste en l'illusion éphémère d'en avoir fini avec le tragique de l'existence : auquel cas la joie n'est pas paradoxale mais est illusoire. Ou bien elle consiste en une approbation de l'existence tenue pour irrémédiablement tragique : auquel cas la joie est paradoxale mais n'est pas illusoire.

On ne sera pas surpris que je donne pour ma part la préférence au second terme de l'alternative, persuadé non seulement que la joie réussit à s'accommoder du tragique, mais encore et surtout qu'elle ne consiste que dans et par cet accord paradoxal avec lui. (*La force* 24)

[Either joy consists of an ephemeral illusion of having gotten rid of the tragic nature of existence in which case joy is not paradoxical but illusory, or it consists of an approbation of existence which is held to be irremediably tragic, in which case joy is paradoxical, but it is not illusory.

It will come as no surprise to hear that I give my preference to the second alternative, persuaded as I am not only that joy succeeds in accommodating itself to the tragic but, in addition and especially that it exists only in and by this paradoxical agreement with the tragic. (*Joyful* 17)]

Such a joy is "attentive" to the "malheur" of misfortune (*La force* 25 / *Joyful* 17), which leads to Rosset to highlight the way in which joy only emerges in and as contradiction: "il n'est de joie véritable que si elle est en même temps contrariée, en contradiction avec elle-meme: la joie est paradoxale, ou n'est pas la joie" (*La force* 25) ["there is no true joy unless it is simultaneously thwarted, in contradiction with itself. Joy is paradoxical, or it is not joy" (*Joyful* 17)]. Because of its contradictory nature, Rosset claims that it is "of an illogical and irrational essence," that it is "necessary cruel, by virtue of the carefree attitude it exudes when faced with the most fatal destiny as well as the most tragic considerations." He specifies that the cruelty of the real can be seen by appeal to the etymology of cruel in the notion of *cruor*:

> *Cruor*, d'où dérive *crudelis* (cruel) ainsi que *crudus* (cru, non digéré, indigeste), désigne la chair écorchée et sanglante : soit la chose elle-même dénuée de ses atours ou accompagnements ordinaires, en l'occurrence la peau, et réduite ainsi à son unique réalité, aussi saignante qu'indigeste. Ainsi la réalité est-elle cruelle—et indigeste—dès lors qu'on la dépouille de toute ce qui n'est pas elle pour ne la considérer qu'en elle-même. (*Le principe* 18)

> [*Cruor*, from which *crudelis* (cruel) as well as *crudus* (not digested, indigestible) are derived, designates torn and bloody flesh, that is, the thing itself stripped of all its ornaments and ordinary external accoutrements, in this case skin, and

thus reduced to its unique reality, as bloody as it is indigestible. Thus reality is cruel—and indigestible—as soon as one removes from it everything which is not reality in order to consider it in itself. (*Joyful* 76)]

Furthermore, joy "consists of a madness which paradoxically permits one [...] to avoid all other madness, which preserves one from neurotic existence and permanent untruth" (17–18). If joy is contradictory to the point where it is simultaneously thwarted, one could ask whether the concept has been stretched so far beyond its given meaning as to necessitate a different label for it. For while Rosset sometimes seems to affirm the immediate joy of common existence, it is only by a complex mental operation that we can see that immediacy as operating in full contradiction with itself, which requires a kind of thinking that could only stand not just in contradiction but in opposition to the joyful immediacy of a moment.

It is, in other words, not so simple to escape mediation as Rosset's paradoxical formulations of joy would let on, since to understand how, or even why, we might want to label the experience of tragedy as joy requires a complex move which necessarily cancels the kind of immediacy, simplicity, or "idiocy" Rosset seeks to hold out for joy. To redefine joy in this way while still preserving the term invites an attempt to seek some sort of continuity with more common understandings of joy, in which case the term itself, if it both bears the trace of the common understanding and undermines it by necessarily including an understanding of the tragic, is complex rather than simple. This is so any time one takes the nature of joy or of the real as an object of thought, at which point even what is claimed to be singular becomes divided by entering the object relation of thought for a subject. Rosset's focus on resolution comes to the fore in his treatment of joy, since it remains unspecified what it would mean to live the contradiction of joy dialectically, opening oneself to the immediacy of an experience while remaining conscious of the tragic perspective he has outlined. At best, one would need temporarily to forget the tragic, in moments such as those Cioran describes when listening to music for instance,[6] or to hold the contradiction explicitly in tension, which requires an act of thought which Rosset seems to see as antithetical to the immediacy of joy. One would also need to abandon the notion of the subject, at least temporarily, as Rosset indicated on at least one occasion in an interview: "C'est « on » qui est joyeux, ce n'est pas « je ». La joie implique une disparition complète du « je »" ["It is 'they' who are joyous, it is not 'I.' Joy implies a complete disappearance of the 'I'"] (in Tellez 85).

The contradiction that defines joy may also be said to operate in Rosset's characterization of the real as well. As Charles Ramond indicates:

[Rosset] ajoute : le réel est invisible parce qu'il est donné comme singulier et simple. Mais, objecterons-nous alors, n'est-il pas doublement contradictoire que le réel soit à la fois « donné » et « invisible » (à quoi, à quel sens aurait-il été « donné » ?), et à la fois « singulier » et « simple » ? On ne voit pas du tout, en effet, pourquoi ce qui est « singulier » devrait être « simple » (Ramond 26)

[[Rosset] adds: the real is invisible because it is given as singular and simple. But, we would then object, is it not doubly contradictory that the real would be at the same time "given" and "invisible" (to what and in what sense would it have been "given?"), and at the same time "singular" and "simple?" We do not at all see, in fact, why what is "singular" should be "simple."]

Both joy and the real, as redefined by Rosset, risk incoherence unless he can articulate the way in which the contradiction animates these conceptions in a way that makes them available to thought. My claim is that Rosset's conception of both joy and the real pays insufficient attention to the subject-object distinction by which we come to know the contradiction of the real and which implies a split that defies the singularity of the real.

To experience the real or joy is to experience ourselves experiencing it and conceptualizing it as such, a point of which Ramond takes account in his critique:

Si Rosset a raison de déterminer le « réel » comme « invisible », ce n'est donc pas, comme il le pense à tort, parce qu'il n'y aurait pas de miroir possible pour lui, mais c'est parce que le réel est toujours déjà miroir … non qu'il serait trop « simple » pour être vu, mais parce que c'est toujours nous que nous voyons en lui. (Ramond 27)

[If Rosset is right to determine the "real" as "invisible, this is not, as he wrongly thinks, because it would not have any possible mirror for him, but because the real is always already a mirror … not that it would be too "simple" to be seen, but because it is always us that we see in it.]

Rosset, by wanting his claims about the real to satisfy the conditions of universal knowledge that is often philosophy's goal, invites difficulties that the situated writings of Cioran and Bataille avoid because of the way their very structure calls into question the universality of any of the claims the writings contain and can thus better account for contradiction. By developing his anti-ontology and then claiming that lived experience necessarily makes no headway in describing or interpreting the real because the real does not give itself to be interpreted, Rosset resorts to joy as a fundamentally aberrant response to the tragedy that he outlines while all the same implicitly denying that such an emplotment is an interpretation. The moment in which one wants to affirm joy is a passing moment, given that joy is precarious and not a permanent state of being;[7] perhaps the moment in which the real presents itself as singular is also such a passing moment of thought, a possibility supported by Rosset's later rethinking of the relationship of doubles to reality.

Rather than doubles being a falsification of reality, he comes to think of them, in his late work, as equivalent to the real itself: "le réel est peut-être la somme des apparences, des images et des fantômes qui en suggèrent fallacieusement l'existence" ["the real is perhaps the sum of appearances, images, and phantoms which fallaciously suggest its existence"] (*Fantasmagories* 66).[8] This new affirmation of a certain kind of double forces Rosset to make a distinction between "les doubles de *duplication*" ["doubles of *duplication*"], positively valued, and "les doubles de *remplacment*" ["doubles of *replacement*"] (*Fantasmagories* 73).[9] Rosset's commitment to an either/or by which the real would either be opposed to its doubles or synonymous with them underemphasizes the dialectical relation between the real and the double by seemingly not admitting their mutual dependence on each other in order for either the real or the double to be conceived at all. Momentarily affirming the real as singular necessarily provides a point of departure for thought rather than a resting place or goal, since it puts a thinker in the paradoxical position of asking about the consequences one might draw for thought from an affirmation of the impossibility of interpretation of the real, a question which itself demands interpretation or risks incoherence.

Rosset acknowledges that philosophy is interpretive and creative:

> Le regard philosophique est ainsi et nécessairement interprétatif, par le simple fait qu'il « mesure »—comme le suggère joliment Nicolas de Cuse dans *Le profane*, rapprochant le mental du mesurable, le fait de penser du fait de mesurer. Et il est toujours aussi créatif, puisque les images qu'il propose de la réalité n'en sont pas des photographies mais des recompositions, lesquelles diffèrent de l'original autant qu'un roman ou un tableau. Il est vrai que le caractère spéculatif et intellectuel de la philosophie en fait parfois oublier l'aspect fabriqué, ouvrier, qui est pourtant primordial. Car une philosophie consiste d'abord et avant tout en une *œuvre*, une création—création dont les caractéristiques ne diffèrent pas fondamentalement de celles de toute espèce d'œuvre. L'originalité, l'invention,

l'imagination, l'art de la composition, la puissance expressive sont l'apanage de tout grand texte philosophique comme ils sont celui de toute œuvre réussie. (*Le principe* 9–10)

[Every philosophy is a *theory of the real*, that is, in accordance with the Greek etymology of the word *theory*, the result of looking at things. This gaze is both creative and interpretive and attempts in its own manner and according to its own means, to render an account of an object or asset of given objects. [...] A philosophical gaze is thus necessarily interpretive by virtue of the simple fact that it "measures" [...]. And it is always creative also, since the images of reality that it proposes are not photographs of it but recompositions which differ from the original as much as a novel or a painting might. True, the speculative and intellectual character of philosophy sometimes makes one forget the fabricated, workmanlike aspect of it, which is nevertheless primordial. A philosophy consists first and foremost of a *work*, a creation—a creation whose characteristics do not differ fundamentally from those of any other type of work. (*Joyful* 71)]

Rosset thus seeks to differentiate his own anti-ontology from philosophical projects more generally by undermining the legitimacy of any representation or interpretation of the real, effectively shutting down the philosophical enterprise.

It is unclear, however, how Rosset's representation of the real would, precisely, be removed from representation and interpretation as he needs it to be in order to differentiate his approach in this way. He goes on to claim that what differentiates philosophy from other kinds of theorizing is the level of generalization at which it seeks to account for reality:

Il s'agit, pour le philosophe, de rendre compte d'un regard porté non sur telle ou telle chose, mais sur toute espèce de choses, y compris celles qui se situent hors de portée de sa perception. [...] Encore une fois, [la philosophie] ne consiste pas essentiellement à être plus « théorique » ou « abstraite » qu'une autre, mais à être plus *générale* : à être une théorie de la en général et non une théorie de telle ou telle réalité particulie (ou ensemble de faits particuliers) comme le sont par exemple un tableau, un roman, un théorème mathématique ou une loi physique. C'est bien toujours le même réel qui est visé. (*Principe* 10–11)

[The philosopher must give an account not of an act of looking at this or that thing but of looking at every type of thing, including those which are outside his or her field or perception [...]. Let me insist: philosophy consists essentially not in being more "theoretical" or "abstract" than any other activity but in being more *general*. Its aim is to be a theory of reality in general and not a theory of this or that particular reality (or set of particular facts), unlike, for example, a painting, a novel, a mathematical theorem, or a law of physics. The same real is indeed always the goal. (*Joyful* 71–2)]

While such a view may seem to give primacy to philosophy in that it seeks to account for the real at its most general level, it does not account for the way in which philosophy depends on representation and interpretation. It is not unproblematic to assume that "reality in general" is or even could be the right object of philosophy; assuming this may well lead us to false assumptions about the extent to which the whole may be grasped at all. Rather, we should be suspicious that perhaps, as Adorno famously claimed, "the whole is the false" (*Minima* 54) and be wary of the totalizing impetus behind a characterization of philosophy as accounting for reality in general. If that remains philosophy's goal, one can only celebrate the fact that it cannot achieve it. The particularity of paintings or novels could in that sense serve as the critique of a certain approach to philosophy, which is falsifying because it is totalizing. To recognize the gap between art and philosophy as ways of knowing is to see the role of thought as attempting to negotiate that gap while never confidently asserting that it has bridged it. The whole can only exist as a dialectical moment by which we affirm the falseness of the whole, precisely on account of the fact that it is always itself a term in the dialectic.

To account for the real as unrepresentable and uninterpretable is to make a totalizing claim about it and to resolve the problem of interpreting the real by simply foreclosing the problem entirely. To do so, however, is to remove the real from the very domain that Rosset claims is that of philosophy, the question of the real in general, because he claims, curiously, that definitive truths are by their nature unphilosophical. Here we are in the fully paradoxical situation of the philosopher who proposes an anti-ontology. Is such an approach still to be considered philosophy because it addresses itself to the question of the real in general, or is this approach outside the domain of philosophy because it claims that philosophy is to be grouped with art and all other forms of interpreting a real which cannot be interpreted? If it is still to be considered philosophy, then Rosset is constantly operating against his own claims about interpreting the real by claiming anti-ontology as a variant of ontology, and in this case he could be accused of the same sort of medicinal function he associates with philosophy, of attempting to shield us from the real by the very fact of writing about its unrepresentable nature. In neither case, then, can a simple acknowledgment of a supposedly definitive take on the real install us comfortably in a certainty that could or should shut down further reflection and further questions and, necessarily, further meaning-making.

This paradoxical situation calls for a reevaluation of the relationship between tragedy and meaninglessness. That relationship is primary for Rosset; tragedy springs from what he labels a double meaninglessness:

> Je définirai sommairement ce mécontentement comme le sentiment de l'insignifiance, la pensée permanente—pensée qu'on oublie parfois mais qu'on ne chasse jamais, car elle revient invariablement se rappeler à la conscience au moment où l'on serait tenté de se laisser conquérir par telle joie du monde—de l'égale et morne insignifiance de toute chose. A la considérer philosophiquement, toute chose qui vient à exister est, pour le dire en gros, doublement insignifiante : par elle-même (insignifiance « intrinsèque ») et par son rapport avec les autres choses (insignifiance « extrinsèque »). (*La force* 95–6)[10]

> [I will summarily define that discontent as the feeling of insignificance, the permanent thought—thought that we sometimes forget but that we never chase away, since it invariably returns to remind consciousness of itself at the time when we would be tempted to let ourselves be conquered by some joy in the world—of the equal and dreary insignificance of all things. Considered philosophically, every thing that comes to exist is, to say it generally, doubly insignificant: by itself ("intrinsic" insignificance) and by its relation to other things ("extrinsic" insignificance).]

Like Cioran, Rosset poses the condition he describes as a question of lucidity, here expressed in terms of consciousness at the surface or sometimes forgotten. But unlike Cioran, he makes no room for creation, whether intellectual or artistic, as a manifestation of lucidity or response to it, since any meaning-making can only mire us further into the realization that there is no meaning or significance to the real. Paradoxically however, such a realization, the coming to consciousness that was the effect of the gadfly or the electric ray in Hannah Arendt's characterization of Socrates, functions rather to shut down both philosophical reflection and artistic creation in Rosset, unless we make room for a dialectical opposition that gets us, once again, out of the either-or situation between consciousness and unconsciousness of insignificance and allows us to articulate the dynamic relation by which both depend on the other.

Simply to articulate our relationship to the insignificant as tragic is already to posit an interpretation and a meaning, and it is arguably not a mere deviation from the real to do so; even the meaningless reveals itself to the understanding through structures and patterns of meaning, a fact which Rosset both implicitly endorses by his characterization of the tragic and explicitly opposes insofar as attempts to impose meaning move us farther from the real. It is the attempt to think in and through the contradiction, as opposed to resolving it, that animates readers' engagement with Rosset and their way of interpreting "le paradoxe de l'existence" as Rosset describes it in explicit dialogue with Cioran, which is "tout à la fois d'être *quelque chose* et de *compter pour rien*" ["at the same time to be *something* and to *count for nothing*"] (*La force* 96). While for Cioran this would be the "horreur" of existence (*La force* 96), it does not preclude what Rosset calls joy, which proceeds from *allégresse*, which for Rosset is an "amour du réel" ["love of the real"], "le fait que le réel exite, qu'il y ait quelque chose plutôt que rien" ["the fact that the real exists, that there is something rather than nothing"] (*La force* 78).[11] It is a more genuine kind of happiness which he distinguishes from what he labels *bonheur*. Joy is different from standard happiness because, if it makes subjects forget what they know about the tragic nature of our relation to the real, the knowledge is forgotten "pour mieux se faire reconnaître par la suite" ["in order then to make itself recognized all the better"]: "ce savoir allègre se différencie de la gaieté ordinaire en ce qu'il implique une prise en compte des aspects les plus tragiques de l'existence : pour cette simple raison qu'il se donne comme prise en charge globale du réel" ["this joyful knowledge differentiates itself from ordinary gaiety because it implies a taking into account of the most tragic aspects of existence for this simple reason that it gives itself as global support of the real"] (*L'objet* 101). It is not quite clear how this kind of joy, the one which takes full knowledge of meaninglessness and suffering into account, would be any different from "la gaieté ordinaire" from which Rosset seeks to distinguish it.

What I will ultimately argue about Rosset's thought is beginning to become clear: because he claims the real is unthinkable, Rosset impoverishes thought as experience by refusing to acknowledge mediation and, along with it, the possibilities that it brings in terms of accounting for thought as a kind of experience. We ultimately end up, as we shall see, either in tautology, a simple affirmation of the real as the real and equivalent to itself, or in ineffable joy, a knowledge that cannot truly be said to be knowledge because it lacks the necessary distance from its object. By canceling the subject-object relation, this approach cancels the possibility of thought while substituting a passing and literally inconceivable joy in its place. What Rosset claims as the fullness of the experience of the real can only seem empty from the perspective of thought as experience. Rather than allowing us to act in accordance with the real, Rosset's cancelation of mediation impoverishes thought not by bringing the real out of its domain but by substituting a problematic concept of immediacy, which is no less mediated a concept than any other, for the mediated concepts by which thought operates and constructs its world. A purported freedom and joy to be found in the immediacy of the real can only, from the point of view of thought, produce anguish once we begin to ask questions about this joy which is purportedly compatible with full realization of suffering, and to posit the real as unthinkable is to leave us without resources in the face of the tragic. Far from provoking joy in the face of the unity of the real, this move to eliminate non-identity leaves us bereft of ways of understanding anything at all and denies experiential status to thought. Rosset's thought ends up, despite itself, in a proto-theological mode that evokes silence as a mode of the real without attending to the way that silence can only be thought as non-identical to itself once we are aware of silence *as* silence, labeled thus as a concept. It remains open to question whether the real can indeed be posited as identical to itself, a question which necessarily leads back to thought as a way not just of representing the world but of creating it.

The instability of this way of thinking is manifest in Rosset's own writings, which appeal to altered definitions of common terms in order to reinvent our understanding. Far from inclining toward the silence of tautology, his works proliferate in a series of rethinkings of his fundamental questions, further anchoring themselves in the double of reality that he conceives thought to be. His confident assertions exist side by side with tentative attempts to define terms or to find "approximations" for the concepts, as in this discussion of *allégresse* in *L'objet singulier*:

> L'allégresse implique un savoir tragique mais ne se confond pas avec lui. Elle ne connaît du tragique que dans la mesure où elle connaît du réel en général, dont le tragique n'est qu'une qualité parmi d'autres. On la définirait donc plus justement, en attendant une meilleure approximation, comme *savoir du réel*. Une telle définition reste évidemment insatisfaisante : non qu'on ait à s'émouvoir de la question qui consisterait à exiger une définition préalable du réel ici invoqué—question à laquelle on répondrait que c'est justement ce dont connaît l'allégresse—mais parce qu'il existe un certain nombre de savoirs du réel qui apparaissent comme très différents de l'expérience de l'allégresse. (*L'objet* 102–3)

[Happiness, *allégresse*, implies a tragic knowledge but is not synonymous with it. It only knows the tragic to the extent that it knows the real in general, of which the tragic is only one quality among others. We would thus define it more accurately, while waiting for a better approximation, as *knowledge of the real*. Such a definition obviously remains unsatisfactory: not that we would have to be moved by the question that would consist in demanding a pre-given definition of the real evoked here—a question to which we would answer that it is precisely what happiness knows—but because there are a certain number of knowledges of the real which appear as if very different from the experience of happiness.]

It is notable that Rosset leaves room here for knowledges of the real in the plural, of which happiness would be only one, which implies that there are potentially competing kinds of knowledge about the real, a fact which decenters happiness and moves away from the unity at which Rosset sometimes aims by including the tragic within happiness. Questions of interpretation re-emerge at every turn along the way of Rosset's explorations of the consequences of his fundamental premise that the real is not available for interpretation. In a later work, *Le réel: Traité de l'idiotie* (1997), he claims that the real presents itself as a text but insists that this manifestation as a "kind of text" only serves to reveal the insignificance of the real (in the sense both of unimportance and of meaninglessness):

> L'insignifiance du réel ne se manifeste naturellement pas seulement lorsque la réalité se présente de manière visiblement incohérente et désordonnée, à l'état de pure et arbitraire contiguïté. Elle apparaît aussi, et mieux encore, lorsque le réel se présente de manière cohérente, ordonnée et continue, constituant une sorte de texte, plus ou moins rudimentaire ou élaboré. Car le réel est en ceci assez semblable aux mauvais écrivains : il a finalement peu à dire, mais donne volontiers à lire. Et le silence, s'il est bien le dernier mot dont ait à nous faire part la réalité, n'apparaît jamais de manière si éloquente que lorsque le réel est précisément en train de parler. Car le silence déguisé, habillé en parole, est plus révélateur que le silence simple. (*Le réel* 23–4)

[The insignificance of the real does not manifest itself only when reality presents itself in a visible incoherent and disordered manner, in the state of pure and arbitrary contiguity. It also appears, and better still, when the real presents itself in a coherent, ordered, and continuous manner, constituting a sort of text, more or less rudimentary or elaborate. For the real is in that rather similar to bad writers: in the end it has little to say, but gives itself willingly to be read. And silence, if it is really the last word that reality would have us participate in, never appears in such an eloquent way as when the real is precisely in the process of speaking. For silence, disguised, dressed in words, is more revealing than simple silence.]

To say that the real has little to say is already to make room for the mediation and interpretation necessary for the real to have any sort of existence at all for us; to assign it agency as Rosset does, allowing it to appear in this way, is already to construct the real, and Rosset's formulation points up the fact that all of his writing on the real is necessarily this kind of construction of it rather than an unmediated description. There is all the difference in the world between a real that has nothing to say and a real that is like a text in that it has "little to say." To indicate that the real speaks in order to speak silence, that it is silence disguised as speech, calls out for elaboration which in no way, one could argue, distances us from that real but rather draws us in to its mediated nature. To speak of a "revelation" on the part of this kind of silence is to see this sort of silent speech as operating in a way akin to a work of art, "speaking" to us in ways that require conceptual mediation which will perhaps help us understand part of the work's truth but will also reveal that that understanding can only ever be partial and tentative, precisely because works of art are non-identical to their conceptual elaboration and thus always surpass them.

Rosset's understanding of meaning as something to be found inherently in a phenomenon as opposed to created in a dialectical subject-object relationship commits him to a view whereby an engagement with meaning translates to embarking on a quest for what can never be found because it does not exist: "dans le cas […] de la question du sens, il est clair qu'un tel intérêt existe : le refus, de la part de beaucoup, de se rendre à l'évidence du non-signifiant, d'admettre que ce qui existe ne veuille rien dire" ["in the case […] of the question of meaning, it is clear that such an interest exists: the refusal, on the part of many, to admit to the obviousness of the non-signifying, to admit that what exists means nothing"] (*Le réel* 53). Rosset links this to the structure of desire with reference to Lacan, and indicates that "si l'objet visé existe on risque de l'atteindre, interrompant du même coup la recherche et le désir" ["if the object we're aiming at exists, we risk attaining it, thereby interrupting the search and the desire"] (*Le réel* 53). Since we are unable to arrive at a full understanding of meaninglessness or insignificance (*insignifiance*), that meaninglessness becomes equivalent to meaningfulness in the sense that both reveal themselves as negative by being impossible to attain in terms of representation and both are implicitly always projected onto an undefined future:

> Le messianisme du sens—« le sens que je vous annonce n'est pas encore très clair, mais vous verrez, tout cela s'éclairera par la suite »—se double ainsi, du côté où l'on s'efforce de contester le messianisme et de dire l'insignifiance, d'une facile et assez ironique caricature. (*Le réel* 54)

> [The messianism of meaning—"the meaning that I am announcing to you is not yet very clear, but you will see, everything will be clear later"—is thus doubled, from the point where we strive to contest messianism and to say insignificance, by a facile and rather ironic caricature.]

Rosset associates this both with the "à venir" most familiar from deconstructionist approaches and the Kantian regulatory ideal; this approach takes meaningfulness not as an object of knowledge but rather of faith, which is by definition separate from the realm of knowledge. Rosset's refusal of a dialectical model of creation of meaning via mediated experience shuts down the possibility of meaning and also commits him to the view that life cannot be lived *consciously*, in the double French sense of being conscious of reality and of living life in good conscience.

> Nous ne posons pas ici la question de savoir si la vie a un sens, si elle vaut la peine d'être vécue, ou toute autre question du même genre. Nous demandons si elle est possible *en conscience*, dans le double sens, psychologique et juridique, du terme : c'est-à-dire en toute sincérité et en toute connaissance de cause. Question qui revient au fond à demander, assez naïvement, si tant est qu'on tienne pour encore valable la définition académique qui voit dans l'homme un animal conscient.
>
> Demander si la vie de l'homme est possible *en conscience* serait une question non seulement naïve mais encore superfétatoire s'il n'y avait cette circonstance particulière que la réponse est, dans tous les cas et quel que soit le biais par lequel on envisage la question, résolument négative. [...] Sans doute savons-nous par *expérience* [...] que la vie en conscience est possible ; mais nous sommes incapables d'établir le *comment* de cette possibilité, qui n'est confortée par aucune sagesse, autorisée par aucune philosophie. (*Le réel* 72–3)

> [We are not posing here the question of knowing whether life has a meaning, if it is worth living, or any other question of the same kind. We are asking if it is possible *consciously*, in the double meaning of the term, psychological and juridical: that is, in all sincerity and in full knowledge. It's a question that comes back to asking, rather naively, if we still take as worthwhile the academic definition that sees in man a conscious animal.

> To ask whether the life of man is possible *in consciousness or conscience* would be not only a naïve question but also a superfluous one if there were not this particular circumstance that the answer is, in all cases and from whatever angle we view the question, resolutely negative. [...] Undoubtedly we know by *experience* [...] that conscious life is possible; but we are incapable of establishing the *how* of that possibility, which is not comforted by any wisdom or authorized by any philosophy.]

Here again, Rosset's rejection of mediation forces him into a split between experience and thought whereby lived experience is entirely divorced from philosophical justification. By returning to his earlier articulation of a philosophy of the tragic, we can account for thought itself as a kind of experience, the anti-systematic approach to tentative meaning-making that emerges from a subject-object relationship between the thinker and a "world" that can be expanded to include conceptual worlds as well. This approach allows for a self-critique of thought that does not at the same time reject its entire enterprise. While it may well be true that "il n'y a pas, il n'y aura jamais de « consolation de la philosophie »" ["there is not, there will never be, any 'consolation of philosophy'"] (*Le réel* 73), thought taken as an object of its own reflection keeps the possibility of a construction of meaning (even as a form of meaninglessness) alive in a way that is foreclosed when the object is eliminated in an act of supposed faithfulness to the impossibility of representing the real.

If one is not able to think "against oneself," to borrow Cioran's formulation, we risk paralysis and dead ends at every turn, along with all of the dangers of non-thinking, including quietism and fanaticism, that we have identified in earlier chapters. Rosset sees escape routes from the unbearable nature of the real both in joy and in the rather unlikely notion of grace, which includes but is not limited to an atheological theological connotation:

> Il semble à première analyse—une fois écartées les fausses solutions du divertissement et de l'aveuglement volontaire—qu'une seule notion permette de rendre compte de ce paradoxe de la perpétuation de la vie au sein de la mort, de la volonté de vivre malgré la connaissance de la mort : la notion de *grâce*— dans tous les sens du terme. (*Le réel* 75)

> [It seems on first analysis—once the false solutions of diversion and voluntary blindness are eliminated—that only one notion permits us to account for this paradox of the perpetuation of life in the heart of death, of the will to live despite the knowledge of death: the notion of *grace*—in all senses of the term.]

These senses of the term include the juridical, the "magnifique," the esthetic, and the theological (75). These are what allow us to go on living life according to the Rosset of *Le réel: Traité d'idiotie*. These moments of grace provide temporary escape from the real without being a true forgetting of it; as we have seen, Rosset's unconventional conception of joy includes the tragic and is even rooted in it. It is unclear, then, why thought (as opposed to systematic philosophy) would not be a viable alternative, since it too participates in what we might call the "as if" of an imagination that continues to treat the world as if meaning could be created from it, while also continuing to recognize the mediated nature of all of our conceptual experiences, even those that claim to posit the immediacy of the real. Marc Alpozzo indicates that, for Rosset, "l'allégresse est une grâce. La joie est une délivrance. Les deux n'effaceront rien bien sûr, mais nous empêcheront de sombrer dans la désespérance, dans un nihilisme passif morbide et atrophiant" ["happiness is a grace. Joy is a deliverance. Both of them will erase nothing, of course, but they will prevent us from sinking into despair, into a morbid and atrophying passive nihilism"] (61). But as I have suggested, there can be no release from the dead end of the paralyzing nihilism to which Rosset's premises lead except for this quasi-magical escape hatch that he enlists grace to provide. This can hardly be a satisfying conclusion, and it is a rather traditional one in the sense that it reproduces a secularized Christian logic of being saved from despair by a divine force for which we cannot account, which we are powerless to obtain on our own, and which yet arrives with remarkable power to give us a kind of triumph that does not reject suffering but comes about only through it. Such an approach both evokes contradiction (joy through suffering) and rejects it by providing some kind of resolution (and lending a plot structure and a meaning to Rosset's account which at other times he claims to dismiss). By refusing mediation, Rosset also attempts to install tautology as a model for the real, which is identical to itself. In the last part of this chapter, I will claim that to conceive the tautology already implies that we are out of the absolute identity that it posits, and that this mediation via conceptual thought is a more viable way of conceiving experience than the miracle of grace. A return to the earlier Rosset's emphasis on dissonance and the tragic nature of thinking will help illustrate the way that thinking as experience allows us to avoid the diametrically opposed and equally undesirable options of nihilism and grace.

Rosset begins his first book, *La philosophie tragique*, by a gesture of purification by which he hopes to build his thought in a way that avoids certain errors of those who have gone before him and some misconceptions that have become commonplaces:

> Avant de penser, il faut commencer par se purifier ; disons même que tout effort de purification est toujours dans son essence un effort de pensée qui commande le plus grand respect. Cette nécessité de pureté, mère de toutes les philosophies, me force ici à commencer l'exposé de la mienne par la description critique de cette idole anti-tragique à laquelle je prétends que toutes les philosophies antérieures ont plus ou moins sacificé. (*La philosophie* 1–2)
>
> [Before thinking, it is necessary to purify oneself; let us even say that every effort at purification is always in its essence an effort of thought that commands the greatest respect. This necessity of purity, mother of all philosophies, forces me here to begin the exposition of mine with the critical description of that anti-tragic idol to which I claim that all prior philosophies have more or less sacrificed.]

Rosset proposes to provide only a description of the tragic rather than an interpretation because, for him, an essential feature of the tragic is that it defies interpretation: "nous pourrions donner comme première définition du Tragique la révélation d'un *soudain refus radical de toute idée d'interprétation*. Non qu'on doive s'interdire de réfléchir ensuite sur la signifcation du tragique, mais il faut d'abord connaître ce sur quoi nous allons faire porter notre réflexion. D'abord donc, se garder d'interpréter" ["we could give as a first definition of the Tragic the revelation of a *sudden radical refusal of every idea of interpretation*. Not that we should forbid ourselves from reflecting afterward on the meaning of the tragic, but we must first be familiar with that on which we are going to focus our attention. First, then, let's keep ourselves from interpreting"] (7). The tragic lies, according to Rosset, in the coincidence of the idea of death with the time of death; he illustrates this with the example of someone who witnesses a man falling to his death. The death is more tragic for the witness than for the man's loved ones, since the latter preserve a notion of him alive, whereas for the witness there is a revelation of a tragic temporality, "l'idée de l'immobilité introduite dans l'idée du temps" ["the idea of immobility introduced in the idea of time"] (8) which reveals the illusion of linear time and allows for the coincidence of the time and idea of death. This discovery of the full impact of death ("ce que certains appellent poétiquement du nom 'd'absurde'" ["what certain people call poetically by the name of 'absurd'"] (16) is one of the three domains of the tragic for Rosset; the other two are "l'échec de l'activité" ["the failure of activity"] and "la découverte de la bassesse inhérente à la nature humaine" ["the discovery of the baseness inherent in human nature"] (16).

Attempting to describe the tragic leads naturally to an attempt to conceptualize it, to take it as an object of thought, but it is just that conceptualization that Rosset refuses as impossible, leading him to affirm that "nous considérons le tragique comme un mystère que l'on ne peut que constater. Notre interrogation portera sur l'homme tragique, sur l'homme face au tragique, non sur le tragique" ["we consider the tragic as a mystery that one can only observe. Our investigation will concern tragic man, man faced with the tragic, not the tragic itself"] (19). Such a conception makes of the tragic a kind of thing-in-itself, whose reality is self-evident for Rosset but unavailable to our urge to interpret it, which entrenches the thinker in a condition of impossibility, whereas to attempt to grasp the tragic as an object of thought only moves the thinker further away from it. Rosset claims that most prior attempts to engage with the tragic have had precisely that effect: "s'interroger sur le tragique, c'est nier le tragique" ["to investigate the tragic is to negate the tragic"] (19), which is why he began with a gesture of ground-clearing in order to gain, in the book that follows, a better understanding of our non-understanding of the tragic and of the impossibility of ever taking it as an object of thought.

He criticizes Christianity for evoking the tragic only to eliminate it by explaining it through original sin. That attempt to interpret and account for the tragic invalidates it completely: "tragique justifié, tragique interprété, ne voit-on pas que ce n'est plus le tragique ?" ["the tragic justified, the tragic interpreted, do we not see that this is no longer the tragic?"] (19). By presenting the tragic as always already explained and interpreted, Christianity blocks awareness of the full extent of the tragic itself by presenting it in a pre-digested form. So what is at stake for Rosset is an unwarranted resolution of the tragic rather than a view that would expose the full force of the tragic and not cancel it by an explanation. At this point it becomes clear that by "interpretation," Rosset perhaps means something more akin to explanation, a definitive account of the tragic rather than an interpretation in the larger sense of the construction of some kind of meaning. One could argue that his characterization of the tragic as uninterpretable or ineffable stems from his non-dynamic understanding of what it would mean to think or know the tragic or, rather, to conflate knowledge with what I have been labeling thinking, the open-ended attempt to construct meaning or understanding that is forever susceptible to reevaluation. Thought as I have been characterizing it is a process in which a realization of the unknowability of the object of thought does not necessarily shut down the possibility of interpreting or conceiving it in that precarious sense by which we would think *with* the unknowability of the tragic rather than opposing thought to the tragic.

As we will see, however, Rosset could be said to engage in the same kind of move for which he criticizes the Christian narrative, namely, of needing to move toward resolution and thereby canceling the tragic. While he upholds the notion of dissonance, he does so in a way that moves toward resolution or synthesis, a synthesis that would account for and include dissonance, but nonetheless his own engagement with the tragic comes far closer to the move he criticizes in Christianity (and indeed in most conceptual engagements with the tragic) than he is ready to admit. Rosset's analysis also reveals the difficulty of avoiding interpretation the way he claims one would need to in order to encounter the tragic. But we are getting a bit ahead of ourselves. Rosset continues to elaborate his characterization of the tragic in a Nietzschean vein, indicating that morality is a forgetting of the tragic:

> L'oubli du tragique, c'est l'oubli de nous-mêmes, c'est l'oubli de la joie. La dimension tragique, dès lors, est abolie, remplacée qu'elle est par la dimension de la petitesse humaine qui se révèle trop peu pour le tragique, en deçà du tragique. Voilà pour nous le désespoir le plus affreux qu'il nous soit possible d'imaginer. (30)
>
> [The forgetting of the tragic is the forgetting of ourselves; it's the forgetting of joy. The tragic dimension, from that point on, is abolished, replaced by the dimension of human smallness that proves to be too little for the tragic, below the tragic. That is, for us, the most awful despair that it is possible for us to imagine.]

The tragic includes joy, which Rosset opposes to happiness: "l'ennemi de la joie n'est pas le pessimisme ou le désespoir, mais *l'optimisme et le bonheur*; l'expression de la joie n'est pas dans une affirmation de la joie, mais dans une affirmation des données tragiques avec lesquelles nous nous déclarons irréconciliables" ["the enemy of joy is not pessimism or despair, but *optimism and happiness*; the expression of joy is not in an affirmation of joy, but in an affirmation of the tragic givens with which we declare ourselves irreconcilable"] (33). Happiness is thus "le refus de la joie" ["the refusal of joy"] (33), and joy remains resistant to the tragic even while being included within it: "toujours aussi vive, toujours aussi jeune, elle pose toujours aussi pleinement la question tragique" ["always just as lively, always just as young, it always poses just as fully the tragic question"]

(34). There is a contradiction in the way Rosset discusses joy, since at times he suggests that joy includes the tragic while he also suggests that they are opposed to each other, as in the claim that life is "un duel" between joy and the tragic "dont l'issue est éternellement remise au lendemain" ["of which the way out is eternally put off until the next day"] (34). How does this opposition square with the claim that the tragic would not be the tragic without the joy which the tragic provokes and threatens?

> La joie à laquelle nous faisons appel pour expliquer l'irréconciaible est déjà présente dans la définition initiale que nous avons donnée : il ne saurait y avoir de tragique, de surprenant par essence sans que quelque chose soit surprise, sans qu'une idée se trouve ruinée ; et il ne s'agit de rien d'autre que de cette joie même, qui nous permet ultérieurement de nous déclarer irréconciliables. (36)

> [The joy to which we appeal in order to explain the irreconcilable is already present in the initial definition which we have given: there could not be anything tragic or by essence surprising without something to be surprised, without an idea finding itself ruined; and it concerns nothing other than this very joy, which permit us ulteriorly to declare ourselves irreconcilable.]

Joy is thus both in opposition to the tragic and irrevocably allied with it as a constituent part of it; they are, to an extent that Rosset never quite fully affirms, indivisible, a fact which requires a dialectical approach to them which suggests that joy and the tragic are never quite self-identical, because they are always implicated in the other. Thus their relation both is and is not a dichotomy, and Rosset's definitions of joy and the tragic are also split against themselves because they affirm joy and the tragic as both separate and indivisible.

To make sense of such claims necessitates going beyond description toward interpretation, at least in the tentative sense. Given Rosset's resistance to interpretation, however, the irreconcilable nature of his descriptions is neither labeled paradox nor further elaborated. Rather, Rosset affirms, as what he labels his "essentielle définition du tragique" ["essential definition of the tragic"], that it is:

> d'abord ce qui nous permet de vivre, ce qui est le plus chevillé au corps de l'homme, c'est l'instinct de vie par excellence, puisque aussi bien, sans tragique, nous ne pourrions pas vivre : nous n'estimerions pas qu'il vaut la peine de vivre, si la voie tragique nous était bouchée. Aux caractéristiques de l'insurmontable et de l'irresponsable, il faut ajouter celui de l'indispensable. (49–50)

[first of all what permits us to live, what is the most pegged to the body of man, it is the life instinct par excellence, since we could not live without the tragic: we would not be able to sense that life is worth living, if the way of the tragic were blocked. To the list of characteristics that includes the insurmountable and the irresponsible, we need to add the indispensable.]

It is at this point that Rosset explicitly credits Nietzsche as the originator of this view of joy and tragedy and as the first to affirm that "la joie doit être recherchée, non dans l'harmonie, mais dans la dissonance !" ["joy must be sought, not in harmony, but in dissonance!"] (50). Rosset goes on to develop a theory of dissonance that is closely bound to his notion of the tragic; it deserves a careful exposition here. He begins by asking how we can account for the pleasure that musical dissonance can afford us:

La notion de « dissonance », qui remplace au terme de mon étude la notion de « surprise », répond à la troisième et essentielle caractéristique tragique : l'indispensable .... [...] Quel est le sens de la dissonance en musique ? Elle met en valeur l'accord parfait, et cette vérité musicale n'est que le reflet d'une vérité plus profonde, une vérité philosophique. Mais la dissonance ne met pas seulement l'accord en valeur, elle est aussi la *révélation* de l'accord : l'accord est inconnaissable sans dissonance, l'accord est inconnaissable en tant que seul accord. (66)

[The notion of "dissonance," which replaces at the end of my study the notion of "surprise," responds to the third and essential characteristic of the tragic: the indispensable .... [...] What is the meaning of dissonance in music? It valorizes perfect consonance, and this musical truth is only the reflection of a more profound truth, a philosophical truth. But dissonance not only valorizes consonance; it is also the *revelation* of consonance: the consonance is unknowable without dissonance; consonance is unknown as just consonance.][12]

Rosset establishes a dialectical relationship between consonance and dissonance with the claim that consonance is only revealed as consonance on account of its negative and mutually constitutive relation to dissonance. As Rosset extends the analogy, he uses the term "harmonie" rather than "consonance," although the two are not, strictly speaking, synonyms, and his notion of a chord aligns better with consonance than with harmony, since the latter can be understood as the whole system of harmonic tension and resolution upon which Western tonal music is structured.

The point is well taken if we consider the discussion in light of functional harmony, whereby a chord gains its harmonic function, and thus its relative stability or instability harmonically, only in its relation to the tonality in which it is functioning. Rosset sums up the point in a verbal equation: "Harmonie + Dissonance = Révélation de l'harmonie perdue" ["Harmony + Dissonance = Revelation of lost harmony"] (66). Dissonance thus allows us to understand consonance retroactively as consonance, as what has been lost, as what is experienced now as lack. Rosset continues in a Nietzschean vein in order to posit that this dissonance yields a new kind of harmony or "accord," a musical chord understood metaphorically here in the usual sense of the English word "accord," between humanity and dissonance, which he sums up in another verbal equation:

> Tout le mystère tragique est renfermé dans cette expression banale du langage musical—expression pourtant si extraordinaire, si paradoxale, si l'on veut bien se donner la peine d'y réfléchir— : l'accord dissonant, … *Dissonance* fondamentale, parce que la révélation de l'irresponsabilité a fait voler en éclats la dernière chance de l'anti-tragique, la dernière possibilité de justification. *Accord* fondamental parce qu'au moment même où la responsabilité et la justification sont mortes, au moment où l'insurmontable a achevé de faire table rase autour de lui, a surgi une nouvelle valeur qui éclipse tout le reste : l'accord entre l'homme et la dissonance, l'homme amoureux de sa propre dissonance !
> Harmonie + Dissonance = Accord tragique (67)

[The whole tragic mystery is contained in this banal expression of musical language—an expression that is, however, so extraordinary, so paradoxical, if we want to make the effort to think about it—: the dissonant chord, … fundamental *Dissonance*, because the revelation of irresponsibility has blasted to pieces the last chance of the anti-tragic, the last possibility of justification. Fundamental *accord* because at the very moment where responsibility and justification died, at the moment when the insurmountable has finished making a *tabula rasa* around it, a new value has emerged which eclipses all the rest: the accord between man and dissonance, man in love with his own dissonance!
Harmony + Dissonance = Tragic accord]

The moment of simultaneous recognition and affirmation of dissonance is a nearly magical one for Rosset: "c'est lorsque nous sentons et affirmons le tragique que nous communions à la vie ! […] C'est alors que nous saisissons le secret de la vie" ["it is when we sense and affirm the tragic that we commune with life!

[…] That is when we grasp the secret of life"] (67–8). But it remains unclear how Rosset's affirmation of the tragic as dissonance, which he characterizes as a new kind of harmony, could be anything except the resolution of dissonance, as opposed to maintaining the dissonance *as* dissonance.

If it was the presence of dissonance that allows us to hear consonance as consonance and dissonance as dissonance, the acceptance of the tragic can only remove some aspect of the dissonance of dissonance, so to speak, by subsuming it into a revised kind of harmony. Would this not be akin to precisely what he criticizes Christianity and indeed most of philosophy for doing, that is, accounting for and explaining the tragic in a way that makes the tragic itself disappear in what Rosset would label an illicit move, given that for him the tragic can never be overcome? To say that there is, at this final stage, a harmony between a human person and dissonance is ultimately to reaffirm harmony, albeit a harmony that is conscious of dissonance. Rosset might contend that this new understanding of harmony-with-dissonance is precisely the kind of experience that cannot be interpreted without the experience itself disappearing, but to affirm this is to leave open to question and doubt the entirety of the metaphor Rosset is constructing here, since metaphors depend on the interpretive act in order to function as metaphor. To attempt to draw the conclusions from Rosset's musico-metaphysical framework is to be drawn back to thinking and to a sense of dissatisfaction with the simple affirmation or description of some kind of new harmony that accounts for joy and yields the "secret of life." There is, I would argue, a dissonance between Rosset's claim that the tragic is uninterpretable or inaccessible to thought and his metaphorical elaboration of dissonance as a manifestation of the tragic, and the dissonance in Rosset's claim cannot be explained away by some higher level consonance. The split within harmony by which harmony comes to include dissonance means that harmony cannot be self-identical; it exists in Rosset both as a sense of lack revealed by the tragic and as the plenitude of the recognition and affirmation of dissonance. To account for this, Rosset would need to allow for non-identity rather than affirming tautology.[13] Otherwise, his terms risk seeming paradoxical to the point of carrying no meaning whatsoever, rather than providing the vehicle for thinking contradiction *as* contradiction rather than as a step on the way to resolution or synthesis.

Rosset's approach takes all of the sting out of the tragic, domesticating it, so to speak, by relegating it to a fact of life that no longer causes anguish or prevents joy. Again, how could we read this move as anything but similar to the redemption of the fall that Rosset sharply criticizes in Christianity? While he would uphold a distinction between eliminating the tragic and embracing the tragic, they amount to the same in that both fundamentally neutralize the profoundly disturbing character of the tragic. For Rosset there even comes to be a sense of familiarity about the tragic:

> C'est lorsque nous sommes en état de *dissonance* que nous connaissons la joie et le sens de la vie, par l'intermédiaire de l'accord tragique qui implique la pleine possession de deux certitudes fondamentales, d'une part de *l'irresponsabilité de la chute* (c'est-à-dire la dissonance poussée au bout d'elle-même), et d'autre part de la *nécessité* de cette épouvante tragique pour que la vie ait un sens et que s'instaure le règne de l'homme. [...] Aussi notre attitude humaine fondamentale est-elle une *reconnaissance* face au tragique [...] parce que :
>
> 1. On reconnaît le tragique, il ne paraît plus étranger.
> 2. On a pour lui de la *gratitude*. (69)

[It is when we are in a state of *dissonance* that we know joy and the meaning of life, by the intermediary of the tragic chord which implies the full possession of two fundamental certitudes, on one hand the *irresponsibility of the fall* (that is, dissonance pushed to its furthest extreme), and on the other the *necessity* of this tragic terror in order for life to have a meaning and so that the reign of man be established. [...] Thus our fundamental human attitude is a *recognition* in the face of the tragic [...] because:

1. We recognize the tragic; it no longer seems foreign.
2. We have *gratitude* for it.]

Such a transformed understanding of the tragic is a sort of magic key for Rosset; he claims it is "une réponse définitive à l'à quoi bon" ["a definitive answer to the question 'what's the use'"] (73) that can guard against suicide, which Rosset associates with the misguided focus on happiness (of which he says that it "n'est autre que l'oubli de la joie" (107) ["none other than the forgetting of joy"]) rather than on the tragic (and on the joy which he allies with the tragic: "l'amour de la vie, c'est la négaton du bonheur de la vie, car le contraire de l'amour de la vie (le suicide), n'est autre que l'affirmation du bonheur de la vie, l'affirmation anti-tragique par essence ... " ["the love of life is the negation of the happiness of life, for the opposite of love of life (suicide) is none other than the affirmation of the happiness of life, the essential anti-tragic affirmation"] (74). In what can only be considered yet another redemptive move, Rosset traces the following path to an acceptance of life as it is given, with a neutralized sense of the tragic: "le Tragique (le non radical à la vie) → L'Estime (L'héroïsme qui ridiculise la vie: je *vaux* beaucoup plus que la vie) → l'Enthousiasme (le oui à la vie, définitif)" ["the Tragic (the radical no to life → Estime (heroism which ridicules life: I am *worth* much more than life) → Enthusiasm (the definitive yes to life)"] (75). While Rosset posits this schema of what we could call a reconciliation of non-reconciliation, he continues to develop his critique of a rationalism that is guided by a notion of happiness rather than the tragic and is thus led to reconciliatory approaches to thought which are blind to the tragic impulse that gave birth to the thought in the first place:

> L'homme rationaliste prétend ne pas choisir et se propose de garder à la fois la valeur et la compréhension, niant par-là qu'il existe un conflit insurmontable entre ces deux domaines, refusant donc la donnée tragique initiale. Pour réaliser ce tour d'adresse, il est obligé *d'inventer* des idées réconciliatrices : il invente la liberté, il invente la providence, pour comprendre la valeur, pour la réconcilier avec la compréhension. Tel est le sens du rationalisme moral inhérent à l'idée du bonheur : il ne s'agit pas de choisir pour le rationalisme, ce qui serait parfaitement valable, mais d'allier indûment ce rationalisme avec la valeur irrationnelle ; et ce n'est nullement le rationalisme qui préside à cette alliance, nullement un besoin de rationnel, mas bien une immense puissance affective qui refuse de considérer le conflit tragique précédant toute démarche intellectuelle, un instinct affectif antérieur à toute pensée morale et que nous avons baptisé l'instinct anti-tragique. (114)

> [Rational man claims not to choose and proposes to keep both value and comprehension, negating thereby that there is an insurmountable conflict between these two domains, thus refusing the initial tragic given. To bring this about, he is obliged to *invent* reconciliatory ideas: he invents freedom, he invents providence, to understand value, to reconcile it with happiness: it is not a question of opting for rationalism, which would be perfectly worthwhile, but of unjustly allying this rationalism with irrational value; and it is not at all rationalism that presides over this alliance, not at all a need of the rational, but an immense affective power that refuses to consider the tragic conflict preceding all intellectual moves, an affective instinct prior to all moral thought and which we have baptized the anti-tragic instinct.]

But here again, there is an either/or logic to Rosset's thought that blocks the possibilities for thought inherent in contradiction and leads him to remain focused on resolution even as he criticizes that same notion. While he is critical of the invention of reconciliatory ideas, his own description of tragedy participates in that same logic by moving toward a synthetic incorporation of the tragic into an affirmation of life that refuses the kind of thought that could attempt to account for and interpret contradiction rather than claiming that the dissonance of the tragic is simply absorbed into the "accord tragique."

While he is certainly right to identify blind rationalism as a "rationalisme totalitaire" whereby "l'homme rationnel choisit *contre la raison*, puisqu'il renonce à une raison dont il ne veut pas s'accommoder, parce que trop tragique" ["rational man chooses *against reason*, since he renounces a reason which he does not want to accommodate, because it is too tragic"] (115), Rosset's solution stops short of a full elaboration of the paradoxes and contradictions to which the tragic leads because he appeals to the joy of reconciliation as a way of suspending engagement with it. He approaches contradiction but backs away from it in what tends to look like an unjustified appeal to joy and to the affirmation of life. He pities those who are unable to abandon a conception of happiness: "nous définissons par là la *conscience malheureuse*, condamnée au déchirement paradoxal et perpétuel entre un état de fait et un état de désir" ["that is what we define as *unhappy consciousness*, condemned to being perpetually and paradoxically torn between a state of fact and a state of desire"] (126). To this he opposes "la conscience tragique" ["tragic consciousness"], which "proclamerait la mort du bonheur et le triomphe du tragique et par conséquent ne serait pas une conscience déchirée, en butte à un conflit dévorant : loin d'être angoissée, elle aurait la sérénité de la certitude tragique" ["would proclaim the death of happiness and the triumph of the tragic and thus would not be a torn consciousness, exposed to a devouring conflict: far from being anguished, it would have the serenity of tragic certainty"] (126). The tragic comes to look suspiciously like a stepping stone on the way to a resolution into something like serenity, with the narrative arc of Rosset's study resolving into the dominance of a no longer antagonistic notion of the tragic, which we could say is no longer tragic at all. By refusing to retain the dialectical tension inherent in the tragic, Rosset simply nullifies it while continuing to claim that the tragic still has some role to play. Without the move to interpretation that would seek to understand just how one could retain labels such as joy and tragedy while completely transforming their content, we are left with questions and no conceptual tools by which to address them. While he claimed that to conceptualize the tragic is to neutralize it and that he sought to do the opposite by giving tragedy its due, the end result ends up reproducing exactly the move he sought to avoid. It is no wonder that, in his later works, Rosset has recourse to a notion of grace, an inexplicable and unjustified manifestation of an escape from the tragic; such a move is already prefigured in *La philosophie tragique* and its unwarranted secular redemption of tragedy that backs away from the contradictions it claims at first to embrace.

Rosset's dissonance is, ultimately, not a dissonance at all, or it is a dissonance at odds with itself as dissonance. By insisting, in his earlier work, on a kind of resolution in spite of himself and, in his later work, on tautology, Rosset ends up demonstrating the dead end that nondialectical thought ends up reaching; the totalitarian nature that he sees in an overly faithful commitment to rationalism could be said to apply to his own insistence on tautology. By claiming to maintain the tragic but then identifying a structure by which it is absorbed into something that includes it but which emphasizes living with joy in the tragic world, he implicitly puts in place a structure that refuses the kind of thoughtful engagement with the world which can be just as enabling of living well in the world as the ultimately anti-intellectual contention that the tragic cannot be conceptualized without being negated or denied. The experience of thought as Rosset characterizes it leads away from thought but does not put an end to the discursivity of his elaboration of his thoughts. He paradoxically goes on to affirm the impossibility of thoughtful engagement with the real but resists the vital experience of engaging paradox and contradiction in order to maintain the vitality of the tension rather than coming to rest in a putative "tragic consciousness" that is not marked by rupture or internal division. In so doing, he reveals, unwittingly no doubt, the way that thought needs to work in and through contradiction rather than affirming the inaccessibility of the real in an undialectical redemptive move that needs recourse to a presumably unconceptualizable and ineffable joy. The ineffability of Rosset's resolution points, inevitably, to thought's ever-renewed role in articulating what we might mean by joy, tragedy, or any of the other concepts by which Rosset claims we live but which, by coming to rest in tautology or totality, posit an impossible split between thought and experience that denies the very contradictions that Rosset's thought had the potential, at first, to maintain.

Conclusion

How, then, to think "after everything?" In the wake of the intellectual, historical, and political undoing of notions of teleological progress, the unity of the subject, the division of the known world into clearly defined subjects and objects, and a basic harmony between thinker and world, the thinkers with whom I have engaged attempt to articulate what remains for thought. I hope to have demonstrated the way in which thought takes on a dramatic structure that implicates the thinker by retaining, but redefining, the conceptual terrain of subjects and objects of thought as well as implicating the thinker in an affective stance toward thinking as experience. Such a view rejects a model of thought as representing the world, not in order to close off the thinking subject in an apolitical solipsism but to acknowledge the thinker's status as fundamentally at odds with the world and thus with the smooth workings of common sense which, left unexamined, lead to totalitarian, uncritical acceptance of things "as they are" and the calamities that result from firmly held convictions. On this view, thought is reinvested with a sense of urgency, doubt, and questioning that necessarily leads the thinking subject to anguish, not in the sense of any privatized drama but in a way that engages in an act of creative destruction of seemingly firmly established "worlds," in order to attempt to conceive of a world that is in fact never static and never reducible to the status of an object. To attempt to think in this way is to undo both thinker and thought and thus to reconfigure a notion of stable subjectivity. It is not, for all that, to reject the notion of subjectivity altogether, for to do so, even if it were possible, would be to deny the role of the thinker who animates and is animated by the dialectical play of subject and object, and thus to put an end to the dialectical process of thinking through contradictions whose opposite always holds out the danger of stasis.

To engage contradiction in this way is to leave oneself open to torment and to resist the facile, reassuring, or comforting conclusions that come with focus on a fixed goal or a reversion to received opinion. Such a view actively resists the temptation of nondialectical thought. To consider that the anguish of thought is perhaps wrongheaded is itself part of the drama, given that the skepticism engendered by turning answers into questions and being nowhere at home in one's thought risks turning back on itself. As Adorno noted in a lecture on metaphysics:

> As a metaphysical thinker, that is, someone who cannot do otherwise than seek to understand, one is sometimes overcome by the eerie suspicion that understanding itself is an illusion that one ought to be rid of, and that precisely the superficial mind which merely registers facts, which one resists with every fiber of one's being, may in the end be right. One must, as it were, include common sense and human triviality in metaphysical meaning; one must incorporate it in speculation as the principle which ensures that the world merely is as it is and not otherwise, if the depths of speculation is not to be false, that is, a depth which confers an *illusory* meaning.
>
> On the other hand, however, the joy of thought, which motivates us to think on metaphysical matters in the first place and to raise the questions I have discussed in the course of these lectures, is simply the joy of elevation, the joy of rising beyond what merely is. (*Metaphysics* 114)

To be caught up in the anguish of thought as experience is, then, to resist the temptation of affirming facile or self-evident interpretations of the world that come to rest in definitive factual answers. It is to remain faithful to the notion of thought as divided against itself by its perpetual non-identity with itself and to the divided self that is both reflected and produced in the notion of thinking against oneself as the motor of thought as drama. The subject of this drama, who stages and is staged by the act of thinking, remains at odds with the world and, through that distance, engages with it from a point of participation by non-participation that sets up thought as perpetual critique.

While it is perhaps surprising to see Adorno discussing "the joy of rising beyond what merely is," we should not lose sight of the fact that thought remains in a state of productive contradiction such that the joy is never permanent, never separated from its opposite through which it is constituted. To rise beyond what merely is, is to attempt a kind of necessarily provisional interpretation that remains keenly aware of the dark rather than being blinded by the light. It is a rising that contains within it its own return, a grounded rise that attempts to make sense, not so much of the world of lived experience so much as the very effort to conceptualize the world as a kind of experience. It has been my claim that the authors I have considered write not in order to provide a record of those attempts but to enact them in the process of writing. In fact, to write at all is to give voice to the problem of conceiving experience, to highlight the constructed nature of any attempt to reproduce a purportedly immediate experience conceptually and/or through writing. Bataille's "inner experience" reorients thought away from a goal in order to transform the subject-object relations implicit in thought; the failure of the attempt to obliterate the thinking subject reanimates the experience by reinforcing the intensity of the newly reconfigured relation to the world and to one's thought as objects. Bataille's thought experiments illustrate the necessary failure of an appeal to inner peace or quietude which, paradoxically, ends up playing the role of end goal which thought by its nature must reject as structurally equivalent to a position of strong commitment to firmly held dogmatic principles which pave the way for the literal violence of ideological conflict.

The appeal to impossible quietude thus becomes political by implication as a way to stave off action in the world that would take its distance from thought via an appeal to deeply held convictions. The consequences of such intellectual restlessness are also played out in Cioran, whose work foregrounds, works through, and plays out the notion of "thinking against oneself," whereby the absence of an Archimedean point for evaluating truth reorients thought and reinvigorates the question of what it would mean to avoid the temptation of a goal-oriented thought. The often aphoristic or page-length forms in which Cioran's writing subject stages this drama encourage the participation of the reader in assembling those forms into dialectical constellations where their contradictions can be engaged rather than dismissed or resolved. As in Bataille, the subjectivity that emerges from the text is fueled by the impossibility of what it seems to want, an eternal and undifferentiated nothingness which, by virtue of the concept's non-identity to itself, automatically depends on its other, a fact which precludes the possibility of undifferentiation except as negation.

A different sort of drama emerges in Clément Rosset, one that I have argued ultimately reaches a dead end because it is not animated by the motor that operates within and across Bataille and Cioran's writings and thus abdicates the role of thought as experience by re-establishing each as an isolated experience and opting in favor of a rejection of thought. While he engages a tragic approach to thought and experience that maintains a focus on dissonance, his thought nonetheless moves toward a resolution of dissonance that is incompatible with the thinking of and through contradiction that allowed for the rich terrain of a thinking subject's experience in Bataille and Cioran. He appeals to a tautological affirmation of the real as the real that does not make room for the non-identity of the concept to the thing and moves his thought instead toward an affirmation of joy or grace that, I would claim, is untenable precisely because it is unthinkable if we are driven back at every step to tautological affirmation rather than engaged in the critical negation that proved so fruitful in Bataille and Cioran.

To think against oneself, then, requires the persistence of subjectivity and the refusal of a unified notion of the thinking subject as clearly distinct from the object of its thought. To think "after everything" is not so much a salvage operation among the ruins as a reevaluation of the simplified notion of a subject-object relation which had been dominant in the more reductionist forms of Cartesianism that had at times guided notions of a positivistic science. It is not so much to rethink the clear subject-object distinction as to reveal the dissonance that had already been at the heart of such a conception, which ignores the non-identity of the concept to the reality it purports to represent, whether that be an object in the external world or the thinking subject as object of thought for itself. Thinking against oneself enacts, via a creative destruction, the emergence of a subject that both constitutes and is constituted by its experiences in the historical world and allows for thought to function as an intervention in that world in a way that resists totalizing or dominating relationships to it. To think through the disconcerting effects of the necessarily unending process of thought is to guard against the temptation of subscribing to a false notion of unity, totality, or quietism that is a greater danger for the thinking subject than the breakdown of the simpler subject-object relation to the world would be.

To remain alive as a thinking subject is constantly to enact the potential destruction of the thinking self while remaining conscious of the impossibility of the task and to account ever anew for the contradiction which feels like an obstacle but is in fact the life of thought, in both senses of that term: it is what allows for thought to constitute experience as opposed to a representation of, or abstraction from it, and to remain vital apart from any systematic or goal-oriented approach. This enactment captures what Adorno identified, in a 1958 lecture, as the "essential task" of dialectical thought: "that happiness and suffering may be revealed as an immanent condition, as an immanent concept of thought itself, that thought and life alike may be redefined and reinterpreted, that this task be undertaken with all possible rigor and seriousness" (*Introduction* 44). I hope to have shown that Bataille, Cioran, and Rosset attempt to give form to such a redefinition and reinterpretation in their writing, which seeks, through a form which resists a false wholeness of an implied systematic approach, to construct the thinking subject in such a way that the affective dimension of thought is neither primary to it nor an afterthought but rather is coextensive with the redefinition and reinterpretation of what it would mean to be a thinking subject in the wake of the intellectual and historical catastrophes of the mid-twentieth century. To think against oneself is to recognize oneself as a situated, historical subject even, or perhaps especially, through configuring one's thought as out of order. It is to be subject to an aporia which is profound and destabilizing, but which does not and cannot remain at the level of aporia precisely because, as was most clearly visible in Bataille, the void becomes one moment in a process of thought that, by attempting to account for aporia, transforms it so that it becomes an element of thought's transformation rather than the cancelation or shutting down of thought.

To think against oneself is also, then, to conceive thought as the negation of the world as it seems to be given, not in the hope of reconstituting some kind of higher order or unity, but to attempt to resist that temptation in favor of eternal shaping and reshaping of the constellations of concepts from which thinkers can attempt to construe provisional meanings. In so doing, thinkers and writers might then remap the terrain of a viable relation to the world to which they attempt to give form.

Notes

Introduction

1. "Perhaps no term has been as heatedly contested in recent Anglo-American cultural debates as 'experience.' Historians concerned with the issues of agency and structure, epistemologists seeking a ground for reliable knowledge, anthropologists anxious about the sources of ethnographic authority, political theorists wrestling with the implications of identity politics, literary critics grappling with the intricacies of representation and discourse, all have struggled to make sense of a term that Hans-Georg Gadamer has rightly called 'one of the most obscure that we have'" (Jay, "Limits" 155).
2. The kind of thought I have in mind here is akin to David Sherman's characterization, in his study of Sartre and Adorno, of a subjectivity that does not disappear by virtue of being mediated because it is at the same time mediating, which becomes necessarily evident when the thinker is operating from a first-person perspective: "Subjectivity is not just passively mediated, which is how it invariably appears when one's philosophical perspective is limited to the third-person standpoint. Due to the continuing historical existence of the subject—that is, the first-person standpoint, which, by virtue of its historical legacy, continues, however tenuously, to presuppose the freedom of its choices in the face of the political totality—subjectivity is also active or *mediating*" (6).
3. As Jeremy Biles notes, "the concept of *Aufhebung* […] is seen by some as the resolution or cancelation of contradictions, and by others as the lifting up and preserving of these contradictions" (13).
4. As Andrew Bowie puts it: "Rather than seeking a reconciliation by working through the contradictions between thought and reality to a philosophical conclusion in the manner of Hegel, then, Adorno thinks that the claim to resolve such contradictions in philosophy will mask real contradictions, whose solution does not lie within philosophy" (70).
5. See *Negative Dialectics*: "The difference between subject and object cannot be simply negated. They are neither an ultimate duality nor a screen hiding ultimate unity. They constitute one another as much as—by virtue of such constitution—they depart from each other" (*Negative* 174).
6. On the role of interpretation and its relationship to experience in Adorno's thought, see Roger Foster: "Interpretation is […], for Adorno, a linguistic practice that

seeks to reverse the severing of communication from expression, a process that is at the root of the narrowing of cognitively significant experience. [...] Adorno understands that process [...] to be one involving the constant self-correction of concepts" (17).

7   "The movement of the concept is not a sophistical manipulation that would insert changing meanings into it from the outside but rather the ever-present consciousness of both the identity of and the inevitable difference between the concept and what it is supposed to express, a consciousness that animates all genuine knowledge. Because philosophy will not relinquish that identity, it must accept this difference" (Adorno *Hegel* 71).

8   See Susan Buck-Morss' characterization of this aspect of Adorno's method: "Adorno didn't write essays, he *composed* them, and he was a virtuoso in the dialectical medium. His verbal compositions express an 'idea' through a sequence of dialectical reversals and inversions. The sentences develop like musical themes: they break apart and turn in on themselves in a continuing spiral of variation. The phenomena are viewed as Freud viewed dream symbols: They are 'overdetermined,' so that their contradictory complexity needs to be disentangled through interpretation. But there is no affirmation, no 'closing cadence.' The contradictions are unraveled; they are not resolved" (101).

9   For a succinct overview of the similarities and differences in Adorno and Arendt's fundamental assumptions and approaches, see Rensmann and Gandesha 8–9; for a fuller treatment, see Benhabib.

10 See *The Life of the Mind* 179–93.

11 "Thinking deals with insivibles, with representations of things that are absent; judging always concerns particulars and things close at hand. But the two are interrelated, as are consciousness and conscience. [...] The manifestation of the wind of thought is not knowledge; it is the ability to tell right from wrong, beautiful from ugly. And this, at the rare moments when the stakes are on the table, may indeed prevent catastrophes, at least for the self" (Arendt 193).

12 Cf. "perhaps the everlasting paradox" of philosophy according to Adorno, which is that it "must proceed interpretively without ever possessing a sure key to interpretation: nothing more is given to it than fleeting, disappearing traces within the riddle figures of that which exists and their astonishing intertwinings. The history of philosophy is nothing other than the history of such entwinings. Thus it reaches so few 'results'" ("Actuality" 126).

13 For a more recent defense of the creative destructive power of thought and politics, see Eric Cazdyn: "Just as revolutionary consciousness is snuffed out by the logic of the chronic (in which the possibilities to imagine and desire a radically different future are suppressed by the promise of management), the already dead flashes the

radical possibility of usurping dominant discourses of life and death and reigniting revolutionary consciousness" (Cazdyn 189).

14 On Kierkegaard's reception in France in the early twentieth century, see Teboul. For Nietzsche, see Schrift, especially 1–24.

15 This point of convergence in their prose writings stands in contrast to their divergent approaches to poetry. Fondane polemicized against Valéry's abstract, conceptual approach to verse. See Salazar-Ferrer 70–71.

16 See Zalloua on skepticism and theory. In the context of an analysis of Montaigne and the essayistic form of thinking, he writes: "Not amenable to self-immunization, essaying produces monsters, exploding the ideals of sovereignty and self-containment, astonishing its dutiful practitioner at every turn. The essay form continually grapples with these anxieties of unsettlement and vulnerability. In other words, pure heterology meets the demands of essaying—of interpretation" (54).

17 The double period, here and in other citations, is Valéry's own punctuation.

18 All unattributed translations from French are my own.

19 On Shestov and Fondane, see Arta Lucescu-Boutcher.

20 See Olivier Salazar-Ferrer on Job's importance for Fondane as a figure of lived, experienced thought: "L'herméneutique existentielle construit des personnages concrets-abstraits qui par leur double nature invitent précisément à vivre leur pensée. [...] Tous les personnages conceptuels fondaniens (Abraham, Philoctète, Kierkegaard, Rimbaud, Baudelaire), remarquons-le, sont des variations (historiques, littéraires, poétiques) autour du personnage [...] de Job, que nous pouvons appeler pour cette raison *le paradigme de Job*" ["Existential hermeneutics constricts concrete-abstract characters who by their double nature invite a living of their thought. [...] All of Fondane's conceptual characters (Abraham, Philoctetes, Kierkegaard, Rimbaud, Baudelaire), let us notice, are variations (historical, literary, poetic) on the character [...] of Job, which we could call for that reason *Job's paradigm*"] (96–7).

Chapter 1

1 As Benjamin Noys puts it: "Bataille cannot be either rejected or appropriated: to reject Bataille is to fail to read him but to become an apologist for Bataille, to celebrate him, is also to fail to read him. What Bataille requires is a reading that respects the heterogeneity of his thought, a thought that is of and at the limit" (4).

2 Martin Jay evokes Jacques Derrida's claim that inner experience "is not an experience, because it is related to no presence, to no plenitude, but only to the 'impossible' it 'undergoes' in torture" (Derrida 272), but cautions that "this is not

to say, however, that inner experience is simply the opposite of critical reason [...], but rather that it cannot be ever fully reconciled with it in its positive form" (Jay "Limits" 164).

3   On Bataille's complex relation to Hegel, and on the need for distinguishing between an approach to Hegel via determinate negation, which Bataille could be said to endorse, and an approach via absolute knowledge, which he firmly rejects, see Queneau as well as Noys on Bataille's relationship to Hegel which is "at once so close and so distant" since Bataille is "neither a disciple of Hegel nor is he an anti-Hegelian" (99–100).

4   One of the consequences of the impossibility of the appeal to knowledge is Bataille's recourse to literature, according to Kristeva: "la transposition de « l'opération souveraine » dans du langage exige une *littérature*, non pas une philosophie ni un savoir" ["the transposition of the 'sovereign operation' into language requires a *literature*, not a philosophy or a form of knowledge"] (279).

5   See Patrick ffrench on Bataille's relation to Hegel as implied by the form and content of *L'Expérience intérieure*: "To read *L'Expérience intérieure* is to oscillate from the intransigence of the demand for totality, for the summit, to the collapse, the experience of not being all [...]. While Hegel's book is so constructed as to lead its reader majestically from one moment of the process to the next, while at the same time including within each moment the totality of the process, right to the end, Bataille's book is constantly interrupted, collapses. He falls asleep, he forgets. [...] In both cases the content is inherent in the form. Yet at the same time Bataille's writing is so closely tied to the Phenomenology and to its demand that it reads at times as a commentary, not of the book itself, but on the experience of reading it" (69).

6   As Patrick ffrench indicates, Bataille's emphasis on the persistence of the subject and the human dimension of intellectual experience marks his writing and distinguishes it from that of Blanchot: "Blanchot's writing, I would propose, passes over into, or plays around the limit of the dimension ruled by the disaster, the imperious silence or nothingness (*néant*) which is the condition of thought. Bataille remains at the limit of the exposure of the human, and the human specifically in its bodily suffering and sexual dimension, to this disaster, to the night" (113).

7   For details of this publication history, see Kendall's "Translator's Introduction."

8   See also Robert Sasso: "l'athéologie est donc, tout à la fois, discours de l'absence, et absence du discours en tant qu'ils s'agit d'un discours auto-destructif, négateur : un discours-suicide. A la « forme » nihiliste de l'athéologie correspond un « fond » qui sans cesse s'effondre ou [...] s'ouvre, s'épanche" ["atheology is thus, all at once, a discourse of absence, and absence of discourse since it is a question of a self-destructive, negating discourse: a suicide-discourse. To the nihilistic 'form' of

atheology corresponds a 'content' that constantly melts away or [...] opens itself, pours itself out"] (105–6).

9 Translations from *L'Expérience intérieure* are from Kendall with page references in parenthetical citations.

10 As Kalliopi Nikolopoulou indicates, "we must be very clear not to relegate to Bataille a thoughtless celebration of madness; thinking beyond the concept is still thinking, and actually, a more rigorous and difficult thinking—not madness" (100).

11 Attempts in the secondary literature to define inner experience lead to similarly intriguing but necessarily murky characterizations, such as this one by Kevin Kennedy: "for Bataille, this notion of 'inner experience', is neither internal, nor an experience in the strict sense of the word. It rather represents the paradoxical attempt to put into words, to communicate, what exceeds language and communication; it constitutes, very generally speaking, an attempt to confront the 'nothingness' outside of any subject-object dichotomy" (95).

12 Translations of these notes are my own.

13 As Rodolphe Gasché notes: "the immediacy of experience is a figure that Bataille borrowed from his dialogues with Hegel but also turned it against him" (280).

14 I have explored Bataille's notion of nonknowledge in relation to his writing on poetry in *Poetry's Knowing Ignorance* 85–120.

15 See Angelos Evangelou, who notes that "for one to be able to shift from *I* to *ipse*, one needs the other. One can assume *ipseity* only through reaching the other, which is also in the state of losing itself" (91).

16 As Evangelou notes: "Bataille is not an advocate of madness, or, to be precise, he is not an advocate of any sort of conscious and calculated entering into madness. In other words, he is not calling for a sacrificial plunge into madness, just as he is not calling for a constant state of massacre and total eradication of human life. As he calls for a 'dying while surviving,' he also calls for a reason which can perceive itself as obscure and irrational. [...] In other words, he argues for a reason reasonable enough to embrace not its own complete and irreversible annihilation but the acknowledgement of the possibility of its own annihilation" (126).

17 Joseph Libertson observes the impossibility of either closure or transgression in Bataille: "Closure is more or other than a observation, and transgression is less or other than a liberation from constraint. Closure and transgression are both exigencies, both the exigency, both contaminations and impossibilities. *Expérience* is one principle of this economy of impossibility. Failure and irony are thus permanent factors in its thematization" (255).

18 Likewise, there is a suggestive parallel between Bataille's articulation of his project: "Principe de l'expérience intérieure: sortir par un projet du domaine du projet" (5: 60) ["Principle of inner experience: to get out through a project of the realm of the project" (52)] and Adorno's stated goal in *Negative Dialectics*: "To use the strength

of the subject to break through the fallacy of constitutive subjectivity—this is what the author felt to be his task ever since he came to trust his own mental impulses" (*Negative* xx).

19 Peter Tracey Connor rightly notes that "the terms in which Bataille describes sovereignty and the 'consciousness of the instant' remain very close to those that describe the 'inner experience'" (88–9).

20 As Jean-Luc Nancy puts it, Bataille "never stopped writing, always writing the exhaustion of his writing" (334). For Nancy, Bataille's theorizing of sovereignty is what, paradoxically, makes its achievement impossible: "[Bataille] advanced his thought so far that its seriousness deprived him of that divine, capricious, evanescent sovereignty which nevertheless remains his only 'object'" (333).

21 Kevin Kennedy remarks that "the impossibility to reach God, experience or the ineffable through words leaves philosophical discourse (that nevertheless needs to take these notions into account) with sole possibility of dramatizing, of performatively demonstrating this impossibility" (101).

22 Kalliopi Nikolopoulou notes that in Bataille "dramatization is to experience what language is to philosophy, namely, the mode of its exposition" (107). See also Connor 8–82.

23 For an extended reading of laughter in Bataille, see Amir 105–48.

24 Blanchot returns to the idea of inner experience, limit, and negation in *L'Entretien infini*; see especially 302–20.

25 Robert Sasso illustrates the paradox that consciously animates Bataille's writing on nonknowledge: "il faudrait dire et penser que l'impensable-indicible n'est pas rien. Mais nous voyons aussitôt quelle contradiction contient cette proposition: il n'est pas possible que l'indicible soit objet de la pensée. […] Bataille a été tout à fait conscient du caractère intenable de ses propositions sur le non savoir" ["it would be necessary to say and think that the unthinkable-unsayable is not nothing. But we see right away what a contradiction that proposition contains: it is not possible for the unsayable to be an object of thought. […] Bataille was totally conscious of the untenable character of his propositions about nonknowledge"] (93).

26 For more background on Bataille's engagement with and resistance to Nazism in the context of his writings of the Second World War period, see Irwin 16–20.

27 See also Martin Jay: "Despite its dangerous resemblance to the 'inner experience' celebrated by Ernst Jünger in connection with the war, Bataille's alternative resisted the activist, virile heroism promoted by his German counterpart. *Krieg als innere Erlebnis* was translated, to be sure, into French in 1934 as *La guerre notre mère* and may have had some echo in Bataille's 1938 essay 'The Structure and Function of the Army.' But while Jünger's sado-masochistic fetish of pain and demand for a return to mythic consciousness resemble similar moments in Bataille's thought, his stress on will and ascetic self-mastery did not. Although admitting that asceticism might

be conducive to a certain variant of experience by stilling the desire for objects, Bataille claimed it fell short because it made of experience itself a kind of object—or rather, a blissful state of being—to be desired" (*Songs* 375–6).

28 See also Marasco: "I take Bataille's rejection of actionism to stem instead from the critique of calcuative rationality, the assault on projects, and the refusal to subordinate the play of chance to the empire of profit. And I read the texts that compose the unfinished *Somme Athéologique* as attempts to push political thinking to the outer limits of reason so that praxis may come back into contact with the fugitive principle of freedom. Thought it can be taken as a philosophical doctrine, an interpretive device, a poetic experiment, and an ethical comportment, the will to chance is also a political formula" (117).

Chapter 2

1 Thomas Ligotti pithily presents Cioran by indicating that "contained in his works is an ample stock of quotable outbursts, any one of which could serve as a synopsis of his conviction that human existence was a wrong turn made by the universe" (165). Alexandra Laignel-Lavastine sees in Cioran's fashioning of a voice from nowhere a troubling indication of his inability to come to terms with, or fully denounce, his prior engagement with fascism: "Maintes ambiguïtés subsistent quant à l'authenticité de ses regrets mais aussi […] quant à sa capacité à se défaire des catégories conceptuelles et des stéréotypes judéophobes inoculés dans les années 1920 et 1930. S'il fallait caractériser ces ambivalences d'un mot, on pourrait dire qu'elles procèdent chez lui d'une double impossibilité: de liquider le passé (indifférence) mais aussi de l'affronter" ["Many ambiguities remain concerning the authenticity of his regrets but also […] concerning his capacity to rid himself of conceptual categories and judeo-phobic stereotypes injected in him in the 1920s and 1930s. If we had to characterize these ambivalences in a word, we could say that they stem from a double impossibility in him: to liquidate the past (indifference) but also to confront it"] (518–19).

2 This non-engagement is arguably, as Marta Petreu has claimed, the result of Cioran's shift away from his "total commitment" to extreme right-wing ideology in the 1930s to the thinking against oneself that I explore in his later French writings. Petreu notes: "We do not know exactly why and how this occurred, for there are no documents to reflect this shift. We can only assume that what changed Cioran's mind was the war, the revelation of the Holocaust, the arrest in Paris and the subsequent deportation of the Romanian-Jewish poet B. Fundoianu, the fear of retribution for his involvement in a far-right movement, remorse, and so on" (234).

For details of his involvement in right-wing extremism, see Petreu 94–200 and Laignel-Lavastine.

3   See for instance, among many other examples, this aphorism: "Dévorer biographie après biographie pour mieux se persuader de l'à quoi bon de n'importe quelle entreprise, de n'importe quelle destinée" ["To devour biography after biography in order the better to persuade oneself of the 'what's the use' of any enterprise or destiny whatsoever"] (*Oeuvres* 1696).

4   Throughout this chapter I use "Cioran" as shorthand for the writing voice in the works, as opposed to the biographical author.

5   Patrice Bollon ultimately concludes that this method thought leads ultimately to "un art de vivre évolutif [...], une façon de s'accommoder du monde et de soi [...]: une éthique" ["an evolutionary art of living [...], a way to come to terms with the world and oneself [...]: an ethics"] (Bollon 164). I would claim that such an interpretation closes down the dynamic relation between thought and living by seeing a progression from one to the other, as opposed to keeping alive the dialectical tension by which thought and living cannot be separated.

6   See Sylvain David on the impossibility of Cioran's co-opting ancient wisdom: "en recyclant des récits anciens sans pour autant être en mesure de souscrire à leur fin—tout en étant lui-même bien incapable de proposer une ouverture émancipatrice—le penseur, malgré l'apparent renouveau de sa démarche, ne peut entièrement se déprendre des grandes apories de la modernité" ["by recycling old stories without for all that being able to subscribe to their ending—even while being incapable himself of proposing an emancipating opening—the thinker, despite the apparent renewal of his processes, cannot entirely get loose from the great aporias of modernity"] (136).

7   For more on the refusal of salvation in Cioran, see my *The Fall out of Redemption* 139–69.

8   The intertwining of thought and suffering can be seen in Cioran's earlier work, published in Romanian and known in French as *Le livre des leurres*, where he indicates that one of the most important influences on his thought was not one of the canonical philosophers but the archetypal biblical voice of suffering, Job: "Jamais je n'ai eu besoin de Kant, de Descartes ou d'Aristote ; eux qui n'ont pensé que pour nos heures monotones et nos doutes autorisés. Mais je me suis arrêté sur Job, avec une piété filiale" ["I have never needed Kant, Descartes, or Aristotle; they have only thought for our monotonous hours or our authorized doubts. But I tarried with Job with a filial piety"] (234).

9   My reading opposes itself to that of Nicole Parfait, for whom Cioran seeks, via "une esthétique de la cruauté, une métaphysique de l'échec et une éthique de l'élégance" ["an esthetic of cruelty, a metaphysics of failure, and an ethic of elegance"] to "se

libérer de toutes les entraves qui le rattachent encore au monde, et d'acquérir, à travers la (re)création absolument autonome de soi par l'écriture, cette *unicité de l'Etre* perdue jadis en même temps que l'innocence" ["free himself from all the hindrances that still keep him attached to the world, and to acquire, through the absolutely autonomous (re)creation of self by writing, that *unity of Being* lost in days gone by at the same time as innocence"] (171). Such a recuperative project is, I hope to show, impossible and even undesirable in Cioran in light of the primacy of thinking against oneself.

10 Translations from the *Précis* are from Richard Howard's translation *A Short History of Decay*.

11 As Marta Petreu writes, "a reader familiar with the rest of Cioran's work […] is able to see beyond the author's veiled allusions [in *Précis de décomposition*] and realize that in fact Cioran is placing himself on trial, that this book is the testimony of a fracture" (238).

12 The stakes are important for thinking generally but also of course for Cioran personally, as the reference to ideologies and bloody farces is inseparable from his own early involvement in the fascist Iron Guard in Romania. In that sense, this opening move of the *Précis* is an exploration of ways to prevent, in the wake of impossible quietism, the catastrophic transformation of ideas into dangerous and reprehensible ideology.

13 On "radical passivity" in Cioran's contemporaries or near-contemporaries, see Thomas Carl Wall.

14 On the evasion of failure in Cioran, see Acquisto, "De l'impossibilité."

15 As Alfred Abad indicates: "Malgré le caractère sceptique du *vide* qui abroge le fondement de toute notion ou idée, l'espoir de parvenir à cette condition peut également être considéré comme une fascination, la plus grande de toutes. Cioran lui-même n'accepte pas une telle possibilité mais admet seulement l'expérience opportune que l'accès intermittent au vide peut permettre en nous" ["Despite the skeptical character of the *void* which abrogates the foundation all notions or ideas, the hope of attaining this condition can equally be considered a fascination, the biggest of them all. Cioran himself does not accept such a possibility but allows only the opportune experience that intermittent access to the void can allow in us"] (56).

16 For a reading of Schopenhauer in light of the impossibility of resignation, which resonates with aspects of Cioran's approach to the question, see Acquisto, *Living Well with Pessimism* 37–75.

17 Alfredo Abad notes that for Cioran "le *vide* peut octroyer une libération médiatisée, un état à partir duquel il soit possible d'identifier nos obsessions, nos fantasmagories. Or, penser que le vide pourrait permettre à l'homme de parvenir

à une parfaite lucidité reviendrait à ignorer l'appartenance de l'homme à l'échec comme un sceau de sa condition" ["the *void* can grant a mediated liberation, a state from which it would be possible to identify our obsessions and our phantasmagorias. But to the think that the void could permit man to come to perfect lucidity would mean to ignore the way man belongs to failure as a seal of his condition"] (56).

18 For a reading of Cioran's writing that emphasizes how recognition of personal failure as manifest through misguided action can yield intellectual humility, see Costica Bradatan: "Perhaps to transcend the political failures of his youth, the later Cioran sought to understand their deeper meaning, and to incorporate this understanding into the texture of his thinking. The result was a more nuanced philosophizing and a more humane thinker. His personal experience with failure brought Cioran closer to a province of humanity to which he could not otherwise have had access: that of the ashamed and the humbled" (161).

19 There are echoes here of Hannah Arendt's comments on Socrates as a gadfly: "he knows how to sting the citizens who, without him, will 'sleep on undisturbed for the rest of their lives' unless somebody comes along to arouse them. And what does he arouse them to? To thinking and examination, an activity without which life, in his view, was not only not worth much but was not fully alive" (172).

20 Sylvain David takes a periodizing approach that sees in Cioran's later works an increasing recognition of the necessary failure of the project of thinking against oneself: "le penseur doit constater, dans ses ultimes recueils, que les « exercices négatifs » auxquels il s'est livré, en vue de se purger des valeurs et représentations de l'imaginaire collectif, ont eu pour résultat de faire de lui une enveloppe vide dans laquelle les manifestations du monde extérieur, empirique, peuvent désormais s'infiltrer à leur guise" ["the thinker must observe, in his last volumes, that the 'negative exercises' which he undertook, in order to purge himself of values and representations of the collective imaginary, had as their result to make him an empty envelope in which the manifestations of the external empirical world, can from now on infiltrate themselves as they wish"] (283).

Chapter 3

1 "Je lui reproche ses emballements et jusqu'à ses ferveurs. Il n'a démoli des idoles que pour les remplacer par d'autres. [...] Il n'a observé les hommes que de loin. Les aurait-il regardés de près, jamais il n'eût pu concevoir ni prôner sur le surhomme, vision farfelue, risible, sinon grotesque" ["I reproach him for his flights of enthusiasm and even his fervors. He demolished idols only to replace them with

other ones. [...] He observed men only from afar. If he had looked at them from up close, he could never have conceived or extolled the overman, far-fetched vision, laughable, if not grotesque"] (Cioran *Oeuvres* 1323).

2. Denis Lejeune notes that "the notion of 'tragique' as used by Rosset or Nietzsche is, it should be stressed, quite different from usual definitions of the word. For Rosset, what is at stake in traditional tragedies is not a conflict between freedom and Determinism (or Fatalism), as is often claimed. What such tragedies do illustrate, however, is *man's inability to accept, or deal with, reality*: what Oedipus is told by the oracle in Sophocles's *Oedipus Rex* is what *will happen*, and everything he may try to do to avoid killing his father and marrying his mother will come to nothing" (58).

3. For a more general overview of Rosset's thought, see Amir 328–46 or Lejeune 47–70.

4. He goes on to articulate the difference between the two by way of the kinds of conclusions they aim or do not aim to draw: "pensée tragique et pessimisme diffèrent donc par leur contenu [...]. Ils diffèrent aussi par leur intention. Constat, résignation, sublimation plus ou moins compensatoire sont ici les mots de la sagesse pessimiste. L'intention tragique—l'intention proprement terroriste, telle qu'on la trouve chez Lucrèce, Montaigne, Pascal, ou Nietzsche—diffère sur tous ces points" ["tragic thought and pessimism differ by their content [...]. They differ by their intention as well. Acknowledgment, resignation, a more or less compensatory sublimation are the words of pessimist wisdom. Tragic intention—the properly terrorist intention, as we find it in Lucretius, Montaigne, Pascal, or Nietzsche—differs on all these points"] (18–19).

5. Jean Tellez poses this question as a potential critique of Rossset: "la joie de vivre est-elle indicible parce qu'irrationnelle, ou bien indicible parce qu'inavouable ?" ["is joie de vivre unsayable because it is irrational, or because it is inadmissible?"] (143).

6. For example: "La musique, elle seule, qui apaise le remords propre à toute existence, me console d'avoir jamais été" ["Music, and music alone, which calms the remorse proper to all existence, consoles me for having ever been"] (*Fenêtre* 40).

7. See *L'objet singulier*: "L'allégresse est alors un sentiment de bonheur passager et en grande partie illusoire, puisque procédant de l'oubli provisoire des soucis, et non de leur suppression réelle: un « bon moment » dans la vie et rien de plus" ["The happiness I call *allégresse* is a feeling of passing and in large part illusory happiness, since it proceeds from the provisional forgetting of cares, and not from their real cancelation: a 'good moment' in life and nothing more"] (*L'objet* 100).

8. For more on Rosset's shift in his understanding of reality and its doubles beginning in his 1997 works, see Vinolo 131–57.

9. For a critique of this distinction based on its ultimate untenability, see Vinolo 169.

10 In *Le réel*, Rosset offers this definition of *insignificance*: "Nous appelons *insignifiance du réel* cette propriété inhérente à toute réalité d'être toujours indistinctement fortuite et déterminée" ["What we call the insignificance of the real is that property inherent in all reality of being always indistinctly fortuitous and determined"] (*Le réel* 13).
11 Tellez identifies the following unresolved ambiguity in Rosset's characterization of *allégresse*: "*Le Réel: Traité de l'idiotie* définit très explicitement l'allégresse, ou « amour du réel », comme attachée au *seul* « fait ontologique »: « le fait que le réel existe, qu'il y ait quelque chose plutôt que rien » (78). *La Force majeure* donne une précision importante, hélas quelque peu confuse. La joie de vivre est identifiée au « plaisir d'exister », mas celui-ci est qualifié de « réjouissance assez complexe » ; c'est « un plaisir plutôt pris au fait qu'il y ait de l'existence en général qu'au fait de son existence personnelle » (FM 18). En résumé: l'allégresse dépend-elle de la joie d'exister, ou la joie d'exister de l'allégresse ? Rosset paraît préférer cette dernière option … " ["*Le Réel: Traité de l'idiotie* defines *allégresse*, or 'love of the real,' very specifically as attached to the *only* 'ontological fact': 'the fact that the real exists, that there is something rather than nothing' (78). *La Force majeure* provides an important clarification, which is, alas, a bit confused. *Joie de vivre* is identified with the 'pleasure of existing,' but the latter is qualified as 'a rather complex rejoicing'; it is 'a pleasure caught up with existence in general more than with the fact of personal existence' (FM 18). In sum: does *allégresse* depend on the joy of existing, or vice versa? Rosset seems to prefer the latter … "] (141).
12 I have translated *accord* as "consonance." It also carries the sense of a chord.
13 See Rosset, *Le démon de la tautologie*.

Bibliography

Works Cited

Abad, Alfredo. "La séduction de l'échec" in Aurélien Demars and Michaela-Gentiana Stanisor, eds., *Cioran, archives paraxales*, Tome VI (Classiques Garnier, 2022), 53–62.
Acquisto, Joseph. "De l'impossibilité de l'échec chez Emil Cioran" in Aurélien Demars and Mihaela-Gentiana Stanisor, eds., *Cioran: Archives paradoxales—nouvelles approches critiques*, Tome VI (Classiques Garnier, 2022), 83–94.
Acquisto, Joseph. *The Fall Out of Redemption: Writing and Thinking beyond Salvation in Baudelaire, Cioran, Fondane, Agamben, and Nancy*. Bloomsbury, 2015.
Acquisto, Joseph. *Living Well with Pessimism in Nineteenth-Century France*. Palgrave Macmillan, 2021.
Acquisto, Joseph. *Poetry's Knowing Ignorance*. Bloomsbury, 2020.
Adorno, Theodor. "The Actuality of Philosophy." *Telos* 31 (Spring 1977), 120–33.
Adorno, Theodor. *Critical Models: Interventions and Catchwords*. Columbia UP, 2005.
Adorno, Theodor. *Hegel: Three Studies*. Tr. Shierry Weber Nicholsen. The MIT Press, 1999.
Adorno, Theodor. *An Introduction to Dialectics*. Tr. Nicholas Walker. Polity, 2017.
Adorno, Theodor. *Kant's Critique of Pure Reason*. Polity, 2001.
Adorno, Theodor. *Metaphysics: Concept and Problems*. Tr. Edmund Jephcott. Stanford UP, 2001.
Adorno, Theodor. *Minima Moralia*. Tr. E.F.N. Jephcott. Verso, 2020.
Adorno, Theodor. *Negative Dialectics*. Tr. E.B. Ashton. The Seabury Press, 1973.
Adorno, Theodor. *The New Music: Kranichstein Lectures*. Tr. Wieland Hoban. Polity Press, 2021.
Adorno, Theodor. *Notes to Literature*. Tr. Shierry Weber Nicholsen. Volume 1. Columbia UP, 1991.
Alpozzo, Marc. "Le language du réel ou de la tautologie selon Clément Rosset." *Les Carnets de la philosophie* 12 (juillet-août-septembre 2010), 53–62.
Amir, Lydia. *The Legacy of Nietzsche's Philosophy of Laughter: Bataille, Deleuze, and Rosset*. Routledge, 2022.
Arendt, Hannah. *The Life of the Mind: Thinking*. Harcourt Brace Jovanovich, 1977.
Attell, Kevin. "Language and Labor, Silence and Stasis: Bartleby among the Philosophers" in Jason Frank, ed., *A Political Companion to Herman Melville* (UP of Kentucky, 2014), 194–228.
Bataille, Georges. *Inner Experience*. Tr. Stuart Kendall. State U of New York P, 2014.

Bataille, Georges. *Œuvres complètes*. Gallimard, 1973.
Baudry, Jean-Louis. "Bataille and Science: Introduction to Inner Experience" in Leslie Anne Boldt-Irons, ed., *On Bataille: Critical Essays* (State U of New York P, 1995), 265–81.
Bell, David. "Introduction: Of Silence and Insouciance in Philosophy" in Clément Rosset, *Joyful Cruelty: Toward a Philosophy of the Real*. Ed. & Tr. David F. Bell (Oxford UP, 1993), vii–xvi.
Benhabib, Seyla. "Arendt and Adorno: The Elusiveness of the Particular and the Benjaminian Moment" in Lars Rensmann and Samir Gandesha, eds., *Arendt and Adorno: Political and Philosophical Investigations* (Stanford UP, 2012), 32–55.
Biles, Jeremy. *Ecce Monstrum: Georges Bataille and the Sacrifice of Form*. Fordham UP, 2007.
Blanchot, Maurice. *Faux Pas*. Gallimard, 1943.
Blanchot, Maurice. *Faux Pas*. Tr. Charlotte Mandell. Stanford UP, 2001.
Blanchot, Maurice. *L'entretien infini*. Gallimard, 1969.
Bollon, Patrice. *Cioran, l'hérétique*. Gallimard, 1997.
Bowie, Andrew. *Adorno and the Ends of Philosophy*. Polity Press, 2013.
Bradatan, Costica. *In Praise of Failure: Four Lessons in Humility*. Harvard UP, 2023.
Buck-Morss, Susan. *The Origin of Negative Dialectics*. Free Press, 1979.
Cavaillès, Nicolas. *Cioran malgré lui: Ecrire à l'encontre de soi*. CNRS Editions, 2011.
Cazdyn, Eric M. *The Already Dead: The New Time of Politics, Culture, and Illness*. Duke UP, 2012.
Cioran, Emil. *Divagations*. Tr. Nicolas Cavaillès. Gallimard, 2019.
Cioran, Emil. *Fenêtre sur le rien*. Tr. Nicolas Cavaillès. Gallimard, 2019.
Cioran, Emil. *Œuvres*. Gallimard, 1995.
Cioran, Emil. *A Short History of Decay*. Tr. Richard Howard. Arcade Publishing, 1998.
Cioran, Emil. *The Temptation to Exist*. Tr. Richard Howard. Quadrangle Books, 1968.
Cioran, Emil. *The Trouble with Being Born*. Tr. Richard Howard. Seaver Books, 1976.
Connor, Peter Tracey. *Georges Bataille and the Mysticism of Sin*. The Johns Hopkins UP, 2000.
David, Sylvain. *Cioran—Un héroïsme a rebours*. Les Presses de l'Université de Montréal, 2006.
Derrida, Jacques. *Writing and Difference*. U of Chicago P, 1978.
Evangelou, Angelos. *Philosophizing Madness from Nietzsche to Derrida*. Palgrave Macmillan, 2017.
Faucher, Kane X. "The Transcendental Empiricism of Georges Bataille: The Incommensurable Object." *Culture, Theory, and Critique* 46: 2 (2005), 163–76.
ffrench, Patrick. *After Bataille: Sacrifice, Exposure, Community*. Legenda, 2007.
Fondane, Benjamin. *La conscience malheureuse*. Verdier, 2013.
Fondane, Benjamin. *Le Lundi existentiel et le dimanche de l'histoire. Chronique de la Philosophie vivante*. Non Lieu, 2021.

Foster, Roger. *Adorno: The Recovery of Experience*. State U of New York P, 2007.
Gasché, Rodolphe. *Georges Bataille: Phenomenology and Phantasmatology*. Stanford UP, 2012.
Grossman, Évelyne. *The Anguish of Thought*. Tr. Matthew Cripsey and Louise Burchill. U of Minnesota P, 2018.
Hegel, G.W.F. *Phenomenology of Spirit*. Tr. A.V. Miller. Oxford UP, 1977.
Hill, Leslie. *Bataille, Klossowski, Blanchot: Writing at the Limit*. Oxford UP, 2001.
Hollier, Denis. *Against Architecture*. Tr. Betsy Wing. The MIT Press, 1989.
Irwin, Alexander. *Saints of the Impossible: Bataille, Weil, and the Politics of the Sacred*. U of Minnesota P, 2002.
James, Alison. "Richard Rorty et Clément Rosset face à la littérature." *Littérature* 147 (September 2007), 99–114.
Jarrety, Michel. *La morale dans l'écriture: Camus, Char, Cioran*. Presses Universitaires de France, 1999.
Jay, Martin. "The Limits of Limit-Experience: Bataille and Foucault." *Constellations* 2: 2 (1995), 155–74.
Jay, Martin. *Songs of Experience*. U of California P, 2006.
Kendall, Stuart. "Translator's Introduction: A Debauchery of Thought" in Georges Bataille, ed., *Inner Experience*. Tr. Stuart Kendall (State U of New York Press, 2014), vii–xxiv.
Kennedy, Kevin. *Towards an Aesthetic Sovereignty: Georges Bataille's Theory of Art and Literature*. Academia Press, 2014.
Kristeva, Julia. "Bataille, l'expérience et la pratique" in Philippe Sollers, ed., *Bataille* (UGE, 1973), 267–301.
Laignel-Lavastine, Alexandra. *Cioran, Eliade, Ionesco: L'oubli du fascisme*. Presses Universitaires de France, 2002.
Lejeune, Denis. *The Radical Use of Chance in 20th-Century Art*. Brill, 2012.
Leppert, Richard. "Adorno and Opera" in Peter E. Gordon, Espen Hammer, and Max Pensky, eds., *A Companion to Adorno* (John Wiley & Sons, Inc., 2020), 443–56.
Libertson, Joseph. *Proximity: Levinas, Blanchot, Bataille and Communication*. Martinus Nijhoff Publishers, 1982.
Ligotti, Thomas. *The Conspiracy against the Human Race*. Penguin Books, 2018.
Lucescu-Boutcher, Arta. "Shestov and Fondane: Life beyond Morals." *Cardozo Studies in Law and Literature* 6: 1 (Spring-Summer 1994), 79–86.
Lurson, Guillaume. "Georges Bataille: mystique et expérence intérieure." *Revue de Métaphysique et de Morale* 3 (2018), 307–22.
Mansfield, Nick. *The God Who Deconstructs Himself: Sovereignty and Subjectivity between Freud, Bataille, and Derrida*. Fordham UP, 2010.
Marasco, Robyn. *The Highway of Despair*. Columbia UP, 2015.
Marcel, Gabriel. *Homo Viator*. Éditions Montaigne, 1944.

McGowan, Todd. *Emancipation after Hegel: Achieving a Contradictory Revolution*. Columbia UP, 2019.
Nancy, Jean-Luc. *The Birth to Presence*. Stanford UP, 1993.
Nikolopoulou, Kalliopi. "Elements of Expérience: Bataille's Drama" in Andrew Mitchell and Jason Kemp Winfree, eds., *The Obsessions of Georges Bataille* (State U of New York P, 2009), 99–118.
Noys, Benjamin. *Georges Bataille: A Critical Introduction*. Pluto Press, 2000.
Parfait, Nicole. *Cioran ou le défi de l'être*. Editions Desjonquères, 2001.
Petreu, Marta. *An Infamous Past: E.M. Cioran and the Rise of Fascism in Romania*. Ivan R. Dee, 2005.
Popescu, Gabriel. "De l'athlétisme intérieur dramatique de Cioran et Loyola" in Aurélien Demars and Mihaela-Genţiana Stănişor, eds., *Cioran archives paradoxales*, Tome II (Classiques Garnier, 2015), 65–72.
Proust, Marcel. *A la recherche du temps perdu*. Gallimard, 1989.
Proust, Marcel. *Time Regained*. Tr. Andreas Mayor and Terence Kilmartin. The Modern Library, 2003.
Queneau, Raymond. "Premières confrontations avec Hegel." *Critique* 19: 195–6 (1963), 694–700.
Ramond, Charles. "Préface" in Stéphane Vinolo, ed., *Clément Rosset: La philosophie comme anti-ontologie* (L'Haramattan, 2012), 9–35.
Rensmann, Lars and Samir Gandesha. "Understanding Political Modernity: Rereading Arendt and Adorno in Comparative Perspective" in Lars Rensmann and Samir Gandesha, eds., *Arendt and Adorno: Political and Philosophical Investigations* (Stanford UP, 2012), 1–27.
Ribeiro, Brian. *Sextus, Montaigne, Hume: Pyrrhonizers*. Brill, 2021.
Rosen, Michael. *Hegel's Dialectic and Its Criticism*. Cambridge UP, 1982.
Rosset, Clément. "Despite Everything, Happiness Is Still Happiness: An Interview." *Angelaki* 82: 2 (August 2003), 73–83.
Rosset, Clément. *Fantasmagories*. Minuit, 2006.
Rosset, Clément. *La force majeure*. Minuit, 1983.
Rosset, Clément. *La philosophe tragique*. Presses Universitaires de France, 1960.
Rosset, Clément. *L'objet singulier*. Minuit, 1979.
Rosset, Clément. *Le choix des mots*. Minuit, 1995.
Rosset, Clément. *Le démon de la tautologie*. Minuit, 1997.
Rosset, Clément. *Le principe de cruauté*. Minuit, 1988.
Rosset, Clément. *Le réel: Traité de l'idiotie*. Minuit, 2004.
Rosset, Clément. *Logique du pire*. Presses Universitaires de France, 1971.
Salazar-Ferrer, Olivier. *Benjamin Fondane et la révolte existentielle*. Editions de Corlevour, 2008.
Sartre, Jean-Paul. "Un nouveau mystique" in *Situations* I (Gallimard, 1947), 143–88.

Sasso, Robert. *Georges Bataille, le système du non-savoir: une ontologie du jeu.* Minuit, 1978.
Schrift, Alan. "French Nietzscheanism" in Alan Schrift, ed., *The History of Continental Philosophy* (U of Chicago P, 2010), Vol. 6, 19–46.
Sherman, David. *Sartre and Adorno: The Dialectics of Subjectivity.* State U of New York P, 2007.
Sorensen, Asgar. "The Inner Experience of Living Matter: Bataille and Dialectics." *Philosophy and Social Criticism* 33: 5 (2007), 597–615.
Stoekl, Allan. *Agonies of the Intellectual, Commitment, Subjectivity, and the Performative in the Twentieth-Century French Tradition.* U of Nebraska P, 1992.
Surya, Michel. *Georges Bataille: An Intellectual Biography.* Tr. Krzysztof Fijalkowski and Michael Richardson. Verso, 2002.
Teboul, Margaret. "The Reception of Kierkegaard in France, 1930–1960." *Revue des sciences philosophiques et théologiques* 89: 2 (2005), 315–36.
Tellez, Jean. *La joie et le tragique: Introduction à la pensée de Clément Rosset.* Germina, 2009.
Thacker, Eugene. *Cosmic Pessimism.* U of Minnesota P, 2015.
Valéry, Paul. *Cahiers.* Gallimard, 1973.
Vinolo, Stéphane. *Clément Rosset: La philosophie comme anti-ontologie.* L'Haramattan, 2012.
Wall, Thomas Carl. *Radical Passivity: Levinas, Blanchot, Agamben.* State U of New York P, 1999.
Zalloua, Zahi. *Theory's Autoimmunity: Skepticism, Literature, and Philosophy.* Northwestern UP, 2018.

Index

Abad, Alfredo 200 n.15, 200 n.17
action 5, 58, 78–80, 97–8, 137, 147
   creative 132
   passivity and 104
   and thought 57, 105, 118
Adorno, Theodor 4, 6–8, 11, 13–15,
      17–18, 20, 23, 39, 48, 56, 95, 166,
      192 n.2, 192 n.4, 192–3 n.6, 193 n.8,
      193 n.12
   "The Essay as Form" 12, 16, 24
   essential task of dialectical thought
      11, 190
   Introduction to Dialectics 9–11, 48, 57
   metaphysics 188
   Negative Dialectics 12, 192 n.5,
      196–7 n.18
   "Why Still Philosophy?" 6
Alpozzo, Marc 174
Arendt, Hannah 4, 17, 23, 27, 39, 143, 167,
      201 n.19
   creative and destructive thought 18, 22,
      24, 30, 151
   The Life of the Mind 17–18
   non-metaphorical language 21
   nowhere of thinking 19–20
   political relations 22
   thinking and art-making 18
Aristotle 18–19
Attell, Kevin 22

Bataille, Georges 16, 23, 45, 97, 104,
      110, 114–15, 120, 123, 129, 141,
      153, 158–9, 163, 189–91, 194 n.1,
      195 nn.3–6, 196 nn.10–11, 196
      nn.13–14, 196 n.18, 197 n.19, 197
      n.22, 197 n.26, 197–8 n.27, 198 n.28
   dialectics 49
   L'Expérience intérieure (see *L'Expérience
      intérieure* (Bataille))
   nonknowledge 59–60, 71, 73, 85–6,
      197 n.25
   Œuvres complètes 50

   sovereignty 69–70, 197 nn.19–20
   'The Structure and Function of the
      Army' 197 n.27
Baudelaire, Charles 101, 106
Baudry, Jean-Louis 72
Bell, David 153, 160
Biles, Jeremy 192 n.3
Blanchot, Maurice 47, 57, 76, 82, 195 n.6
Bollon, Patrice 100, 199 n.5
Bowie, Andrew 192 n.4
Buck-Morss, Susan 8, 193 n.8

Camus, Albert 23
Cavaillès, Nicolas 108
Chestov, Léon 31
Christianity 42, 114, 174, 176–7, 181–2
Cioran, Emil 41–2, 78, 88, 95, 97, 115,
      153, 158–9, 162–3, 168, 189–90,
      198 nn.1–2, 199 n.6, 200 n.9,
      200 n.15, 201 n.18, 201 n.20
   Cahiers 98–100
   "condition séparée" 139
   De l'inconvénient d'être né 98, 146
   duality, mitigation of 105–7, 115,
      137–8
   form of wisdom 103–4
   "Généalogie du fanatisme" 109
   humans and devil 106
   impossibility 98, 103–4, 110, 124–5,
      137, 147
   insomnia 42, 130, 143–4, 147
   La Tentation d'exister 98, 100, 137
   Le livre des leurres 199 n.8
   passivity 101–2, 104, 107, 109
   Précis de décomposition (see *Précis de
      décomposition*/*A Short History of
      Decay* (Cioran))
   skepticism 41–2
   "thinking against oneself" 41, 98,
      100–1, 107–8, 114, 116–17, 119–21,
      125, 139, 143
   well-being 99

common sense 17–20, 187
Connor, Peter Tracey 197 n.19
conscience 142–3, 172–3, 193 n.11
consciousness 10, 46, 83, 109, 142–3, 167, 173, 184, 193 n.7, 193 n.11
contradiction 5–7, 9, 12, 23–4, 26, 42, 48–9, 54, 89, 95, 97, 130–1, 161–3, 174, 181, 184–5, 187–9, 192 n.4
creative and destructive thought 18, 21–2, 24, 30, 119, 151, 187, 190, 193 n.13

David, Sylvain 100, 199 n.6, 201 n.20
Derrida, Jacques 194 n.2
Descartes, René 1, 9
dialectical subjectivity 95
dialectical thinking/thought 5, 7–12, 14–15, 17, 24, 29, 32, 35, 41, 72, 98, 101, 110, 137–8, 142, 151, 187
 antithesis of 131
 characterization of 48, 56
 in historical terms 17
 and writing 12
dialectics 7, 75
 characterization of 7
 reciprocal relation for 8
dissonance 42–3, 104, 174, 177, 179–82, 184–5, 189–90
Dostoyevsky, Fyodor 101
drama/dramatization 1, 5–6, 16, 42, 50, 76–7, 85, 106, 114–17, 122, 124, 146, 187–9, 197 n.22
 contradiction 6
 of dialectical thought 137
 reconciliation 12

engagement 5, 15–16, 131
Evangelou, Angelos 196 n.16
experience 4, 19–20, 24, 32, 36, 45, 52–3, 56–7, 61, 65, 71, 74, 76, 84, 92–3, 95, 112, 116, 124, 129, 131, 145, 151, 154, 158, 168, 185, 187, 192 n.1, 196 n.17
 inner experience 8–9, 29, 40–1, 45–50, 52–4, 58–60, 61–4, 70–2, 77, 79, 82–3, 88, 91, 123, 189, 194 n.2, 196 n.11, 197 n.27
 intellectual experience 13, 15–16, 54, 56, 195 n.6
 isolated 189
 and knowledge 59–60
 known and unknown objects 67
 lived 10, 31, 35, 60, 62, 66, 114, 118, 124, 132, 144, 153–4, 156–7, 164, 173, 188, 194 n.20
 sui generis 7
 and thought 2–4, 34–5, 62, 114, 118, 173

Faucher, Kane 47–8
ffrench, Patrick 95, 195 nn.5–6
Flaubert, Gustave 152
Fondane, Benjamin 24, 30, 194 n.20, 198 n.2
 La conscience malheureuse 31, 36–8
 Le Lundi existentiel et le dimanche de l'histoire 31–4
 metaphysical and dialectical concerns 39
 philosophy and religion 31–3
 poet and existential thinker 34–6
 thought and politics 40
Freud, Sigmund 134, 193 n.8

Gadamer, Hans-Georg 192 n.1
Gasché, Rodolphe 196 n.13
goal-oriented thought 64, 94, 119, 139, 189–90
Goffey, Andrew 151
Grossman, Evelyne 16

Hegel, G. W. F. 5–7, 11, 14, 16, 30, 36, 48–50, 192 n.4, 195 n.3, 195 n.5, 196 n.13
 Phenomenology of Spirit 4
Hill, Leslie 47, 69
Hollier, Denis 51
humanity 13, 27, 34, 36, 106, 109–11, 114–15, 118, 138, 180, 201 n.18

identity thinking 15, 134, 139, 146
Ignatius of Loyola 77, 108
 Spiritual Exercises 16
immediacy 2, 4, 54, 61, 63, 65–6, 70, 141–2, 154, 162, 169, 196 n.13
 of joy 162
 personal 3

inconscience 134
inner experience 8–9, 29, 45–8, 52, 54, 57, 62, 71, 79, 123, 189, 194–5 n.2, 196 n.11, 197 n.19, 197 n.27.
  See also *L'Expérience intérieure* (Bataille)
  authentic 65–6, 72, 78
  self and 49–50
Irwin, Alexander 94

James, Alison 159–60
Jarrety, Michel 149
Jay, Martin 194 n.2, 197 n.27
Jünger, Ernst 197 n.27

Kant, Immanuel 3, 6, 120, 172
Kendall, Stuart 51
Kennedy, Kevin 196 n.11, 197 n.21
Klossowski, Pierre 47
knowledge 9–10, 18, 25, 41, 55–6, 71–2, 75, 82, 95, 134, 147, 157–8, 163, 168, 170
  experience and 59–60
  subject and object 9–12, 14–15, 24, 67–8, 86
  thought and 119
Kojève, Alexandre 49
Kristeva, Julia 49, 75, 195 n.4

La guerre notre mère 197 n.27
Laignel-Lavastine, Alexandra 198 n.1
Lao-Tse 101
Lejeune, Denis, 'tragique' 202 n.2
Leppert, Richard 9
L'Expérience intérieure (Bataille) 2, 23, 29, 40, 45–6, 48–51, 95, 195 n.5
  anguish 50, 60, 64–5, 76–9, 81, 83–5, 88, 91
  asceticism 73
  communication 59, 62, 80, 84, 88
  discursive reason 48
  "Draft of an Introduction to Inner Experience" 45–6, 53
  experience and knowledge 59–60
  goal of experience 55–6
  of happiness 64–6
  immediacy of experience 54, 61, 63, 65–6
  irresolvable enigma 52–3
  known/unknown objects 67
  laughter 81, 83
  le ravissement 60–1
  logic of sacrifice 68–9
  mysticism and ecstasy 53–5
  "A New Mystic" 90
  rational thought and concepts 47
  reading and writing 50–1, 63, 72, 94
  reconceptualizing 57
  "Seconde digression sur l'extase dans le vide"/"Second Digression on Ecstasy in the Void" 85
  self-negation 88–9
  Somme athéologique 50, 94, 198 n.28
  sovereignty and subjectivity 69–70
  state of intoxication 51–2
  subject-object relations 70–1, 74, 76, 81, 86–7, 91–2
  thinking and knowing 58
  transcendence 91–3
  violence of war 78–80
  words and concepts/meaning 47–8, 51, 53
Libertson, Joseph 196 n. 17
Ligotti, Thomas 198 n. 1
lived experience 10, 31, 35, 60, 62, 66, 114, 118, 124, 132, 144, 153–4, 156–7, 164, 173, 188, 194 n.20
Lucretius 158

Mansfield, Nick 69
Marasco, Robyn 3, 198 n.28
Marcel, Gabriel 88–9
Marx, Karl 36–7
McGowan, Todd 5, 9
meaning-making 20, 159, 167, 173
Méthode de Méditation 50
Meville, Herman 23
Montaigne, Michel de 24, 158, 194 n.16
mutual constitution 13
mystical experience 53–4, 89, 92, 141

Nancy, Jean-Luc 197 n.20
  "writing *against* meaning" 49
negation 12, 22, 49, 57–61, 63–4, 104, 147, 149–50, 152, 189, 191, 195 n.3
Nietzsche, Friedrich 101, 149–50, 177, 179–80, 202 n.2

Nikolopoulou, Kalliopi 196 n.10, 197 n.22
non-conceptuality 70, 76, 81, 85, 142
non-identity 5, 9, 11, 15, 17, 42, 95, 141, 152, 181, 188–90
  importance of language 13
  subjectivity and objectivity 20
Noys, Benjamin 69–70, 194 n.1, 195 n.3

Parfait, Nicole 199 n.9
Pascal, Blaise 158
personal immediacy 3
pessimism 42, 149–50, 155–8
pessimist philosophy 154–8, 160
Petreu, Marta 198 n.2, 200 n.11
philosophy 6, 14, 29, 37, 46, 72, 77–8, 107, 119–20, 122, 124, 143–4, 146, 151, 153
  art and 35, 166
  interpretive and creative 164–5
  modern 105, 136
  "perhaps the everlasting paradox" 193 n.12
  pessimistic and tragic 154–8, 160
  and religion 31–3
  systematic 5, 23, 35, 55, 139, 143
  and thought 123, 145, 157
Plato 8, 17
Précis de décomposition/A Short History of Decay (Cioran) 1, 97–8, 100, 107, 109–10, 112, 200 nn.11–12
  contemporary thought and ancient models 135
  "contre nature" 141
  dogmatism and quietism 117–18, 137
  esthetics and metaphysics 127
  "Hantise de l'essentiel"/"Obsession of the Essential" 122–3, 128–9
  history and skepticism 112–14, 117
  homosexual 139–40
  humanity 115–16, 118
  "Invocation à l'insomnie"/"Invocation to Insomnia" 143–4
  "L'animal indirect" 115
  "Le décor du savoir" 133–4
  "Le penseur d'occasion"/"The Second-Hand Thinker" 129–31
  lived experience 118, 124, 142, 144
  "Merveilles du vice"/"Wonders of Vice" 139, 142–3
  night's revelations 144–6
  "Non-résistance à la nuit"/"Non-Resistance to Night" 120
  philosophers 121–2, 125
  radical passivity 113
  secular idolatry and catastrophe 110–11
  self-torturing 132
  sickness and sterility 125–6
  truth 119–20, 134, 139, 147
  violence and salvation 144
  "Visages de la décadence" 132–3
Proust, Marcel, *A la recherche du temps perdu* 65–6, 68

Ramond, Charles 163
reality, nature of 42–3, 149–50, 165
  betrayal of the real 153
  conscious of 167, 172–3
  cruelty of 161
  immediacy of 154, 169, 174
  joy 150, 154, 160, 162–4, 168, 173, 177–8
  meaninglessness 152, 158, 170–1, 173
  negation 149–50, 152
  relationship of doubles 164
  and suffering 150, 169
  tautology 42, 152–3, 168–9, 174, 181, 185
  unrepresentability 160
Ribeiro, Brian 114
Rosen, Michael 7
Rosset, Clément 31, 42–3, 150, 189–90, 202 n.2. *See also* tragedy and real
  allégresse in *L'objet singulier* 168–70, 202 n.7, 203 n.11
  anti-ontology 165–6
  consonance and dissonance 43, 179, 181
  creative work on language 159–60
  "essentielle définition du tragique"/"essential definition of the tragic" 178–9
  humanity and dissonance 180
  idea of death 175
  Joie de vivre 152, 203 n.11
  Joyful Cruelty 160–2, 165–6

La Force majeure 160, 203 n.11
La philosophie tragique 174–5, 185
Le choix des mots 151
Le principe de cruauté 151, 161, 164–5
Le réel: Traité de l'idiotie 170–4, 203 n.10
Logique du pire 154–5
meaning-making 159–60, 167
musico-metaphysical framework 181
rationalism 183–4
reconciliation of lucidity 153, 160, 167
tragedy and meaninglessness 167–8
tragic/tragic consciousness 167–70, 175–83, 185

Sartre, Jean-Paul 23, 88, 90–3, 192 n.2
    "crise de l'essai"/"crisis of the essay" 90
Sasso, Robert 195 n.8, 197 n.25
Schopenhauer, Arthur 157, 200 n.16
self-identity, thought and 101
sexual transgression 75
Sherman, David 192 n.2
skepticism 188
    history and 112–14
    and theory 194 n.16
Socrates 17, 167, 201 n.19
solitary thinker 5
Sophocles, *Oedipus Rex* 202 n.2
Sorensen, Asgar 48
Stoekl, Allan 50
subject-object relations 1–2, 5, 15–16, 24–5, 29, 40, 45, 56, 70–1, 74, 76, 79, 81, 84–7, 91–2, 108, 132, 135, 143, 171, 173, 189–90
    Cartesian approach to 10
    dialectical 24, 73, 171
Surya, Michel 93

Taoism 100–2
teleological progress 187
Tellez, Jean 150, 153, 202 n.5, 203 n.11
Thacker, Eugene, crying, laughing, and sleeping 149. *See also* pessimism
"Théorie de la bonté"/"Theory of Goodness" 136–8

thinking against oneself 41, 95, 98, 100–1, 103–4, 107–8, 114, 116–17, 119–21, 125, 133–5, 139, 143, 158, 188–91, 198 n.2, 200 n.9, 201 n.20
thought/thinking 1–2, 4, 16, 19–21, 29, 61, 97, 112, 129, 142, 146, 160, 166, 174
    and action 57, 105, 118
    anguish of 2–3, 5, 16, 40, 59–60, 64, 76–9, 83–4, 88, 91, 97, 129, 188
    experience and 2–4, 34–5, 62, 114, 118, 173 (*see also* experience)
    and knowledge 119
    limits and limitations of 9, 22
    and living 199 n.5
    philosophy and 123, 145, 157
    and politics 39–40, 193 n.13
    and reality 192 n.4
    and self-identity 101
    thinker and 3, 10, 132, 141–2, 187
    writing and 3, 5, 21–3, 107
totality 6, 15, 37, 41, 60–1, 72, 80–1, 88, 139, 185, 190, 195 n.5
    to knowledge 60
    subjectivity 192 n.2
tragedy and real 42–3. *See also* reality, nature of
tragic philosophy 154–5, 158, 160
tragic thinking 158–9, 174

Valéry, Paul 24
    approach to truth 27
    Cahiers 24, 26
    foreignness 26–7
    layered approach to thought 28
    philosophy of destruction 29–30
    self-variance 26
    subject-object relation 24–5, 29
    veritable art of thinking 28
vita activa and *contemplativa* 2

writing 2–5, 11–15, 55, 63, 66, 100, 102, 114, 166, 189
    reading and 63, 72
    thinking and 3, 5, 21–3, 107